TAKING CHARGE

CHARGE
of Infertility

TAKING CHARGE
CHARGE
of Infertility

Patricia Irwin Johnston

Perspectives Press
P.O. Box 90318
Indianapolis, IN 46290

Also by Patricia Irwin Johnston

Perspectives on a Grafted Tree
Understanding: A Guide to Impaired Fertility
 for Family and Friends
An Adoptor's Advocate (out of print)
Adopting after Infertility

Perspectives Press
P.O. Box 90318
Indianapolis, IN 46290-0318
U.S.A.

Manufactured in the United States of America

hardcover ISBN 0-944934-07-2
paperback ISBN 0-944934-08-0

Library of Congress Cataloging in Publication Data:

Johnston, Patricia Irwin
        Taking charge of infertility / by Patricia Irwin Johnston.
                p. cm
        Includes bibliographical references and index.
        ISBN 0-944934-07-2 cloth -- ISBN 0-944934-08-0 paper
        1. Infertility--Popular works.   I. Title.
    RC889.J55   1994
    616.6'92--dc20   93-44146
                                                              CIP

This book is dedicated

with grateful thanks to Barbara Eck Menning,
who established the trailhead,

and with love to my friend Judith Calica,
infertile woman, patient advocate, and therapist,
for the inspired thinking which helps so many continue to grow
and for her willingness to make brave (and personally expensive)
professional choices which have benefitted thousands of people
with a fertility impairment.

ACKNOWLEDGEMENTS

This is the book that, logically, should have preceded *Adopting after Infertility*, which was released in the fall of 1992. While that book was being written and afterwards, friends and colleagues from all over North America kept niggling me to get this one done, too.

What they knew was that much of the process that I had developed on decision making and had shared in workshop format but not in writing over the last ten years still would not reach a significant segment of its infertile audience who simply weren't yet able to pick up a book with the word *adoption* in its title.

They were right, of course. But *Adopting after Infertility* just wouldn't wait. Its time had come, and it needed to be poured out to make room for the space that *Taking Charge of Infertility* would need to occupy in my thinking, in my office, on my computer.

There is never an end to learning, and I continue to be inspired by the hundreds of infertile couples to whom I speak each year. They are the real teachers and the real authorities. I am awed by the challenges they face in this complex time. To the couples in Chicago, Lancaster, Columbus, Louisville, Newark, Lexington, New York, Richmond, Houston, San Francisco, Indianapolis, Halifax, Miami, Winston-Salem, Milwaukee, Cincinnati, Raleigh, and Winnipeg who have allowed themselves to be experimented upon during the year this book was in process, my special thanks! You polished the stone!

Patricia Irwin Johnston
Indianapolis, November, 1993

TABLE OF CONTENTS

	Acknowledgements	6
	Introduction	9
1	The Journey	15
2	Nobody Understands	35
3	Creating a Plan	55
4	Choosing Service Providers	95
5	Making Medical Treatment Choices	119
6	Beyond Finding the Cure	151
7	Embracing Life without Children	163
8	Collaborative Reproduction	171
9	Adopting	193
10	Pregnancy	215
11	Parenting after Infertility	223
12	What Should We Tell the Kids?	233
13	Life Goes On	253
	Index	261

INTRODUCTION

Everyone who writes on a topic as specialized as infertility does so from a unique perspective. Some of the authors of the most widely recommended and useful books which readers are likely to come across are medical professionals with a wealth of experience in drug therapy and surgery to share. Others are mental health professionals sharing their valuable expertise on psychological and social issues, from dealing with loss to learning communication skills to making decisions. In a few cases these authors who work professionally in this field are also consumers of infertility services; they have themselves dealt with a fertility impairment. Some books have been written by individuals sharing their personal journeys through infertility in hopes that others can learn from their travails.

An author's viewpoint certainly colors what he or she has to say, and understanding an author's perspective can help a reader decide just how valuable that experience is likely to be for him. And so, before you begin this book, you should know something about my perspective on infertility and its alternatives.

I am not a medical or mental health professional. I do not treat patients or engage in counseling. By training, certification, and professional experience I am a teacher, writer, and librarian. Among the skills this background has given me is an interest in pulling together the thinking and writing of many people in a number of allied areas, repackaging it, and offering it in a manner that is sometimes more easily understood than it was when its originator presented it. That's what good teachers do: they present the discoveries of inventors and researchers and explorers and philosophers in a manner that is not really simplified, just clarified.

As a self-described infertility and adoption educator (there are no university courses, degrees or certifications in such a field) I am one of a very few individuals who really are teachers rather than those who are skilled in another field who are called upon to speak or to write, when what they do much better is practice medicine or counsel.

I am also an infertile person. And more than that, my husband and I are members of a family that has faced infertility in two successive generations and extended itself through three generations by adopting its children rather than giving birth to them. This long-term experience with intergenerational infertility, I believe, gives me a perspective that is unique among those who are working with infertile people today.

Aside from this, my husband's and my story is not particularly unusual for people our age. Dave and I married in 1965. We were very young. He had just graduated after five years of pharmacy school and I had just completed my second year of college. I'm sure that some of our friends from college assumed that we "had" to get married, so that most were probably surprised to learn years later, through holiday cards or reports from mutual acquaintances or as we bumped into one another at homecoming football games, that while we had acquired advanced degrees, a lovely home, a boat, nice cars and were taking great trips, the Johnstons had no children until the year of our tenth anniversary. Our family of five was not completed until we had been married for nineteen years. As most of our college friends sent their children off to college, the Johnstons were still dealing with diapers and day care. As we sent our oldest off to college last fall (with our youngest just entering fourth grade) most of our high school and college classmates had emptied their nests and several had become grandparents.

When Dave and I discovered in 1969 that we had a fertility problem, we felt a little like pioneer explorers. There were no guides available, no maps to read. We just plunged into the thicket and hacked away to blaze our own trail, letting it grow up again behind us (there was no going back, anyway.) We were aware that occasionally we were going in circles, but there was no one, really, of whom to ask questions.

Oh, yes, Dave's parents had dealt with infertility and multiple miscarriage and neonatal death back in the 1930s and '40s before finally adopting Dave and his younger sister, but the continent they had explored had been quite different from the one on which we found ourselves. The tools available to them were obsolete (thank goodness!) They could empathize (an important comfort), but they could not guide us. My parents, on the other hand, though very supportive, had had the opposite problem. They had produced five pregnancies in close succession, and when we began our attempts to start a family were still worrying about the possibility of having a "change of life baby" as my mother's parents had had.

Finally, in the very early '70s Dave and I did stumble upon a book written for consumers about infertility. It had been written by a physician. I can't remember his name or the book's title now, but I do remember how very grateful we felt that there was something out there to offer us guidance, something to explain what these tests we had been repeating and repeating with no answers were all about, something to suggest new tests about which we could ask our doctor. With this book in hand, several years into testing, we asked about a laparoscopy. (Yes, I really did write that. We had to ask for a laparoscopy.) I got one, and we discovered that my fallopian tubes had been badly damaged by adhesions formed after a previous abdominal surgery. Surgery in 1973 to correct that was unsuccessful. There was micro surgery being done then, but we'd never heard of it. Laser surgery and *in vitro* fertilization were still in the future. We were told that we were permanently infertile, and we grieved for the children who would not be born to us.

That grieving was harder, somehow, for me than it was for Dave. Perhaps part of the difference was that, as an adoptee raised happily in a loving family, he knew from personal experience that adoption could be a wonderful alternative. I was, initially, more afraid of adoption than he was. Besides, the experience of growing up in a large extended family where the genetic connections were so interesting and obvious among the cousins gave me a different perspective on genetic connection than Dave had. And part of the difference was the basic difference between how women brought up when I was growing up and men who grew up when Dave did perceived infertility, family building, relationships, themselves.

But part of the difference was also the lack of support. We felt isolated. The significance of our infertility was unacknowledged by the counseling community in 1973. A well respected family therapist actually said to me that if "something as insignificant as infertility" was causing such stress in our marriage, something else must be wrong with the marriage. I thought of myself as "crazy" for feeling so much pain. I truly feared for my sanity. I wallowed in grief for a full year, my loving but helpless husband hovering nearby, before I could think about moving on.

When I was, finally, ready to move on, we talked and read and asked questions, and adoption became the right choice for us. Our son was born in 1975. But we wanted to parent more children, and when we lost our place on an agency waiting list after being transferred to a new city in 1977, I began to re-explore all of the options for becoming parents again: adoption, new treatments, etc.

Around Thanksgiving of 1978 (a few months after the miraculous birth in England of the first IVF baby, Louise Brown) I stumbled upon a rather boring looking little blue book in the public library: *Infertility: A Guide for the Childless Couple*, by Barbara Eck Menning, the founder of the still very young RESOLVE, Inc.. Reading that book changed my life, because it was the first to discuss the psycho-social impact of infertility, the first to give credibility to the pain and anguish that the infertility experience had rained upon me.

With a friend, Carol Hallenbeck, and a supportive physician, W.R. "Bud" Keye, I started a RESOLVE chapter. I began to see RESOLVE as something like a National Geographic Society of infertility— an organization begun by experienced explorers as the baby boomers began to reach childbearing age, its purpose to help the boomers through the thickets of infertility. Over the years RESOLVE has become more and more sophisticated at doing just that, but it hasn't been easy. The existing territory had been thoroughly explored and found wanting, and modern day exploration of infertility treatment demands a willingness to experiment and to be experimented upon, to set out as if on a new planet with an unfamiliar atmosphere, and to be comfortable with a kind of star wars technology which expands and changes at blinding speed.

In my era as a patient, the most difficult thing about infertility may have been its isolation. In my opinion the most difficult aspect of being infertile today is the hurricane speed at which the process of testing and treatment hurls patients along. While patients of Dave's and my era hated the waiting and stalling, the fact is that one benefit of that was that it forced us to think carefully about what our next step might be. Today's patients pitch downhill, caught up in a forward momentum which seems difficult to stop. On the other hand, patients also become afraid to stop—afraid of disappointing their partners and their families, of letting down their medical team, of looking "chicken," of failing.

Of course, since the beginning of human society infertile people have always been out of control of their reproductive lives. But for the baby boomers and those who followed them, one of the complications of that kind of loss of control is that they expected to be in control of their fertility. The first boomers came to sexual maturity just as The Pill had been perfected. "Everyone" was using it, and so everything had changed.

It seems to me that what infertile people need most today is a way to regain control of their reproductive lives while at the same time learning the difficult lesson that life can't be controlled. The purpose of this book is to offer them a method for doing just that. This book is not meant to be a medical guide to infertility. Medical and surgical advances are so rapid today that a book purporting to deal specifically and exhaustively with testing and treatment for a fertility impairment would be outdated before it even hit the shelves. The best sources of up-to-date information about testing and treatment and options today are to be found by attending consumer-oriented seminars, in reading newsletter articles and easily updated fact sheets, and in talking to and asking questions of consumer advocates and specializing professionals. In the course of this book, I hope to help you learn to find all of those resources.

One unusual factor in the way this book has been formatted is that it does not contain a collected bibliography at the end. Most such bibliographies, it seems to me, simply serve to let the reader know that the author has done a lot of reading herself. As a librarian and an educator, on the other hand, I see books as practical tools. So I have created a short and very selective resource section at the end of each chapter. Each of the organizations and books and tapes in these resources sections will provide you with specific tools of value for making decisions and finding professional help about that chapter's topic.

With this kind of information in hand, patients must then learn to be their own consumer advocates. They must work diligently to keep their own focus while not becoming tunnel-visioned. They must think carefully about how various personal, political, financial, and ethical pressures influence the organizations, the institutions, the volunteers and the professionals who purport to want to help them find their way.

So, rather than attempting to add to the jumble of technical jargon plentifully available, this book is meant to offer a framework for individuals who need to make important decisions, for partners who need to communicate effectively with one another. Using this framework demands honesty and a willingness to avoid denial. It requires respecting differences in needs and wishes and reactions. It enjoins you to refuse to allow anyone—self, partner, care providers—to engage in reductionism concerning either the experience and consequences of infertility or any of its treatments or lifestyle alternatives.

Finally, this book contains flat-out opinion, some of it jarring. Because my purpose is to make you think for yourselves rather than accept the thinking of others, I've not been afraid to question the infertility "establishment" in order to startle you from complacency and a tendency to move in lock step. And who is this "establishment" today? Doctors and nurses and technicians, of course, but also manufacturers of medications and equipment and vendors of alternative services such as donated gametes and adoption. And, yes, I'm not beyond saying that I believe that even some of the national leaders of the once proudly-independent consumer groups have let go of some of the important components of their role as consumer advocates in an effort to appease significant donors and potential political allies.

I cannot make your journey for you or identify a right road. The path must be your own. I can, though, reassure you from hard experience that a well made journey is worth the effort. On the other side of infertility life is good and sweet again. And while my path would not reach your goal, I can offer you tools crafted from experienced exploration for making your own trailblazing easier.

Here are those tools. You need only reach out for them.

Chapter 1

THE JOURNEY

*There are only two ways to approach life—as a
victim or as a gallant fighter—and you must decide if
you want to act or react... a lot of people forget that.*
Merle Shain

Most of us spent many childhood days curled in warm laps
reading fairy tales and nursery stories with happy endings.
Surrounding us was the firm shape of a parent who would keep us
safe and secure. The fairy tales gave way to more realistic stories,
but the themes remained substantially the same: for those who are
good and noble and true, for those who try their best, the
dangerous unknown is only a fairy tale. Those who try hard will
succeed. This was the background into which we were launched
into adulthood.

Yet those born as a part of the post war baby-boom have
also been part of momentous social change that has involved huge
shifts in our thinking about marriage and family and reproduction.
Men and women are equal and women should see themselves as
more than "just" mothers, taking the time to study hard, to develop
careers before thinking about starting a family. We should feel
comfortable with ourselves sexually and feel entitled to
experiment, to use birth control to avoid the danger of becoming
pregnant too soon. You can always become a parent *later*. These
were equally loud messages for many of those growing up in the
'50s and '60s and '70s.

Our expectations about love and family building were
initially idealistic and simplistic. Two people fall in love. They
commit to one another. They establish a firm foundation on which

to build a secure home. They have a planned number of children. They live happily ever after.

In biology class, in family living class, in health and sex education there were drawings and diagrams and a lot of warnings about the danger of premarital sex. The message was that our maturing bodies were time bombs set to go off. Growing up in the pre-AIDS era, we heard a great deal about certain demons related to our emerging sexuality: about damaging our reputations, about getting sexually transmitted diseases, and most of all about unplanned pregnancy. Yet in all of those classes in all of those years nobody told most of us about infertility. All of which contributes to a general denial that infertility is important.

But you and I know that infertility _is_ important, and it begins with a crisis.

Like the dragons which confronted the princes and princesses in those childhood fairy tales, infertility roars into our lives finding us totally unprepared. When this dragon rears its head, we tend first to play ostrich, burying our heads in the sand and pretending not to see. For months we may deny the possibility of a problem. We're under a lot of stress at work. Our timing is off. The travel schedule has gotten in the way. Looking back on those early months now and remembering your own denial, you may wonder why it took so long for you to realize that you needed help, why you wasted so much time at the wrong doctor, why you refused to acknowledge the fact of infertility.

The answer is not so difficult. You were afraid. Somewhere, in the back of your mind, you sensed that a dragon was there, and you hoped to avoid the crisis of facing the dragon by ignoring it.

But finally, because it wouldn't go away, because it didn't just disappear in a magical flash, you were forced to acknowledge that this dragon—infertility—was real, and it needed to be reckoned with.

The crisis of infertility is a profound one for many of those for whom it is a part of the life experience—a crisis of proportions that, at least at the time of the experience, seems legendary.

The Chinese, an ancient and philosophically sophisticated culture, write not with an alphabet, but with complex word pictures. Interestingly, in Chinese the written expression of the concept of _crisis_ is drawn by putting together the characters for two other words: _danger_ and _opportunity_.

Because we sense danger in the face of any crisis, we often seek to deny the reality of what we are facing. And so it is with infertility. To acknowledge a fertility impairment is to face imminent danger. Though at first we might not be able to clearly identify precisely what we fear, our subconscious senses the possibility of loss ahead.

Remember that childhood friend who moved away when you were four? The special toy lost irretrievably on the plane to Grandma's? The cat that ran away? The math test you failed? The first love who unceremoniously dumped you? The college which turned you down? Getting fired from that great job? Losing that important business deal?

Every day we experience losses. Some of these losses are painful and etch themselves on our memory and our being. Some pass by nearly unnoticed because we have become so accustomed to dealing with them. But every loss—the large and the small—is one of the lessons which contribute to the development of a unique pattern of coping with loss, a pattern which becomes so familiar, so automatic, that over time one rarely even realizes it has begun and is going on again.

Do you recall, for instance, having found yourself in a situation like this?

Having spent a day shopping, you arrive at home with your house key in your pocket and your arms loaded with packages only to hear the insistent ringing of your telephone on the other side of the door. Twentieth century North Americans have a terrible time allowing a phone to go unanswered, so as a typical member of your generation you struggle with the packages you are juggling in order to fish out the key and rush inside to answer the phone.

As you put the phone to your ear you hear yourself saying, "Hello? Hello?" to a dial tone (<u>denial</u>.) You're <u>surprised</u> to hear that dial tone. How could they have hung up? You begin a litany of "if only's" (<u>bargaining</u>) ("If only I had had my key out and ready."... "If only they'd let it ring one more time.") Feeling frustrated and disappointed and maybe even a little <u>angry</u> at somebody because of the loss of this call ("Doggone it, they should have let it ring one more time"... "Darn it, won't I ever learn to make more than one trip"), you look at the packages strewn in your foyer and subconsciously begin the familiar process of coping with (<u>accepting/resolving</u>) the loss.

Perhaps you shrug it off with an "Oh, well, if it was important, they'll call back" and go about your business of picking up the packages and putting away the groceries. Or perhaps you allow the ice cream to melt on the floor while you pick up the phone and call a friend. "Hi. did you just call?... No?... Yeah, well, I missed a call just as I got in from shopping... So, what're ya doin'?..." Perhaps your reaction to the frustration of an accumulation of lost phone calls would inspire you to rush right back out to the electronics store to buy an answering machine.[1]

There are many styles of coping with loss. Some people are routinely more comfortable than others in accepting loss as normal and natural—as a part of their fate. Some people cope with loss by seeking substitutions for the lost item or issue. Some people aggressively seek to avoid loss by assuming as much control as possible over every situation.

---

1.   This scenario has been borrowed and then significantly adapted and embellished from 1976 version of *How to Survive the Loss of a Love*, by Melba Cosgrove, Harold Bloomfield, and Peter McWilliams. The 1991 revised version (Bantam Books) no longer contains this clarifying anecdote. Too bad! But the book remains a good resource for those dealing with loss of any kind.

Beyond this general personal style of handling loss, how we cope with a particular loss is colored to a large extent by a variety of factors related to when the loss occurs: the solidity of our self esteem, the memories the new loss triggers of earlier losses about which it reminds us, the unresolved losses it dredges up for us, the support systems we have available to us at the time of the loss, the reactions of people who are important to us, and more.

Because infertility is an experience which involves multiple losses, each with its own degree of significance, taking the time right now to determine how it is that you and your partner each cope with loss is an important step toward deciding what alternatives are right for you. Please consider taking the time to pause and reflect on that before continuing to read.

Acknowledging Infertility's Losses

Having talked about your personal styles of reacting to loss you may feel ready to think about the series of losses built into the infertility experience. Over many years of thinking about it, reading about it, talking with hundreds of couples about it, I have come to see six distinct areas of significant loss, most of which encompass several other related losses.

Losses Perceived to Be a Consequence of Permanent Infertility

1. Control over many aspects of life
2. Individual genetic continuity linking past and future
3. The joint conception of a child with one's life partner
4. The physical satisfactions of pregnancy and birth
5. The emotional gratifications of pregnancy and birth
6. The opportunity to parent

Perhaps most clearly and immediately felt by those of us who experience infertility is the loss of **control** over numerous aspects of our lives. Today's couple, who came to sexual maturity and selected a partner after the birth control revolution precipitated by the wide availability of the birth control pill in the mid sixties, have always had the distinct expectation that they would be able to control their fertility. Unfortunately, because infertility was not discussed as they grew up, this expectation included not just the expectation that they would be able to avoid pregnancy when they so desired, but that they would be able to achieve pregnancy when they so desired.

Naive as it may seem in retrospect, most people begin the journey toward parenthood with plans like these: "We'll get pregnant in September so that the baby will be born in May and I'll have time to get back into my bikini by summer," or "You can go off birth control right in the spring before we get our degrees and then take the board exams in the summer before your pregnancy starts to show." Losing control of a part of life which their peers take so completely for granted is devastating and, for many people, precipitates a humiliating blow to self esteem.

And this loss of control takes on an even greater dimension now, in the 1990s, than it did a decade or two ago. According to Judith D. Schwartz, author of *The Mother Puzzle: A New Generation Reckons with Motherhood*, in her June 29, 1993 *New York Times* article "The New Mommy Trap,"

> "Reproduction has taken on a new cachet, and savvy marketers have taken note. In advertising, fantasy has traditionally implied sexual imagery, unattainable luxury or exotic settings. The new message is that the nuclear family is better than all that...Reproduction (implicitly meaning biological parenthood) has become a trope for individual success."

Schwartz goes on to point out that recently advertisers have begun to take this tack in promoting everything from ovulation detectors to fragrances (DNA, Eternity, etc.) to clothing (The Gap) and food products (Tyson Chicken.) The resulting implication that controlled family building is the ultimate sign of success creates extraordinary pressure on the one in six couples experiencing a fertility impairment.

Yet treating infertility demands that couples give up even more control. Control of their sexual privacy and spontaneity, for example, is forfeited to a medical team which asks them to chart their intercourse, supply semen samples, appear within hours after intercourse for a post-coital test, etc. Months of counting days, reading basal thermometers before our eyes are even in focus, plotting little x's on a graph to represent when we had intercourse (and sometimes wondering with some embarrassment whether we should add a couple so that the doctor won't think we're not "really trying"!) takes its toll. Couples who explore adoption often complain that they feel that they've lost control of other areas usually seen as private to a social worker or attorney or prospective birthparents.

Control of calendars is given over to treatment. An ill-timed out-of-town business trip can ruin a whole month's chances. A social invitation to share a rustic and noisy cabin for the weekend involves a check to see whether the date falls on a "fertile weekend."

Many infertility treatments involve therapy with various hormones which may, along with the general stress of being a "patient," contribute to massive mood swings and shifts, making both patient and partner feel out of control of emotions. Too often patients have too little information and develop unrealistic expectations about their ability to control these shifts. They become angry and ashamed of their inability to exert control over their emotional reactions.

What type or size car to buy depends on whether or not it will be carrying children. Accepting a new job or a promotion can become dependent on how travel impacts on the treatment program, whether or not the new company has excellent health care benefits which cover infertility treatments, as well as whether or not the new employee's coverage for infertility treatment would be excluded because it was defined by the insurance company as a pre-existing condition. Continuing education may be put on hold when a woman expects that any day she will become pregnant, so that finishing a term might be difficult or impossible. Whether to buy a house in the suburbs with sidewalks for Big Wheels or a condo in the city close to work and cultural events is controlled by infertility. Even the most private and seemingly simple of decisions—how much time to spend in a hot tub, how much coffee to drink, how many miles to run each week, whether to buy briefs or boxer shorts—can be controlled by the infertility experience.

Couples often comment that with infertility they feel that they have lost control of every aspect of their lives. To many individuals for whom being in control is an important part of their ability to feel confident and competent, infertility represents a devastating loss, but this is not infertility's only loss.

Potentially, infertility means the loss of our **individual genetic continuity**—our expectation that we will continue the genes of our families in an unbroken blood line from some distant past into a promising future. For those raised in blood-is-thicker-than-water cultures, this loss is significant enough to be avoided at all costs.

Genetic connection seems to be less important in general among people who are several generations removed from their immigrant grandparents in "melting pot" or "patchwork quilt" cultures such as that of the U.S., Canada, and Australia. And as we become a more transient world, wherein large numbers of people live far removed from their families of origin, it has become increasingly accepted that people build kinship communities which substitute for genetic families from among the people with whom they feel a common bond.

Still, in many countries, in many ethnic communities, in some religions, and in many families genetic connection remains a cultural imperative! Why we feel this way is not so important as is the fact that we acknowledge that we do indeed feel this way. Further, as we'll discuss later, for infertile individuals for whom this loss is central and powerful, pursuing family building alternatives which allow only one partner to retain genetic continuity can be devastating to some relationships.

Some families are entirely comfortable with the idea of adopting in order to carry a family into the future, while others believe strongly that the family blood line cannot be grafted onto. Moreover, as a whole society defines parent-child relationships primarily by blood ties, and clearly devalues as second-best or second-rate parent-child relationships which do not include genetic connection such as those in adoption, stepparenting, fostering, mentoring. We are fascinated in a macabre way by stories of babies switched at birth, fathers who discover that the children they were parenting were in fact products of adultery, adoptees who murder their parents. It can be frightening to consider that in order to have the parenting experience we may need to accept a "social handicap" in this role and deal with being seen as "odd" for a lifetime.

And the loss of our genetic continuity is not just our own loss. To experience this loss for some means to let one's family down. More than just offering our parents the social opportunity to be grandparents, some infertile people fear that being unable to carry forward the family's genes may cause them to be seen as failures or disappointments to their parents or grandparents.

Our dreams about parenting included the expectation of our parenting a **jointly conceived child**. In choosing a life's partner all of us do at least a little fantasizing about what our children might be like. Will he have her intellect and his sense of humor? Grandpa's red hair and Aunt Wilma's athletic prowess? Gosh, think of the medical expenses if she inherits both her mother's crossed eye and her father's terrible overbite!

For some, accepting this loss means little more than throwing away the romantic notions fed by years of movies and novels in favor of what we define as a more practical and realistic view of relationships. But for others, this dreamed-of child who represents the blending of both the best and the worst of our most intimate selves also represents a kind of ultimate intimacy—an eternal bonding of partner to partner.

After all, in giving our genes to one another for blending, we offer our most vulnerable and intimate and valuable sense of ourselves—a gift that is perhaps the most precious we can offer. Losing that dream and so feeling forced to consider alternatives such as donor insemination, hiring a surrogate mother, adopting, etc. can be painful indeed for those for whom this expectation was particularly important.

There is also the loss of the **physical satisfactions of the pregnancy and birth experiences**. Many people see the loss of a pregnancy as belonging entirely to women, but this is not true. Though the physical changes and challenges of pregnancy and birth are experienced by women alone, producing a child, as any counselor of pregnant teens will verify, is the ultimate rite of passage for both men and women—the final mark of having reached adulthood. You're grown up now, man, and your parents aren't in charge anymore. Beyond that, the physical ability to impregnate a woman or to carry and birth a child represents the ultimate expression of maleness or femaleness—our bodies at work doing what they were built to do. For many people, losing such capacities challenges their feelings about their maturity or their sexuality or both—about their competence as adult men and women. And to make it worse for couples of the '80s and '90s, an era when physical fitness has achieved almost a cult-like status, the loss of the physical expectations we have about becoming or making pregnant may represent an even more deeply felt loss of body image than it did for couples just a generation older.

Such feelings are based again in societal expectations. It is their own discomfort with and fear of the loss of the physical aspects of getting/making pregnant which generates from outsiders the tasteless humor which relates infertility to sexuality in comments such as, "Do you need a little help there? Happy to offer my services!" or "Let me show you how it's done." or "Hey, all Steve has to do is look at me and I'm pregnant. It must be something in the water!"

And then there are the **emotional gratifications of a shared pregnancy, prepared childbirth, breast-feeding experience** which were a part of our expectations about having children. Over the last two decades, a substantial element of our society, fearful of the impact of massive changes in family structure, has mysticized the experience of birth to an exaggerated extent. In search of the perfect "bonding" experience (a kind of magical super glue without which many fear that families will disintegrate) couples carefully choose specific kinds of childbirth preparation, attend classes together, read books, practice breathing, etc. They expect to experience a magical closeness in spousal relationships, an irreplaceable wonder in sharing the birth experience, an instant eye-to-eye bonding between parents and child. Hospitals market to the expectations of these couples in expensively done and romantically scripted television commercials and display ads. They compete with one another to provide perfect preparation and birthing rooms with the perfect equipment (birthing beds, chairs, tanks) and the perfect atmosphere (music, guests allowed, champagne after, etc.) Certainly the new pronatalist advertising trend Judith Schwartz has identified, which urges parenthood on both sexes, welcoming men to the "fun" and tuning in to women's reproductive anxieties about timing, is simply a new twist on the same old theme.

This set of expectations about the emotional gratifications of a shared pregnancy, prepared childbirth, breast-feeding experience, though far too often unrealistic, is widely held, and may contribute to our own unrecognized prejudices about family life. To risk losing such an experience is much more significant to today's couple than it would have been to their parents and grandparents—many of whose mothers gave birth anesthetized in sterile operating rooms while fathers paced in waiting rooms outside, who often didn't see and hold their children until hours after their births, who bottle-fed formula to their infants (but who did indeed manage to bond with us, their children!)

And finally, to be permanently infertile threatens the **opportunity to parent**, which is a major developmental goal for most adults. The psychologist Eric Erickson has identified a series of developmental milestones humans work toward throughout the life span. In adulthood, the major goals are regenerativity and parenting. To be infertile, on the surface, threatens our ability to achieve that goal, so that for many people this represents a devastating blow.

Erickson and others have clearly demonstrated that it is possible for individuals to achieve the developmental goal and to satisfy the need for parenting without actually becoming biological or legal parents. Many adults find ways of redirecting or rechanneling their need to nurture—through interaction with nieces and nephews and family friends; by choosing work which brings them in frequent contact with children; by volunteering as religious class teachers, scout leaders, or for a group such as Big Brothers/Big Sisters; by becoming active in non-child centered volunteer work; by nurturing the earth through nature hobbies such as gardening, etc.

This is not to imply that lists of possible redirections like these are seen as equivalent substitutions or as realistic direct replacements for the lifelong experience of parenting a child jointly conceived and birthed with a much loved partner. While some adults can and do actively choose to meet their developmental needs to nurture without becoming parents, for couples who have once made the choice to become parents and have then been thwarted by infertility, the choice to redirect that energy is much more difficult. But the exploration of such options is an important part of addressing this loss. Marianne Takas and Edward Warner wrote the valuable book *To Love a Child* (Addison Wesley, 1992) as a way to seriously examine for themselves options for satisfying these nurturing needs.

It is all of these six potential and realized losses and others related to them which tore at your gut during those days or weeks or months when you tried to deny the infertility. These losses were the danger lurking in the crisis, and they were difficult to face. Facing your feelings about infertility's losses can help you find the opportunities in the crisis and in deciding what treatment, what lifestyle alternative is right for you.

Facing the emotional ramifications of infertility will help you to make better decisions about its practical aspects. But facing those emotional ramifications can also be frightening.

Finding Resolution

In the twenty years since the American organization RESOLVE was founded in Boston by Barbara Eck Menning to help infertile people cope effectively, a controversy has swirled around its name and the very concept of resolution. Barbara Eck Menning was a pioneer, the first to call attention to the psycho-social ramifications of infertility. Writing and studying during the period of the early '70s when Elisabeth Kubler Ross' significant work in the area of grief, death, and dying had caught public attention, Ms. Eck Menning empowered millions of infertile people by giving logical structure, words, and labels for their previously unexplained pain. She named her organization RESOLVE because she saw as its goal helping infertile people reach the final stage of grief identified by Kubler Ross as resolution. Her work helped to sensitize thousands of professionals, and generated research and new approaches to treatment and a whole new look at an issue previously relegated to the closet.

Many of those (myself included) who read Barbara Eck Menning's landmark book *Infertility: A Guide for the Childless Couple* (Prentice Hall, 1976, revised 1988) memorized a quote about infertility residing in our hearts as an old friend and always being a part of us and recited it almost like a mantra in our enthusiasm for helping other infertile people find the comfort we had found in RESOLVE.

But as time went by, something began to feel "not quite right" about this approach for some of us. Barbara Eck Menning's pioneering work led to a great deal of reductionist thinking. For many infertile people the goal became resolution—an abstract concept never clearly defined but which far too many couples expected to be identifiable, quantifiable, clearly reachable. Getting pregnant was defined as a resolution. Adopting was defined as a resolution. Choosing to be childfree was defined as a resolution.

Soon we began to see that many professionals—the majority of social work professionals involved in adoption, for example—were being similarly misled. They were judging us by some unagreed upon standard of whether or not we were "resolved" enough to be ready for parenting. As medical treatment became more and more specialized and dependent upon sophisticated technology, and the offices of infertility specialists became busier and busier, thus making contact with our physicians seem less and less personal, medical professionals often dismissed our anger at the milieu of their offices or incidents within the treatment process as a "part of the grief process" rather than justifiable frustration resulting from insensitive practice.

I spent nearly fourteen years as a devoted daily RESOLVE volunteer, beginning as a chapter founder and ending with three years as chair of the national board. (I remain, "in retirement," RESOLVE's ardent supporter!) It took me most of those fourteen years to understand why the concept of infertility always being a part of us was downright offputting to the majority of people dealing with impaired fertility and why the majority of infertile people didn't join RESOLVE or similar support organizations to take advantage of the myriad of valuable educational, advocacy, referral and support services and resources available there.

I get it now, and part of the purpose of my having written this book is to help you move beyond some common, but (at worst) dated and (at best) underdeveloped thinking.

The concept of resolution—or at least the lack of it—has become yet one more way a way to blame the victim.

Becoming a Victim

Unfortunately, many people spend significant amounts of time allowing themselves to become the victims of a crisis, floundering in a sea of despair as they are overwhelmed by waves of decisions that must be made. This tendency to see oneself as a victim is undergirded by a sense of damaged self esteem. Some fertility-impaired people react by feeling that they are somehow less competent than they were before their infertility was discovered. If their reproductive systems aren't working, they somehow illogically reason, then maybe they shouldn't trust their judgment, either. (Maybe Uncle Charlie was right, we're just trying too hard. Perhaps Mom's manicurist's cousin's doctor in Podunk is better than the reproductive endocrinologist at the medical center. Maybe my neighbor who thinks adoption is a sad substitute for real parenting because nobody could ever really love somebody else's reject isn't so far off base!)

Feeling neither confident nor competent, such people become unwilling and unable to make decisions. They begin to abdicate more and more control to others.

These are the people who will slog on obsessively from treatment to treatment, who will drift into a childless future they do not want because they haven't been able to make the decisions that might have helped them consider choices still available to them. It is these people who will fall into a dropped-into-their laps adoption because someone they saw as competent told them it was the next logical step (and, unprepared for the challenging differences in adoptive parenting, will struggle for years with a feeling that things aren't quite right, that this didn't work either.)

I worry about such couples, because when one operates by crisis management—deciding only when one is forced to decide—there is little opportunity for reflection. Caught up in the panic of the situation, such people tend to make decisions only when they must be made, struggling from crisis to crisis. They stumble forward on a conveyor belt carried by a panicky momentum much like that we felt as out-of-control young runners about to skin our knees again.

I worry because fertility-impaired people operating in such a mode tend to act out of desperation. With self conscious laughter, they tell you that they would do <u>anything</u> to have a baby—even drink poison! Sadly, many really would. They beg for one more cycle of a drug their doctor has decided isn't working. They borrow money for yet another in a long string of unsuccessful GIFT or IVF attempts. They risk it all on a not-quite-legal adoption. They juggle two or more potential adoptions or an adoption and a high risk pregnancy at the same time. Obsessively driven toward the goal of bringing a baby home to a waiting nursery, they have thought very little beyond arrival day.

I worry because the self-absorption of people operating as victims won't allow them to feel compassion for others—for birthparents, for people dealing with secondary infertility, for the confused and panicked parents of triplets or quads conceived on fertility drugs or in IVF cycles, for couples dealing with an untimely pregnancy, for pregnant infertiles who can't find a place to "fit in" anymore. For one who has experienced a reproductive loss to have lost compassion for those experiencing other types of reproductive loss is particularly ironic and especially tragic.

I worry about these couples, because by allowing themselves to become victims of infertility, by allowing themselves to avoid thinking about the ramifications of their crisis management style, they almost guarantee that they won't effectively deal with their losses, and that years later those losses will reappear as reopened wounds when new and different losses set a grief reaction in motion losses of jobs, for example, or divorce, or menopause, or the death of a parent or close friend or spouse.

I worry because for victims there is little joy in living.

An Infertile Future?

A significant crisis fraught with loss or the threat of loss nearly always continues to reverberate in our lives in subtle ways. Lost loves, lost opportunities, failed attempts color our world and alter our view significantly.

Infertility is no different. Anyone whose experience with infertility has demanded medical intervention, has caused significant changes in daily life patterns for many months or even years, and has forced reexamination of life goals will come out of the experienced having changed.

Because it touches so many facets of our lives, it is certainly possible for infertility to reverberate negatively in our futures. Yes, some people have had permanent losses of valued friendships, felt unresolvable stresses in family relationships, become addicted to treatment, experienced ongoing sexual dysfunction, become overprotective and unsuccessful parents, and even lost a marriage partner as a result of the experience of infertility.

But these are neither typical patterns of reacting to infertility nor unpreventable ones. Furthermore, the infertility has rarely been the single contributing factor in such disasters. Nearly always these were people experiencing other problems in which the infertility became an exacerbating factor.

We don't have to allow ourselves to become victims of infertility, nor do we have to feel that we must wear its label, like a scarlet letter branded on our foreheads, throughout our lives! Infertility does not, for most people, need to become something akin to addiction or dysfunction for which we need a recovery program. In fact, joining a group like RESOLVE or Infertility Awareness Association of Canada or a local variation is vastly different from the important (and valuable) process of dealing with dysfunction or addiction through the life-changing 12-step programs which proliferate today.

The Alternative

All significant endings and beginnings are indeed crises, fraught with the fear that is a part of facing the unknown. The Chinese concept of crisis consisting of both danger and opportunity is an important one to keep in mind as you do the hard work of making good decisions about infertility.

Our goal in this book will be to learn the psychological facts and the communication skills, the sources of accurate information and the questions in need of answers that can help you to take charge of your infertility and turn a stressful, difficult, and negative episode in your lives into a positive part of who you are and will become, as well as how you will live the rest of your lives.

Having acknowledged and examined and discussed together the dangers that lurk in the infertility experience, you will have readied yourselves for the work of finding opportunity there.

RESOURCES

National and Regional Organizations Offering Support and Information to Consumers about Infertility and Related Alternatives

RESOLVE, Inc. (1310 Broadway, Somerville MA 02144, telephone 617-623-0744) is a U.S. national nonprofit network of 54 chapters offering information, referral, support and advocacy services to infertile people. Dues of $35 annually (includes both national and local chapter membership). Their newsletters, fact sheets and symposia can be indispensable tools. Currently RESOLVE is putting a great deal of effort on a state by state basis into achieving mandated insurance coverage for infertility treatment. They have been successful already in Massachusetts, Maryland, California, and several other states.

Infertility Awareness Association of Canada (523-774 Echo Lane, Ottawa, Ontario K1S 5N8, Canada, telephone 613-730-1322) IAAC is a Canadian charitable organization offering assistance, support, and education to those with infertility concerns by issuance of its bilingual publication *Infertility Awareness* five times a year; establishment of chapters to provide grass roots services; a resource centre; several information packages; and a network of related services. Services are bilingual (English and French) and membership in IAAC is $30 Canadian annually. A complimentary information kit will be sent to interested Canadians upon request.

Ferre Institute (258 Genesee St, Ste 302, Utica, NY 13502, 315-724-4348) is a non-profit organization dedicated to the promotion of quality services in infertility, to the education of professionals and the public about infertility and its treatment and to encourage research in the psychosocial as well as medical aspects of infertility and reproductive health. Although direct services are offered only in a limited geographic region, their excellent newsletter *FerreFax*, directed primarily at professionals, is available to others.

American Fertility Society (1209 Montgomery Highway, Birmingham AL 35216-2809, 205-978-5000) is an international membership organization of professionals—predominantly doctors, but including nurses, reproductive biologists, mental health practitioners and health educators—who have a special interest in family planning and reproductive health. In addition to providing information about local members to consumers seeking a care provider, its special interest group, the Society for Assisted Reproductive Technology, is a membership group of IVF/GIFT clinics who have agreed to report their successes and other statistical data to AFS for dissemination through the annual SART Report. Its Psychological Special Interest Group focuses on the emotional ramifications of infertility. AFS publishes the prestigious medical journal *Fertility and Sterility* and many booklets directed toward patients concerning specific infertility problems and topics.

Endomoetriosis Association (8585 N. 76th Place, Milwuakee WI 53223) is a non-profit with chapters throughout the U.S. The organization publishes a newsletter and offers referrals and support for those dealing with the multiple issues related to endometriosis, only one of which is infertility.

The Organization of Parents through Surrogacy (OPTS) (7054 Quito Ct., Camarillo, CA 93012, 805-482-1566) is a national non-profit, volunteer organization with three regional chapters whose purpose is mutual support, networking, and the dissemination of information regarding surrogate parenting, egg donation, sperm donation as well as assisted reproductive technology including IVF and GIFT. OPTS publishes a quarterly newsletter, holds annual meetings, has a telephone support network, and actively lobbies for legislation concerning surrogacy. Membership is $40 annually.

The Childfree Network (7777 Sunrise Blvd #1800, Citrus Heights, CA 95610, telephone 916-773-7178) is a national organization for singles and couples who have elected a childfree lifestyle. The network publishes a quarterly newsletter, *ChildFree*, containing many helpful articles on the positive aspects of life without children. Though some members made this choice after infertility, most have not experienced infertility, so that one will not necessarily find the newsletter uniformly sensitive to or informed about infertility issues. Subscriptions are $20.00 annually.

Adoption Council of Canada (P.O. Box 8442, Station T, Ottawa, Ontario K1G 3H8. Phone 613-235-1566.) This network collects and disseminates information about adoption throughout Canada, facilitating communication among groups and individuals interested in adoption and promoting understanding of the benefits and challenges of adoption.

Adoptive Families of America (3333 Hwy 100 North, Minneapolis, MN 55422. Phone 612-537-0316.) An excellent source for purchase of books and tapes and of referral to local parent groups, AFA is the largest organization for adoptive families in the world. AFA publishes *OURS: The Magazine of Adoptive Families* bimonthly and sponsors an annual national conference designed specifically to reach out to those considering adopting and adoption-expanded families. Its Annual Adoption Information and Resources packet lists several hundred agencies nationally and offers consumer advice.

Medical and Ethical Information and Emotional Support

Family Bonds: Adoption and the Politics of Parenting by Elizabeth Bartholet (New York: Houghton Mifflin, 1993.) A provocative look at how and why genetic connection is promoted to (in the author's view) the detriment of infertility patients and adoptive relationships stigmatized except when they are quasi or partial adoptions.

Healing the Infertile Family: Strengthening Your Relationship in the Search for Parenthood by Gay Becker, Ph.D. (New York: Bantam Books, 1990) Based on a series of interviews with infertile couples, Dr. Becker presents suggestions for coping and for moving on.

Without Child: Experiencing and Resolving Infertility by Ellen Glazer and Susan Cooper (Boston: Lexington Books, 1988). A collection of carefully linked personal experiences from infertile couples who have pursued the full spectrum of options and experienced a variety of outcomes.

and Hannah Wept: Infertility, Adoption, and the Jewish Couple by Michael Gold (Philadelphia: The Jewish Publication Society, 1988. An infertile rabbi looks at infertility from a religious perspective.

The Infertility Book: A Comprehensive Medical and Emotional Guide by Carla Harkness (second edition, Berkeley: Celestial Arts, 1992) This carefully crafted blend of emotional and medical information is liberally sprinkled with anecdotal information.

Pursuing Parenthood: Ethical Issues in Assisted Reproductive Technology by Paul Lauritzen (Bloomington: Indiana University Press, 1993) A carefully reasoned but complex and academic in tone exploration of the ethics of assisted reproductive technology and other family building options and of the professionals who offer them to the infertile written by one who has himself dealt with infertility and chosen donor insemination.

Infertility: A Guide for the Childless Couple by Barbara Eck Menning (second edition, New York: Prentice Hall Press, 1988) The classic in the field. How could it not be a part of a bibliography on infertility!

Surviving Infertility: A Compassionate Guide through the Emotional Crisis of Infertility by Linda P. Salzer (New York: HarperCollins, rev. 1991) A well regarded handbook dealing with the psychological and social aspects of infertility.

The Infertile Couple by Beth Spring. (Elgin, IL, David C. Cook, 1987.) A guide to the practicalities and ethics of making decisions about infertility written from the conservative Christian perspective. Written primarily for clergy, consumers, too will find it helpful.

Getting around the Boulder in the Road: Using Imagery to Cope with Fertility Problems by Aline Zoldbrod, Ph.D. (Lexington, MA: Center for Reproductive Problems, 1990). A booklet which offers professionals and consumers practical tools for using imagery to deal with the stresses of infertility.

Men, Women, and Infertility: Intervention and Treatment Strategies by Aline P. Zoldbrod, Ph.D. (New York: Lexington Books, 1993). A carefully researched and referenced discussion of various therapeutic strategies helpful to therapists and medical professionals working with infertile couples, well-read consumers will also find this book beneficial. Order from Dr. Zoldbrod at 12 Rumford Rd, Lexington MA 02173 for $6.50.

The following books are examples of the best in medical materials as of the date of this publication. Call RESOLVE or IAAC for a referral to today's most current consumer oriented discussion of medical information:

The Couples Guide to Fertility by Gary Berger, MD, Marc Goldstein,MD and Mark Fuerst (New York: Doubleday, 1989).

Overcoming Infertility: A Practical Strategy for Navigating the Emotional, Medical & Financial Minefields of Trying to Have a Baby by Robert Nachtigal, MD, and Elizabeth Mehren (New York: Doubleday, 1991)

From Infertility To I.V.F.. by Geoffrey Sher, M.D. (New York: McGraw Hill, 1988).

appropriate fact sheets from RESOLVE (See address/phone above. Order by phone with your credit card)

Coping with Loss

How to Survive the Loss of a Love by Melba Colgrove Ph.D., Harold Bloomfield, M.D., and Peter McWilliams. (Los Angeles, Prelude Press and Bantam, rev. 1991) A simple yet powerful handbook for getting through loss of a person or of a dream.

Living through Personal Crisis by Ann Kaiser Stearns (New York: Ballantine Books, 1984. A practical guide to dealing with grief.

When Bad Things Happen to Good People by Harold S. Kushner (New York: Shocken Books, 1981) A reassuring approach to understanding loss and suffering.

Chapter 2

NOBODY UNDERSTANDS!

When I was a child we had a toy—a clown-faced, child-sized plastic figure filled with air and weighted at the bottom with beans or sand. Its purpose was to be punched, and to rise from the blow grinning, waiting to be punched again.

It has often seemed to me that for a very long time as my husband and I experienced infertility we were like a pair of those punching bag toys placed on a conveyor belt moving through a system punctuated by swing-arm gates. As we moved along that conveyor belt from doctor to lab to bed, to doctor to hospital to bed, to doctor to pharmacy to bed, to doctor to counselor to agency to attorney, and on and on, we found that the belt began to speed out of control (rather like the conveyor belt in the candy factory where Lucy and Ethel scrambled to fill boxes that rushed by).

Grinning madly (stiff upper lip, and all that) we were knocked askew by alternating swing arm gates—the doctor, the lab, the hospital, etc.—and sent separately reeling to cope with new information, new alternatives. Occasionally in swinging upright again from a blow we would bump against each other and provide one another with a momentary steadiness. But each time we were hit again, we went our own separate ways—alone.

One of the most confusing and frustrating aspects of battling infertility is coming to recognize and deal with the fact that partners do not see the struggle in exactly the same way. An important part of who we are and how adaptable or flexible we are able to be is simply inborn. Some people are just inherently more adaptable than others. Certainly you've heard an apt, if cliched, description such as this one before: "You know, Madelyn just seems to see her glass as half empty all the time, while Norm sees his glass as half full!" Our adaptability is part of why we react to challenges, changes, losses as we do.

But our environment and experiences contribute greatly to who we are too. Because each of us is an individual, brought up in separate homes and different families, our backgrounds have taught us different ways of reacting. We probably attended different schools and houses of worship. Most often we lived at least part of our lives in disparate geographic locations. Growing up, our experiences of place in the family, of friendship, with the people who taught and guided us, with the material we read and the music we listened to and the television or movies or theater we viewed were different. It was the combination of our life's experience which made us unique individuals, with separate needs and expectations.

The issues which make us unique and even attractive to one another may complicate our ability to communicate our feelings about infertility. The vulnerability which drew one person to his or her more self-assured and confident partner, for example, may reflect self esteem issues, causing infertility to be much more painful to the less confident partner than it is for the more confident partner.

Most of us understand the impact of such differences only after they are called to our attention, preferring instead to assume that surely two people who have chosen one another to spend their lives with and to form a family with would agree on the most primal of issues and needs.

Though as a society we are acknowledging that there is no one "male" way to look at things and no one "female" way to react to things, it remains true that in general the experiences of men and women have caused them to view challenges differently. Men tend to be inclined to look for logical answers, women tend to feel things from the heart. Men tend to be less inclined to share their innermost fears and women are more inclined to spill them all for many to see and hear.

Deborah Tannen is a linguist who has spent many years focusing on how people communicate in diverse cultures.

Recently her work has focused on the differences in communication between men and women, who, even when raised in the same location, experience different cultures. In her excellent best selling book *You Just Don't Understand: Women and Men in Conversation* Tannen points out that in our closest relationships we look for confirmation and reassurance. "When those closest to us respond to events differently than we do, when they seem to see the same scene as part of a different play, when they say things that we could not imagine saying in the same circumstances, the ground on which we stand seems to tremble and our footing is suddenly unsure. Being able to understand why this happens—why and *how* our partners and friends, though like us in many ways, are not us, and different in other ways—is a crucial step toward feeling that our feet are planted firmly on the ground." [1]

Tannen observes that men tend to operate in a world they view as having a hierarchical social order in which they are either one-up or one-down from others in a group. Through a lens where life is viewed as a contest or a struggle to avoid failure and preserve independence, men tend to see conversations as negotiations, where the goal is to retain the upper hand and protect oneself from another's attempt to push one around. Women, on the other hand, view life as a community, and struggle to preserve intimacy and connectedness within the group and to avoid isolation. [2]

Another communications expert, John Gray, author of the book *Men Are from Mars, Women Are from Venus* joins Tannen in pointing out that when sharing their problems with one another, women tend to look for and offer reassurance and understanding—intimacy. Men in conversations with other men, on the other hand, jockey for position with a competitive kind of problem solving. As a result, when men and women communicate with one another about problems, often women complain that men just "order them around, tell them what to do" which they often interpret as dismissing their problems as unimportant. Men, on the other hand, assume that when a woman shares a problem she's looking for an answer to it, so men are confused when their advice is not welcome.

1. Tannen, Deborah, Ph.D. *You Just Don't Understand: Women and Men in Conversation* (New York: Ballantine, 1990) p. 73.
2. Tannen, Deborah, Ph.D. *op. cit.*, p. 26-27.

On a segment of Phil Donahue's interview show, John Gray and several couples who had taken his communication workshop, read his book, or used his audio tapes talked about these communication styles. In the exaggerated style he often uses to stir up his audience and make a point, Donahue agreed with his guest.

"Take for example," pointed out Donahue, "the situation of several couples who are at a party together—one of those places where the men congregate in one room and the women in another. If somebody walked into the group of women and said 'Say, I was in a terrible accident last month...' the women would all immediately react with comments like 'How awful! Are you all right? Is there anything I can do?' But the likely reaction among the group of men might be 'Oh, yeah? Well let me tell you what happened to ME!'"

Of course many members of the audience were offended by the sexism of such an exaggeration, and rightfully so, but differences in social conditioning and expectations do indeed continue to contribute to differences in communication styles between men and women.

Mike and Jean Carter have chosen a childfree lifestyle and joyfully put their infertility behind them. In their book *Sweet Grapes: How to Stop Being Infertile and Start Living Again* (Perspectives Press, 1989) the Carters offer the only organized material on communicating and decision making in infertility that has been written by a man and a woman together. Their insights will be helpful to anyone making any decision which is colored by infertility. Mike writes about his early approaches to communicating with Jean about their infertility.

It took me a long time to learn that I really wasn't helping. Both of my strategies—silence and problem solving—were actually ways of keeping problems at arm's length. At that distance, I didn't have to feel them. I didn't have to be a part of the

hurt and confusion that come with tough issues...
Infertility changed all that...[3]

If the observations of Tannen, Gray and others regarding
the differences between women and men both in their style of
communicating and in their expectations from communication
are correct, they offer some interesting applications to
communicating about infertility and about choosing options.

Consider, for example, the physical and emotional losses of
the pregnancy experience. The communications differences theory
would suggest that men who feel these two related losses strongly
do so because they experience humiliation in being "one down"
from other men, and therefore see themselves as "less a man"
through these losses, while women for whom this loss is
particularly painful may react more strongly to the pain of losing
the intimacy of the expected connection to partner and to child.

Certainly many couples have observed retrospectively that
they felt out of sync with one another during phases of the
infertility experience when, faced with sudden bad news,
husbands began to problem solve and look beyond the loss to a
next step while their wives were wishing for the comfort of
mourning the disappointment together.

Couples often complain that one or the other partner
(often the woman) seems obsessed with the infertility to the
exclusion of everything else in life while the other partner (most
often the husband) is able to compartmentalize it. Merle
Bombardieri, a Massachusetts-based therapist who served for a
time as clinical director at RESOLVE and has devoted a significant
percentage of her private practice to infertility, has offered a
helpful prescription for such couples which has been circulated
widely within RESOLVE chapters.

> The Twenty Minute Rule is a compromise
> tactic that acknowledges the diverging needs of
> individuals in a couple for talking about infertility.
> Using it, couples adopt a routine that requires that
> only twenty minutes a day be spent discussing
> infertility-related issues. The twenty minutes are

3. Carter, Jean W. and Michael. *Sweet Grapes: How to Stop Being Infertile and Start Living Again.* (Indianapolis: Perspectives Press, 1989) p. 132

mutually agreed upon and preset. They don't get dropped into the middle of one partner's Monday night football game or the other partner's absorption in a good book. The timing chosen takes into account when during the day each partner is likely to be the least stressed, the most relaxed and thus receptive to what the other partner has to say.

During this twenty minutes, both partners agree that each will give undivided attention to listening to and reacting to what the other partner is feeling a need to communicate. The Twenty Minutes should not be spent with one partner listening from behind a newspaper to a monologue from the other, but instead should involve a willingness to engage one another in conversation and dialogue, with the goal being to communicate and work together to make decisions.

The Twenty Minute Rule creates a win-win situation, by offering the partner who most needs communicative interchange the guarantee of a particular time each day during which s/he won't be ignored, rebuffed or rejected but instead will be attentively listened and responded to, and by offering the less verbal partner protection from a sense of being "ambushed" and the opportunity to prepare carefully for what otherwise might be a painful and resented intrusion.

Most of us have not been taught good communication skills. In confronting infertility, good communication is imperative. Now may be an ideal time to commit to enhancing communication skills. There are many ways to accomplish this.

You should begin with a promise to one another to be honest, direct and clear and to be respectful of one another's pain, fears and need for privacy. Adopting Bombardieri's Twenty Minute Rule and using it to deal with infertility in bite-sized pieces may be another useful step. Then you may choose to work even more aggressively on building communication skills. I highly recommend as worth the time and effort Deborah Tannen, Ph.D.'s *You Just Don't Understand: Women and Men in Conversation* and Harville Hendrix, Ph.D.'s *Getting the Love You Want: A Guide for Couples*. Both Dr. Tannen's and Dr. Hendrix' materials are also available on audio tape, as is the material from Dr Gray's *Men Are from Mars; Women Are from Venus*. Additionally, the Hendrix and Gray groups each offer weekend workshops for couples on communication skills.

Stress and Infertility

The medical and advocacy communities of the '70s and early '80s spoke out strongly to reassure patients furious with the "relax, you're probably trying too hard" advice that has for so long been a part of public response to infertility. We realize now that advocates may have been overzealous in their efforts to eradicate this myth. "No," they wrote, "trying too hard does not produce infertility, but the process of dealing with a fertility impairment, does in itself produce stress."

It is true that "normal" stress does impair fertility, but researchers are now seeing an increasing number of patients in whom extraordinary stress is a factor in infertility. And the line between "normal" and "extraordinary stress" is a fine one. Stress causes people to be reactive rather than proactive, causes power issues to escalate, creates an increase in prejudicial or stereotypical thinking, and reduces flexibility. People obsessed with body image may indeed impair their fertility. Patients with eating disorders (a growing population) often have ovulation dysfunction. People who exercise obsessively may look absolutely great, but, through sharp reduction of body fat, through ingestion of muscle mass building drugs such as anabolic steroids, etc., may have caused their brains to suppress the production of hormones vital to fertility. Though these patients represent a small number of people dealing with impaired fertility, the number appears to be growing. In most cases behavior modification can reestablish fertility in such men and women.

But while the stress of normal day-to-day life may not cause infertility, it is clear that the process of dealing with a fertility impairment can in itself lead to stress. Though it is medically defined as a disease, and though it often produces an emotional reaction very similar to that expressed by sufferers of chronic illness, infertility creates none of the outward signs of illness which would prompt outsiders to offer support or sympathy. Furthermore, infertility involves a couple, not an individual.

Leaping into adoption or third party reproductive options will not circumvent or solve the stress which is a part of infertility. Infertility's issues are too significant to bypass. Over a lifetime, addressing these issues head on will prove to have been a valuable part of the process of moving on.

Clear and direct communication is vital to healthy relationships. The stress of any kind of crisis makes this communication much more difficult. Searching for ways to reduce stress for oneself and for one another can be an important part of reinforcing the relationship.

Begin by treating your bodies more kindly. They are being poked and prodded and medicated and forced to perform under the glare of spotlights. Try some of the following reducers of physical stress

1.   Keep regular hours and have regular sit down meals. This is a particular challenge for people who do not have children, since they tend to have developed habits which include eating on the run and sleeping whenever they get around to it.

2.   Cut down on caffeine, salt, alcohol, and sweets, since they tend to make your already overworked nervous system work even harder.

3.   Become aware of your breathing. Learn to control it with deep breathing exercises in order to manage stress.

4.   Begin some form of regular exercise that will relieve tension in order to keep your body and mind tuned.

Other stress relievers are psychological. For example

1.   Reduce the minor irritations in your life that tend to accumulate and cause stress. Oil that squeaky door, clean that dirty window next to your desk, straighten your messy underwear drawer. Even better, rather than work on your own minor irritants, surprise your partner by working on his or hers!

2. Give yourself (and your partner, too) a few minutes absolutely alone each day during which each of you allows himself to regroup.

3. Go easy on yourself. Accept your feelings as legitimate and refuse to allow others to make you feel guilty for feeling the pain and the disappointment of your fertility impairment.

4. Know your limitations and work to avoid people and tasks that irritate you.

5. Treat yourself to something special—a manicure or a massage, a new book you've wanted to read, a weekend away with your spouse.

6. Share with your spouse as much as possible (though remembering the Twenty Minute Rule!) Work at keeping the two of you a family with your own traditions. This is especially important during the holidays, when stress can be magnified by the tendency of others to ignore your pain.

7. Prod your sense of humor. Try to be silly about some things, and, wherever possible, try to find silliness in the things that irk you most. Laugh as often as you can find a good reason to, and create some of those reasons. Avoid melodrama in your T.V. or movie viewing and watch some sitcoms you might usually avoid.

8. Tell people that things are bothering you rather than gunnysacking irritations until you explode. Let others know how they can help you rather than expect them to read your mind.

Who's Infertile Here?—The Couples Factor

Often it is difficult for couples themselves—let alone outsiders—to understand the significance of the fact that infertility is a couples issue. While in about 30% of cases both partners are subfertile (infertile when paired with an equally infertile partner, but fertile when paired with a normally fertile or super fertile partner), in the majority of cases of infertility one partner's reproductive system is flawed and the other partner is fertile enough to reproduce given a more fertile partner.

This dilemma is the root of much angst on the part of less fertile partners—particularly for those who personally feel a strong reaction to the idea of losing their genetic continuity or the pregnancy/birth experience. Such people, while grieving, may test their spouse's commitment to them by suggesting divorce, by insisting on plunging into the use of donor gametes, and so on, suggesting these not necessarily because they sincerely want them, but instead creating challenges which dare the spouse to bail out.

In truth, fertile partners of infertile people most often see themselves as infertile as well. Having made the commitment to a person they chose as a life and parenting partner, fertile partners, too, grieve the loss of their dreams and expectations. Even when they recognize immediately that they retain the option of expressing their fertility with a different reproductive partner (surrogate, semen donor, egg donor), fertile partners of infertile people must seriously address all of infertility's losses, recognizing that even in choosing an option which will prevent themselves from losing genetic continuity, the emotional and physical gratifications of a pregnancy experience and the parenting experience, they will still give up a dreamed for, jointly conceived child.

Concerned about their spouses' battered self esteem, the majority of fertile partners indeed choose to render themselves infertile, too, electing to become childfree or to adopt when they come to understand how important this loss of fertility is to their partner. And the majority of infertile people fail to recognize the significance of such a decision, which, when acknowledged as a sacrificial gift to one's partner, might be the greatest self esteem restorer of all.

That year was the worst of Abby's life. After many years of encouraging infertility testing and treatments, she and Alan were hit with a bombshell: the most recent surgery had not only failed, but her tubes were ruined forever. For several reasons IVF was not an option. Adoption was an option they had already talked about and agreed to pursue, but it would be a long time, they knew, before they became parents that way. Though Abby really wanted to be a parent, she also wanted to be able to give her husband a child, not so much for the pregnancy experience, but because they had dreamed so long about their funny blended baby.

Abby descended into a dark depression that lasted months and months. As she slowly emerged, the sky was brightened by encouraging news about adoption. They threw themselves into that and were thrilled beyond belief when their child arrived a couple of years after that final diagnosis.

As engrossed as they were in parenting, as delighted as Abby was to mother this particular child and not another, a piece of her continued to mourn. She mourned for her body, which didn't work the way it was supposed to. She felt ugly, unattractive, defective. She felt guilty that her husband felt he had to stick with her. Nothing Alan could say seemed to make it any better.

Until one day over five years after the end of treatment, when Abby and Alan were thinking about a second child, Abby attended a RESOLVE conference and heard a male therapist talk about how men grieve differently from women, often silently. Something (she was never sure what) clicked. She went home and talked at length with Alan, a man who finds it hard to share his feelings.

That conversation was startling. No message could ever have been more self esteem enhancing or more important to their marriage. Alan told Abby how carefully he had thought through all of those offers and threats of divorce from years before and how frightening they had been for him. What he wanted, he told her (once again, and for the thousandth time, but this time she heard) was not fertility, but Abby. For him the thought of losing Abby as his wife had been more terrifying than the thought of losing his fertility.

"I've wondered many times," says Abby, "why I couldn't have understood that earlier. We both wanted our fertility, and we wanted it together, but beneath it all what we each wanted most was the other, and in our badly communicated grief we almost lost it all."

What is most important here? Sometimes we forget that it was the marriage that came first and the love we felt for each other that led us to decide to try to add children to our family of two. Vision tends to blur when you're bobbling along on that out-of-control conveyor belt.

Get off! Recommit to one another before deciding how you are going to proceed in taking charge of your infertility.

Dealing with Family and Friends

In a long and beautiful essay titled "Grandchildfree" in the Winter '92-'93 issue of the newsletter of RESOLVE of Washington State Barbara Kastner Roundy writes

> Of all my failures in life, there is none that has cut as deep or left as lasting a scar as the failure of a daughter to produce children. Motherhood is an experience that can link mothers and daughters together in a very special bond. It is difficult for me to let go of that expectation. There was such joy in anticipating the happiness that my child and my mother could bring to each other...
> Infertility can make us feel very isolated and alone. But in fact, our infertility directly involves those closest to us, especially, for many of us, our parents. They may be attempting to cope with their own losses while providing support for us. Infertility is a loss that affects an entire family. By understanding that this is a shared loss, we may find the support we need.

You and I know that it isn't easy to be infertile. In fact, that may be the understatement of the century. Infertility is very hard work—work from which there seem to be no evenings and weekends off, no vacation, not even a real end to the job in sight much of the time. I well remember the period of time when nearly anything and everything could remind me of the loss I was feeling and move me in the span of an instant to fury, to terror, or to tears.

But, then, it isn't easy to be the friend or relative of a couple dealing with impaired fertility either, and, having come out the other side of this long dark tunnel, I feel a responsibility to play devil's advocate on behalf of the people whose lives touch yours. Infertile people tend to be moody, swinging in two week cycles of anticipatory hope followed by crashing despair. They tend to find events that make other people feel excited and celebratory—events like baby showers, a christening or a bris, Mother's Day and Father's Day, little kids' birthday parties, culturally child-centered holidays like Christmas, Chanukah, Easter, Halloween—uncomfortable and even unpleasant.

The couple who is absorbed in a course of testing and treatment can often be pretty inwardly focused. Calendars which record a daily basal body temperature and are punctuated with doctor's appointments, days to begin and end medication, a schedule for intercourse, lab dates, etc., don't leave much room for social engagements and just plain fun.

Sometimes it seems as if the infertile couple is the rain on everybody else's parade, the sore spot that must be nursed and treated gingerly by the family at the expense of their own ability to be spontaneously joyful.

But let's face facts. How much did you know about infertility before you faced it yourself? Not much, I'll bet. Your friends and family are at that point now. Unless you educate them you can't expect them to understand your frustrations. They have, after all, been exposed to the very same cultural expectations as have you, and, if you'll remember, you were somewhat surprised by your infertility at first.

You probably tended to deny it for a while because the idea was frightening. Well, it frightens your mom, too. She had been expecting to be a grandma. So she says the first thing that comes to her mind, "Relax, honey, you're probably trying too hard."

You may have been a little embarrassed by the infertility at first when you didn't understand how common it was. You might yourself have felt that it was somewhat sexual in nature and expressed a little nervous humor about it. Is that what your brother is feeling when he cracks, "Hey, Bub, ya need a little advice on how it's done?"

Before you were educated, you, too, were likely to believe some of those old myths that have now come to be oh-so-much-more-than annoying:

Take a vacation.
Have a glass of wine before bedtime.
Try my doctor.
Adopt—then you'll get pregnant!
It's probably all part of God's plan.
If you <u>really</u> wanted a child you'd...

Come on, admit it, you've been guilty of insensitivity, too—back then, before you knew that infertility has emotional consequences rather than emotional causes, before you knew that it wasn't primarily a female condition, before you realized that one in five couples experiences it.

What changed you? Learning about it! That's the answer for your friends and family, too, and since you've probably learned from experience that the information they are likely to stumble across in the daily newspaper (that important medical journal) or in an interview on *Geraldo* or on *A Current Affair* (first rate consumer advocates) isn't what you want them to believe, you'll have to educate them yourselves.

There are many ways. Subscribe to your infertility group's newsletter for them. Give them a copy of my booklet *Understanding: A Guide to Impaired Fertility for Family and Friends* or RESOLVE's brochure for friends and family, or *How Can I Help?* from Merle Bombardieri and Diane Clapp. Take these significant others with you to an educational meeting or to a consumer group's symposium.

If you decide to pursue adoption, send them Pat Holmes' *Supporting an Adoption* or Linda Bothun's *When Friends Ask about Adoption*. Definitely include a subscription to A.F.A.'s *OURS: The Magazine for Adoptive Families* on your holiday shopping list, and consider *FACE Facts* or *News of FAIR* or *Adopted Child* or *Adoptnet* or *Roots and Wings*. Perhaps you could subscribe to several of these for yourself and pass them along to different friends and relatives.

In the back of the booklet *Understanding: A Guide to Impaired Fertility for Family and Friends* (Perspectives Press, 1983), I provided a list of twelve do's and don't's for caring others to follow in order to provide support for an infertile couple.

1. Do be ready to listen when one or the other partner or both need to talk. Don't, however, offer unsolicited advice unless you are absolutely sure both that your advice is

factual and needed and that you are prepared for the possibility of being seen as a meddler.

2. Do be sensitive. Infertility is a very personal issue and is very important to most couples whom it affects. Don't joke about it or minimize it in any way.

3. Do let the couple know that you realize that infertility can be a difficult problem and that you care about them.

4. Do be patient. The infertile couple's two week cycles of hope followed by disappointment may bring mood swings.

5. Do be flexible. At some points couples will find child-centered activities welcome and will want to be involved. At other times they may need to be allowed to isolate themselves. Don't impose your own behavioral expectations on them.

6. Do be realistic. Don't continue to deny the problem or its diagnosis in an attempt to be kind or optimistic. Support the decision to take time out from treatment or to stop it entirely.

7. Do be supportive. Having satisfied yourself that the couple has access to expert medical care as it is defined by a support and advocacy organization, don't impugn their decision making abilities by implying that you know a better doctor. Don't put down the couple's chosen treatment or alternative.

8. Do be truthful. Don't try to hide your own pregnancy or that of another friend or family member out of "kindness." Instead respect the infertile couple's need to be told as others are learning of it and try to acknowledge, privately, that you know that the pregnancy may be difficult for them at times and you are willing to be understanding of this.

9. Do be an advocate. As you hear other family members and friends react to the infertile couple insensitively, educate these other "carers" to the pain of infertility.

10. Do let the couple know if you are finding it difficult to know what to say rather than saying nothing at all when you can't find the right words.

11. Do remember that infertility is a highly individual condition. When, how, and if the infertile couple reacts to its issues and stages will depend largely on their own circumstances. It is not at all abnormal for some reactions to be severe. These people are grieving.

12. Do recommend RESOLVE, IAAC and groups like them to the couple whom may not be aware of them. Consider as well that such volunteer-run and donation-supported organizations need your financial support as well as the memberships of infertile couples and the professionals who work with them if they are to continue to be able to provide a full range of services.

But having served as your advocate, I'd like to suggest that there are things that your family should be able to expect from you, too:

1. **Information**. People can't be sensitive about something they don't understand. Each time that you diplomatically point out a painful error that a friend, a family member, a medical person, a member of the clergy has made in referring to you or to infertility, you increase the likelihood that this person's sensitivity level will be raised and such errors will not be repeated.

2. **Sensitivity**. Just as you expect that your family members should be sensitive to your pain, you must realize that your infertility may be painful to them, too. Parents, in particular, often tend to feel guilty that they may have done something to contribute to your medical problem. As well, they shared your assumptions that grandchildren would be born who shared the family genes. Just as you mourn the potential loss of your genetic children, so do they. They will, however, feel guilty about publicly mourning such a loss, realizing that you may interpret their mourning to mean that you have failed them and thus adding to your discomfort. Mourners need one another. Be sensitive and

open to each other's pain. Understand, too, how very difficult it will be for your friends and family to enjoy their own pregnancies if you have not given them permission to do so.

3. **Patience**. Your friends and family are at least one step behind you and your spouse in resolving infertility's impact on your lives together. You and your partner will have spent a great deal of private time making decisions before you announce them publicly. Be prepared for the fact that when you announce your decisions, particularly controversial ones, your family will not yet have had the time to adjust to them as you have. They may react with shock, with fear, even with revulsion. They must be given time to adjust, and you must support them in this adjustment, just as you wish them to support you in your decision. Beyond this, it is important to accept that fertile people cannot ever be expected to fully understand such a profound experience as is infertility.

4. **Openness**. Quietly gathering each mistake, each carelessly hurtful remark, each uncomfortable reaction from family members and friends, and socking them away in a gunnysack to be dumped into the middle of Thanksgiving dinner is not fair. No one can be expected to change behavior if not made aware that the behavior is causing pain. Use private moments to sensitize your loved ones.

5. **Clarity**. As you work to sensitize and inform, keep your discussions simple, brief, and factual whenever possible. Most listeners, not absorbed in the daily pain of infertility as are you, are unable to absorb or deal with the heaviness of your situation all at once.

6. **Responsiveness**. Sometimes the people who love you can be a bit more objective about your situation than can you. Once you have educated a friend about infertility you should be able to assume that she will no longer offer advice unless she has thought it over carefully and is prepared to accept a negative reaction to it. Consider that sometimes educated friends who offer opinions may be right. Blinded by your own obsession with a fertility

impairment, you may need to take a step away in order to see clearly. Give some thought, at least, to the opinions of the infertility-educated people who love you.

Yes, you deserve to have your family understand and support your experience with infertility, and when they can't or won't it's <u>perfectly fine</u> to avoid baby showers and child-centered holiday celebrations for a while. In fact, that is often the healthiest thing you can do in finding ways to regain a measure of control.

The challenge is in avoiding the painful situation in a way that does not cause you additional pain or embarrassment. There are some ways to do this

1. Create a conflict in your schedule. Miss Manners reminds us that you are under no obligation to explain what it is, just offer your regrets and don't allow yourself to be sucked into explanations. This works particularly well for showers and christenings, etc., but is more difficult to do for holidays. Consider allowing yourself the privilege of leaving town altogether for the holidays, offering your family the exciting news that you've arranged a special get-away weekend for yourselves without mentioning your infertility-related holiday discomfort at all.

2. Enlist the help of a sensitive friend or family member to serve as your advocate with persistently snoopy and insensitive others. Ask this person to have a quiet heart-to-heart with the potentially offended or offensive host or the guest of honor, enlisting them to become part of your sensitivity team as well.

Finally, understand that some people will never respond well. No matter how carefully you try to educate them, no matter how many copies of *Understanding* you pass out, a few people in your sphere of intimacy are likely to remain insensitive. Don't continue to beat yourself up about this by trying over and over again. The best method for coping with these few, no matter how closely they are related to you, is by avoiding them.

RESOURCES

Enhancing Communication between Partners and with Others

How Can I Help? A Handbook of Practical Suggestions for Family and Friends of Couples Going through Infertility by Diane Clapp and Merle Bombardieri (Lexington, MA: Fertility Counseling Associates, 1991) Order from Wellspring Counseling Center, 33 Bedford St #18, Lexington MA 12173 at $7.25 postpaid)

Understanding: A Guide to Impaired Fertility for Family and Friends by Patricia Irwin Johnston (Indianapolis: Perspectives Press, rev. 1990)

* *You Just Don't Understand: Women and Men in Conversation* by Deborah Tannen, Ph.D. (New York: Balantine Books, 1990). Clearly points out the differences in communication styles and interpretations between men and women, offering manageable techniques for improving communication between opposite sexed partners.

* *Getting the Love You Want: A Guide for Couples* by Harville Hendrix, Ph.D. (New York: Henry Holt, 1988). Practical information on learning to defuse power struggles in relationships by letting go of self-defeating behavior, communicating more accurately and sensitively, and focusing your attention on meeting your own and your partner's needs.

* *Men are from Mars, Women Are from Venus: A Practical Guide for Improving Communication and Getting What You Want in Your Relationship* by John Gray (New York: HarperCollins, May, 1992).

* Denotes materials also available on tape

Chapter 3

CREATING A PLAN

Every successful journey is guided by fixed stars.
Bill Clinton

Having learned to communicate effectively you can now put what you've learned to practical use. In order to conquer an enemy you would develop a battle plan. To manage a business, one would develop a business plan. Dealing with infertility lends itself well to similar strategic planning.

If we are to meet infertility head on, we need a plan of action. And a plan of action demands that we make lots of decisions. The process of decision making involves gathering information, examining long term implications, prioritizing desires, choosing among alternatives, allocating resources, and committing to a course of action. No matter what decision needs to be made, the process is the same.

Each of us has a personal style of decision making, and that style is related to the ways we communicate and the ways we deal with loss as discussed in earlier chapters. Some of us may be more inclined to want to listen to our heads and to try to deal with everything in a logical, straightforward fashion (some people call this left brain thinking.) Others of us experience our emotions so powerfully that we make decisions primarily with our hearts, sometimes not even trying to apply logic (you may see this referred to as right brain thinking.)

The best of decisions, however, are made with both the heart and the head, so that when one partner is more emotional than the other, or when one partner would prefer to squelch emotion and deal with everything intellectually it really is important for both partners to open themselves to listening to one another, and respecting the importance of the views that come from both the head and from the heart.

Making good decisions is a skill that can be learned and applied to both the personal and professional aspects of our lives with amazingly productive results. If you feel that you are in need of some help in learning to make effective decisions, the two of you may wish to do some reading, attend seminars, or listen to some tapes together to build your decision making skills. New materials in this area seem to come out regularly and often. Over the years I've found Theodore Isaac Rubin's work helpful and I have gained insight from Stephen Covey and Spencer Johnston, but as I write (autumn, 1993) the two books (also available on tape) I would most heartily recommend for those who wish to build their decision making skills are *The Confident Decision Maker: How to Make the Right Business and Personal Decisions Every Time* by Roger Dawson (New York: William Morrow & Co, 1993) and *Woulda, Coulda, Shoulda: Overcoming Regrets, Mistakes, and Missed Opportunities* by Dr. Arthur Freeman and Rose DeWolf (New York: HarperCollins, 1989.)

Motivation, says Dawson, comes when the pain of doing nothing exceeds the pain of moving on.[1] In Dawson's experience, great decision makers have nine traits in common. They have a high tolerance for ambiguity (and what could be more ambiguous than making selections about treatment or lifestyle options in infertility?) They have a well-ordered sense of priorities (in this case because they've seriously examined the losses infertility represents to them.) They are good listeners (and making decisions with a partner demands careful listening!) They are good at building consensus. They avoid stereotypes (a tremendous danger when dealing with the myth-filled and rapidly-changing world of infertility treatment or the various traditional and partial adoption alternatives.) They always remain resilient. They are comfortable with both hard and soft (statistical and emotional) input. They are realistic about cost and difficulty (a real challenge with infertility treatment!) They avoid what Dawson calls "decision minefields" (such as "if experts tell you, it must be true" and "if the person pushing it seems enthusiastic, he must be convinced he can make it work," etc.)[2] In his book, tapes, and workshops Roger

---

1. Dawson, Roger; The Confident Decision Maker (New York: William Morrow & Co, 1993) p. 55

2. Dawson, op cit; Chapter 12.

Dawson offers his audience specific skills and inspiration for becoming a confident decision maker.

Arthur Freeman, a cognitive therapist and co-author of *Woulda, Coulda, Shoulda: Overcoming Regrets, Mistakes, and Missed Opportunities*, helps his readers to understand how the very way they process thoughts and information can influence their ability to cope with losses in their lives. This book is of particular value in helping us understand that "resolution" is to a large extent a shift in attitude, so that it is something over which we do indeed have control.

Couples feeling fearful about what to do next, or those who feel stuck in an impasse may find these materials helpful before moving into the laborious and emotion-intensive process of building a plan.

The planning process outlined in this book has been designed so that it could be used by people to examine the infertility experience at any or all of the points in a series of stages:

1.   Beginning to deal with the testing and treatment process and deciding what courses of action to pursue from a list that includes a variety of standard treatment alternatives.

2.   Re-evaluating treatment after basic testing has been done, medical issues identified, and standard treatment has not been successful, in order to decide whether or not to pursue more costly, invasive or experimental procedures.

3.   Re-evaluating the success of treatment, acknowledging the possibility that it may not result in the conception and birth of a child genetically related to both partners, and beginning to explore facts and feelings about options beyond treatment: gamete adoption (donor insemination, egg donation, surrogacy), traditional adoption in all of its variations, or embracing the option of child free living.

4.   Deciding to end traditional treatment and to aggressively pursue an alternative choice: gamete adoption (will require more medical assistance), adoption, or child free living.

What this means is that couples who are introduced to this planning process early in their infertility experience will probably use this planning format once in its most complicated and time consuming form, and, having spent the time to evaluate their feelings and shared them with a partner, to assess and inventory personal resources, and to set a general plan for themselves, they would be in a position to come back to the process again and again in order to make other decisions or the refine the plan. Most couples find that subsequent opportunities to use the system take significantly less time and energy than does the first complicated round—a set up round.

No matter where you <u>think</u> you are in the series of four stages when you pick up this book, please consider taking the time to go back to the first step to review the decision making process at each stage so that you can be confident in the future that you have fully explored and made decisions about all of the options that are open to you. Despite the fact that doing so will be time consuming and may be emotionally difficult, you will be glad, later, that you disciplined yourself in this way.

Humans have a tendency to reflect on decisions made earlier and to wonder if they made the right ones. "If only's" are a common part of our looking backward with 20/20 hindsight. But decisions properly made can last us a life time. When we give our decisions careful thought and focused energy, we can look back on them confidently, knowing that <u>at that time</u> and <u>under those circumstances</u> we made the very best possible decisions. Because infertility will always be a significant part of the people each of you are and become, it is important that you feel comfortable and confident about the decisions you make along the way. For these reasons, the significant expenditure of time and energy required to complete this process will be well worth it!

The facts are these: once upon a time you decided to have a baby, and you expected that to be a relatively simple feat. But then you faced infertility, and that earlier decision to have a baby was complicated by an entirely new set of facts. In light of those facts, you have been placed in the position of needing to make that decision to have a baby all over again—perhaps several times.

Do you still want to become parents if it means exposing your bodies to potent drug therapies and invasive surgical procedures? Do you still want to become parents if it means borrowing money or risking savings put aside for the future in order to pursue treatments with odds of less than 50% success? Do you still want to be parents if in order to do so you need to be prepared to parent several children born at once? Do you still want to be parents if the route to doing so involves arranging to use the reproductive powers or the genetic material of someone outside of your marriage? Do you still want to be parents if it means that the child you parent will not be genetically connected to you? Do you still want to be parents if it will take years more to accomplish? Do you still want to be parents if it means having others determine whether or when or to whom you can be? Do you still want to be parents???

The process described here can help you to decide. But first, a pair of cautions. First, understand that this process is a skeletal format for decision-making rather than a road map. Because infertility testing and treatment changes rapidly, it would be impossible to formulate all of the questions to deal with all of the contingencies that will likely arise during the course of your family planning process. Instead, what I hope to do is show you how to go about predicting the questions you need to have answered, gathering the data you need, following a process for evaluating that data, communicating directly with your partner about these issues, and then deciding together on a specific course of action.

Second, keep in mind at all times that, even when it feels as if you are on an out-of-control conveyor belt, you are not . Each step in the testing and treatment processes is a separate and complete step. Though many around you (including, and perhaps even most especially, the professionals) will simply assume that you will want to go on and on and on until you have a child in your home to parent, in order to take charge of your infertility you must truly believe that each step is self contained and that each new step demands a separate decision. It is always OK to stop, whether it is to rest, to reevaluate, or to change directions entirely.

If you begin with a willingness to remain aware and in control, with a belief that each step in the process is separate and unique, with a respect for one another's feelings as well as opinions, you will be much more likely to feel successful in dealing with fertility impairment, no matter what the ultimate outcome of your medical treatment.

My planning process involves several separate steps:

1. Personal reflection.

2. Sharing your discoveries about yourself with your partner.

3.   Inventorying personal resources—time, money, emotional energy and physical capacity.

4.   Gathering information about each of the options you find of enough interest to merit exploration.

5.   Discussing ways to blend your separate needs and wishes in order to select a course of action which does not compromise the needs or values of either of you and represents either a consensus opinion or a synergistic decision—a decision that you both see as better than either of you would have reached alone.

6.   Building a detailed plan for pursuing that course of action—developing strategies, assigning tasks, allocating resources, setting a time for evaluation.

7.   Following the plan by pursuing the course of action.

8.   Evaluating and adjusting the plan as needed.

To gain control of your infertility for the first time, the process cannot be done in a few hours. Ideally, in fact, it will take a number of weeks. Each of you will spend several hours separately doing some personal homework (reflection) and then follow that by sharing what you have recognized about yourself with your partner. This process should open communication between you which will help you to decide what avenues you wish to explore together.

The goal of those early stages is to prepare to join your partner for one or more long retreat weekends where you will use the data gathering you have already done to create a personal plan (step six). Your overall plan will be one developed after investigation, discussion and compromise. It will allow each of you to feel that the relationship continues to be in balance and that neither of you "wins" at the expense of the other's "loss."

But What If We Can't Agree?—Dealing with an Impasse

Before we even begin the process of decision making, let's directly address what I am certain is your greatest fear: What if you can't agree? What if it feels as if your individual needs and desires are in such direct conflict that there is no route to compromise and consensus?

For many couples it is this very fear that prevents them from communicating directly with one another and leads them slog on through too many years of treatment or to drift aimlessly through too many years of just waiting. The underlying fear is that without clear agreement the marriage itself is in jeopardy, and for some people this fear tends to lead them to acquiesce to options with which they are not really comfortable.

For the decision making process described here to be successful, each of you must agree to lay aside these fears and to be completely straightforward and honest with one another. In return you each must also agree to accept and validate the other's initial feelings without judgment, without argument, and, (hardest to promise, perhaps) without panic.

If you find that you are at an impasse—that your needs are in direct conflict and that together you are unable to see a route to compromise—there are at least two important things to try. First, give yourselves some time and space. Pause to catch your breaths and recall some of the important things you've already covered. You are each unique individuals with different backgrounds and influences. You cannot feel identically. Your very maleness and femaleness have contributed to those differences in needs and feelings. You chose one another to be life partners both because you shared values and dreams and because there were things about each of you that complemented the other's strengths and weaknesses. You are committed to one another and to finding a solution to the problem you face together. The issues you are dealing with are profound, emotional, and life changing. One or the other of you may find that you are experiencing a visceral and wrenching reaction which is, purely and simply, grief. Working through a grief reaction cannot be rushed. The most important thing the two of you can do if either or both of you feels temporarily overcome by the confusion or negativism of grief is to agree to postpone further discussion and planning for an agreed upon length of time-usually several months. During that time try to give yourselves a total time out, feeling confident that on some future date that you have mutually agreed upon, you will examine once again whether it is time to pursue the need to make clear decisions about future family plans.

Second, but no less important than allowing one another time, you may find that several sessions with a mediator or counselor will be valuable. Unfortunately, choosing such a counselor is not always easy. Many human service professionals are not well informed about infertility issues. You may wish to start with someone known to you already—a counselor you have seen for other reasons, someone you have heard good things about, your clergyperson. If you do not know of such a resource or if you find those known to you to be unfamiliar with or insensitive to the unique characteristics of the infertility experience, ask the closest infertility support group for a referral.

And so, let us begin...

Reflecting

The decision making process begins with several days or weeks of self reflection and information gathering. Step one is to be done independently of one another. Find a quiet spot away from your partner where you can spend a significant amount of time privately examining the six losses we talked about before as accompanying the infertility experience and your feelings about them:

Infertility's Potential Losses
1. Loss of control
2. Loss of individual genetic continuity
3. Loss of a jointly conceived child
4. Loss of the physical expectations you have about the pregnancy experience itself and about feeling the power to impregnate
5. Loss of the emotional expectations about a shared pregnancy, birth, breast-feeding experience
6. Loss of the opportunity to parent

Where and when to do this is a matter of personal choice. While some couples prefer to do this separately but at the same time as a first step during a retreat weekend and then to share the results immediately with one another, most couples have found it more useful for each partner to accomplish this step days or weeks before their retreat, at a time personally chosen and unknown to their partner, and then to give themselves at least a few days afterwards to ruminate further upon their self discoveries before sharing them with their spouse. Consider these options—reflecting about infertility's losses days or weeks before a retreat or as a first step in a retreat—and decide together which you feel would be most useful for the two of you.

During reflection the task at hand is yours and yours alone. Without trying to predict how your partner might personally react to these losses, and being especially careful to try to avoid worrying about how you feel your partner would react to your own feelings about these losses and their alternatives, think seriously about infertility's six potential losses and try hard to determine how you might rank them as to their importance to you and to you alone.

Without considering at all the physical realities of your personal infertility diagnosis, ask yourself, "If I had the power to avoid personally experiencing one or more of these losses, which would I choose to avoid?"

Try ranking the losses from one to six (the first is the most significant loss, the sixth is the least significant loss). Then assign a weight to each loss using a familiar one to ten scale, where one represents something of little importance to you and ten represents strong feelings of importance.

You may be wondering why, if you've already ranked the losses from most important to least important, you would need also to assign a weight to each of those losses. In fact, for some couples this step may prove somewhat cumbersome. But this step can be helpful to both emotional decision makers and intellectual decision makers. People whose personal style is rational and logical and so may have tended to try to ignore or bury their gut feelings about infertility, this step is an important part of fully understanding the depth of feeling you and your partner each experience about each of these loss issues so that you can creatively work on compromise and consensus plans for your family. On the other hand people who have been caught up in the emotional pain and loss of infertility may find that in forcing themselves to give structure and logic to the process they are better able to see hope among the options and alternatives available to them.

Let me share an example of how this ranking and weighting system might work on an issue other than infertility. Following is a table which shows how my husband Dave and I might rank the appeal of certain vegetables against one another.

Vegetable	Pat's ranking	Dave's ranking
broccoli	2	3
corn on the cob	4	1
peas	3	2
potatoes	1	4
beets	5	5

Now, looking at this list which has only been ranked, only one thing is entirely clear: Dave and I both like beets the least of the five vegetables, and we don't appear to feel similarly about any others! If we can't agree on what vegetables we like, how on earth will we plan our menus?? Oh my!

But, when Dave and I assign weights to our feelings about each of these individual vegetables on a scale of 0 to 10 (0 means we can't stand the vegetable, 10 means we love it), we have a great deal more information.

P's ranked list	weight	D's ranked list	weight
1 potatoes	10	1 corn on the cob	10
2 broccoli	8	2 peas	8
3 peas	7	3 broccoli	8
4 corn on the cob	5	4 potatoes	5
5 beets	0	5 beets	0

This ranked <u>and</u> weighted list gives us significantly more information with which to work. What we find is that Dave and I will eliminate beets from our household menu (actually, each of us would have liked to have been able to weight beets a -3). Because corn is his favorite vegetable, I eat it fairly frequently, and because potatoes are mine, he eats them more often than he would on his own. But the broccoli and the peas are more in the middle for each of us. We each like them, and so at home we eat them fairly often—more often than either of us gets to eat our favorite vegetable from this list. On the other hand, we have since neither of us actively dislikes the other's favorite, we have found ways to compromise with them, too. My objection to corn on the cob is its messiness, so I cook it and cut my own serving off the cob. He likes some potato dishes better than others, and I serve these occasionally. When we go out to eat, each of us tends to choose that favorite vegetable that we don't get enough of at home. In communicating in this way, we each become "winners" in choosing what we will eat.

Ranking and weighting the losses accompanying infertility is significantly more important to planning your future together than is ranking and weighting your feelings about vegetables, of course, but this exercise can help you understand what can be accomplished with open discussion and a willingness to accommodate and to compromise.

Noelle and Ben really didn't want to bother to do the ranking and weighting. Initially it seemed cumbersome. But Noelle and Ben had read a lot of how-to-get-pregnant" and "new technology" books, and they were willing to take a chance on the process in hopes of naming the fears they had experienced throughout their three years of unsuccessful attempts to expand their family. The tears that began to flow while Noelle was pondering the loss of the emotional expectations she had about being pregnant made it all quite clear. She wanted the nine months of hopes and dreams as the baby grew. She wanted the experience to share with her sisters and friends who had given birth. The subsequent discussion with Ben led to an agreement that using donor eggs would be a viable option for them, but that surrogacy would not. In making the attempt to logically state the pros and cons of each loss, the issues had become clearer to Noelle and Ben, and as a result, so had the solutions.

As you are asked to weight your reactions to the losses you ranked, do you find yourself feeling equally or almost equally strongly about more than one loss? Or do you find yourself ranking only one loss high on the scale in terms of both its impact on you and its importance to you? As you think about your growing up expectations about family building and being a parent, about the messages you received from your own family and the culture in which you grew up about connectedness and parenting, you may be surprised to discover how deeply you feel about some of these losses. The depth of the feelings you experience in reaction to certain of infertility's losses may exaggerate your usual pattern of dealing with loss. You or your partner may very well find yourself grieving.

Though in years past many people dealing with infertility recognized that they were experiencing grief, often they could not quite identify what it was they were grieving. Identifying the cause of grief can be valuable in that it helps one to focus, but identifying the cause of grief does not eliminate the loss that triggers it or put an end to the pain which must be worked through.

It is imperative that you be honest with yourself in completing this step. Don't try to guess how you think your partner will rank and weigh each loss. Don't consider at this point how what you already know about your own relative fertility or your partner's will impact on your choices and rankings. Simply be gut honest here in ranking and weighting how you _feel_ about these potential losses.

Having completed this step and feeling clearer about your own needs, your own values, your own dreams and how they have been challenged by infertility, each of you will be able to think more clearly about four general groups of choices which are open to couples who are dealing with a fertility impairment. And because you will have put "labels" on what for many was previously a rather nebulous set of uncomfortable feelings, you will be able to communicate your needs more effectively to your partner.

The Range of Choices for Planning about Infertility

1. Continuing treatment to the point of having tried every possible option.

2. Using donated eggs or sperm to allow one of you to maintain a genetic connection.

3. Adopting.

4. Embracing a childfree lifestyle.

Choosing options for you and your spouse is a task to be accomplished together, but it will be helpful if, before you discuss them together, each of you has given some careful thought to your personal reactions to each option so that you will have a clear idea of why you feel strongly positively or negatively about any of them. Ask yourself these questions:

1. In light of what you've learned about yourself and your reactions to the potential losses of infertility, how important do you feel it is to you to learn more about further treatment options which would help you to conceive and birth a child genetically related to both you and your partner?

2. Now, while you are still alone, think about the options available through assisted reproduction—using the donated gametes of another man or woman; or hiring a surrogate to carry a child conceived with the husband's sperm and the wife's egg, the husband's sperm and the surrogate's egg, the husband's sperm and donated egg, donated sperm and the wife's egg, donated sperm and donated egg? Are you able to allow yourself to explore these options given what you've identified about your personal needs?

3. What about traditional adoption, whether independent or agency, infant or older child, domestic or international? Is it possible to love, nurture, parent a child not genetically related to you? Do you feel that you might want to explore

any of these options further as an alternative to not becoming a parent at all?

4.   And finally, what about the option of not parenting at all in a permanent way but instead finding alternative outlets for your interest in nurturing? Given what you now know about yourself, are you willing to learn more about and discuss with your partner the idea of electing to follow a childfree lifestyle?

Building a Plan—The Retreat Weekend

After you have given one another plenty of time for reflecting, setting aside a weekend for the purpose of making some careful decisions and formulating a preliminary plan is a worthwhile investment in your family's future. The logistics require your willingness and commitment to giving undivided attention to planning to take charge of infertility. You will need a minimum of 48 hours for this phase of your planning process.

Your time will be most constructively spent without the interruptions of normal routine, so many couples have found it useful to plan such a weekend away from home—camping, in a hotel, in a friend's borrowed vacation home, etc. If your finances do not allow for escape, or if you feel that the pull of an escape location might distract you from the task at hand, your retreat can be successful from home base. Simply be sure that you tell your family and friends and employers (no fair taking call that weekend!) that you have plans for the weekend, hide your cars (so that no one will know that you are home,) unplug your doorbell (so that you won't be tempted to answer the door to friends who drop by unexpectedly,) turn your phone's ringer off and use an answering machine (with the screening feature turned off) to take messages for you.

Whether you are staying at home or leaving for your retreat, free yourselves of all normal weekend "must-do's." Change the laundry, marketing, cleaning and lawn care schedules for the week. Better yet, reward yourselves and one another by hiring these jobs out for this once. Give careful thought to meal planning for the weekend. If you will be staying at home, do all necessary shopping in advance and be sure to plan one or more meals out. You'll need the break. Plan to include time in the 48 hour retreat weekend for exercise and/or entertainment. Plan some walks or a jog together, take in a carefully chosen escapist movie or play or a concert (this isn't the weekend to rent videos like *Immediate Family* or *Steel Magnolias*). If the location retains complete privacy, so that neither of you will be exposed to the observation of others if emotions rise to the surface, some of the talking you will do during the retreat weekend can be done while you are sitting on the bank of a river fishing, walking through a woods, lying on a quiet beach. Holding such intimate conversation in busy public places (city beaches, park benches, while walking down busy downtown streets or through a weekend art fair) is not recommended.

You will need paper and pencils, books and tapes and articles that each of you has already read and wishes to share with the other, staples to ward off the munchies, perhaps some tapes or CD's that you mutually agree are stress-relieving without being sleep-inducing.

This decision making process will be hard work, both physically and emotionally draining. Take breaks as often as either of you feels a need.

Sharing

Many couples plan to make this task the first step in a retreat, while some do it beforehand. At the very least, for this step you need to choose a time and place where you can be uninterrupted for at least two hours.

Hand your partner a sheet of paper on which you have listed only your own ranking and weighting of infertility's losses. Examine one another's lists and then compare them.

Of course it would be ideal if you found that your lists were identical. How much easier making your next choices would be! But, as you will understand from our having discussed the many factors which make individuals so different when responding to the same crisis, you will likely find that your lists differ.

Discuss the differences. If your lists are ranked similarly, you will move quickly from this step to examining specific treatment options or family planning alternatives. If your lists are quite different, your goal will be to search for areas of agreement as you seek to compromise and build consensus about where you will be going together. Expect this discussion to produce deep feelings in each of you.

Often couples discover that what seems like a clear solution to one partner in reality enhances the other's pain. Let's consider some quick examples of situations like this.

Miguel's low sperm count makes his impregnating Sondra unlikely. Sondra, however, seems to be normally fertile. To Sondra a clear, quick, cheap, private solution to the problem is donor insemination. She even suggests that perhaps Miguel's brother would be willing to be the donor so that at least the baby would share Miguel's genes. She is shocked and even angry to hear that Miguel doesn't immediately agree to this solution which even respects Miguel's genetic pool. Sondra has not taken into consideration how important his own ability to impregnate his wife is to Miguel. If Miguel is to seriously consider this option for building their family, Sondra will need to give him time and space to mourn this significant loss and will need to be respectful of his ultimate decision, which may be that this option is rejected and another compromise route to parenthood is selected.

Bill and Sharon want a family, but Sharon's endometriosis has not responded to treatment. Bill has had it with trying to get pregnant. He's ready to adopt and doesn't understand why Sharon is resisting. But Sharon's endometriosis is incredibly painful. Besides being a reproductive problem, it is taking over other aspects of her life as well. While Bill is focused on putting the infertility behind them, Sharon can't yet see beyond solving the medical problem which would continue to consume her. It's too early for Sharon to consider adoption. The endometriosis needs to be managed first.

The answers won't necessarily come easily, and at this stage it is likely to be unreasonable to expect that you will see only one path of choice. You will need to do a great deal of talking, questioning, sharing. If each of you feels able to keep an open mind during these early explorations and is willing to try to reject nothing out of hand; if each of you will allow yourself to hear about options, to try them on and wear them for a while, to explore them with your partner before deciding whether or not this is an option you care to pursue together; you are almost ready to gather information about all the alternatives which you have not agreed to dismiss. But first, you need to understand the resources available to you.

Inventorying Personal Resources

In creating a logistical plan for any purpose, an early step is taking an inventory of the resources available to be budgeted and expended in order to achieve a series of goals and objectives. Planning an assault on the infertility dragon is no different.

Resources at your disposal for this battle are all available in limited quantities and are for the most part nonrenewable, so they must be budgeted. Those resources are **time**, **money**, **emotional energy**, and **physical capacity**.

What you need to gather now is raw data about these resources. You'll organize the details during your strategic planning sessions.

Be aware as you begin this task that it is often emotionally difficult to accomplish this inventory, because listing these resources realistically often forces us to take out and carefully examine facts we may have been trying to deny or ignore, facts which may severely inhibit our ability to accomplish the goals we have initially identified as most important to us. This process of inventorying resources, then, may be another place where loss reactions are triggered. The inventory and subsequent discussions about it may clarify your assumptions or lead you in completely new directions in setting your goals and objectives.

 **Emotional Resources** are not concrete. They cannot be objectively measured. Emotional resources are affected by your ethical, religious, and moral response to an issue and can be assessed only through honest self examination and discussion between partners. Couples who have adequate outside support from family, friends, professionals or a group often find that their emotional reserves are increased as a result.

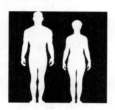 **Physical Resources** are measured by looking at the realities of your diagnosis, your age, and the prognosis for success in treatment. How this prognosis could be enhanced by seeking more specialized care is an important factor. You must also assess what physical effects various treatment options will have on your ability to manage other aspects of your day-to-day life. Your normal physical energy level and how you react to physical discomfort are factors, too.

 **Financial Resources** include your salary, your savings, and the sources from which you might borrow (financial institutions, family members, against life insurance, etc.)? Gather specific information about employee benefit options such as the limitations on health insurance plans which cover you, adoption benefits, etc. After treatment you must have money for raising a family and pursuing other life goals.

 **Time** must be assessed from both day-to-day and long term perspectives. Examine any restrictions imposed by your jobs (availability of flex time, medical leave, parental leave.) Consider how your ages might affect treatment (both physically and emotionally), your access to alternative parenting options, and your parenting ability over the years.

In the section describing some activities for you to do on a
a retreat weekend, you will be asked to "get real" and ask
yourselves some very difficult questions about this resource
inventory. Gathering realistic data is imperative to being able to do
this work.

Lars and Moira had found one another after
each had ended a first marriage of over ten years'
duration. Now in their mid 40s and in the fifth year
of a stable and loving relationship, they wanted very
much to have a baby together. They entered
treatment optimistic. But earlier life choices and life
experiences had vastly altered their resources for
reaching the goal of a shared pregnancy. The two
divorces had left each with meager savings.
(Financial resources were limited.) Moira's
physician had determined fairly quickly that she did
not respond favorably to stimulation of her ovaries
and the quality of the few eggs produced was poor
(Physical capacity was diminished.) They were open
to adoption but quickly found that their options for
infant adoption were hampered by the fact that they
were seen as "too old" by many agencies. (Time was
ticking away.) If it was a baby they wanted, their
options were limited: surrogacy, egg donation,
private adoption. Initially each option seemed
frighteningly radical, and perhaps even financially
unreachable, but Moira and Lars determined that
each deserved careful consideration. They had the
work for their retreat weekend cut out for them.

Information Gathering—Educating Yourselves

Having agreed on whether or not to rule out certain
options, you must obtain as much background information about
each option which remains open to you as you possibly can. So
that you can both feel confident that the final decision is mutually
satisfying, both members of a couple should take responsibility for
participating in the information gathering process. You will find
this an empowering experience, allowing you to regain an
important measure of control. If your partner will not agree to

take responsibility for some of this information gathering, stop the process and ask him or her to join you in some counseling sessions to determine what is causing the impasse.

In the chapters discussing various options which follow, you will find some specific current resources which may help you to gather information. But because treatments and options change almost daily, it is important that you learn where to go for the most up-to-date information no matter when you happen to pick up this book.

Information is available from a variety of sources. Books, tapes, fact sheets, magazine and professional journal articles, seminars and symposia are sources of information. For referral to the most current and accurate written resources on infertility and some information on adoption, contact both the nearest local chapter and the national office of RESOLVE, Inc. in the U.S. and Infertility Awareness Association in Canada. The Organization of Parents through Surrogacy (OPTS) can provide information and referral regarding various forms of surrogacy and donor insemination. For more specific information about various adoption options, your first stop should be Adoptive Families of America (AFA) and their local member groups. The American Fertility Society publishes patient booklets and pamphlets on a number of topics. For a nominal fee your local library can obtain nearly anything they do not carry through the interlibrary loan program. Hospitals and medical schools often make their libraries open to consumers for research. Your physician may be willing to have his staff do a computer search of professional literature on a particular topic for you.

Seminars and monthly meetings held by infertility and adoption support groups are another important source of information. Most RESOLVE and IAAC chapters periodically hold an infertility symposium (often, but not always, cosponsored with Serono Symposia) These are day-long events which offer a menu of presentations by medical, counseling, and social service professionals on most medical issues and treatments and some lifestyle alternatives. Similarly, in most major cities adoptive parent support groups sponsor adoption conferences or fairs. Occasionally you will even find that a university or community college offers a short-term continuing education course on infertility or adoption how-to issues.

Since these are often annual or biennial events, you may find that your own timing doesn't match that of the group. Don't despair! Frequently the sessions have been audio-taped and are available for borrowing or for purchase. Contact your local infertility support group or adoptive parents' group about this possibility. At the same time, it is also important to recognize that such opportunities are difficult to come by, and so to give yourself an added nudge to attend such an event when it is available even if the timing seems just a little off (your favorite team will always play another big game, your vacation can usually be adjusted) or the distance a bit annoying (a two hour drive may be a reasonable investment in order to obtain hard-to-come-by information.)

On a national level, Adoptive Families of America holds an annual two day conference for adoption-built families and prospective adopters featuring national experts in the field and has every session taped by von Ende Communications. AFA makes these tapes available through *OURS: The Magazine for Adoptive Families*. Von Ende Comm also tapes the biennial conferences of Indiana's Adoption Forum Coalition, the annual North American Conference on Adoptable Children, the conferences of Adoptive Parents Committee of New York and many others and maintains catalogs and subject specific lists of their available tapes. Contact Brus and Diane von Ende at 3211 Margaret Dr., Golden Valley MN 55422 (telephone 612-529-4493).

I often speak to couples who are reluctant to reach out to an advocacy group. The excuse most often reported is, "We're feeling fine. We don't want a support group." Such a reply reflects a misunderstanding of what adoptive parent groups and infertility organizations do. While I understand that many people do not wish to seek the support component of such groups, these groups offer much more than support.

Here, among a membership made up of consumers, are the real experts in a field—those whose personal experience with it has taught them how important it is to be well informed. Volunteer leaders of mutual support groups have made it their business to gather as much data as possible and to keep track of the frequent changes not just in their own communities but beyond them. Additionally, A.F.A., RESOLVE, I.A.A.C. and others are becoming more and more involved in legislative advocacy work on behalf of their constituents. RESOLVE's chapters have won the battle for mandated insurance benefits in several states already and have made it a priority to fight for coverage under any national health plan. A.F.A.'s advocates lobby on the national level, monitor state legislation, and connect families sharing similar legal concerns from around the country.

But of course, local groups, which are staffed by volunteers, tend to devote the majority of their time to the issues that are most important to those actually doing the volunteering. Sometimes this means that a group may appear on the surface to be more supportive of treatment than adoption, or more supportive of adoption than assisted reproductive technologies, or intimidated by or critical of childfree living. Usually this is more a perception than a reality, and the facts are that the groups does indeed have access to information that can be helpful or is anxious to build and support a group within the group exploring certain alternatives not currently represented among the volunteer leadership.

I believe that couples do themselves a <u>serious</u> disservice if they do not take advantage of the educational and referral and advocacy opportunities available through volunteer run advocacy and support organizations, not just by subscribing to a newsletter, but by attending the educational events they offer!

As a good consumer, however, you must keep yourself well informed, so that if you see the advocacy group with which you are affiliated appearing to take off on a particular tangent to the exclusion of others or ignoring some of the options open to their constituency, it is your right—and I would even say that it is your responsibility—to investigate what is driving the organization's direction and to make your voice and your objections heard rather than simply leaving the organization.

A successful businessman who became president of a RESOLVE chapter told a workshop audience of his long-term reluctance to come out of the infertility closet by joining RESOLVE. He didn't understand the program, and had an image of a bunch of strange people going around the room and rising in sequence to say something like, "Hi, I'm Lloyd, and I'm infertile. My sperm are all abnormally shaped." Finally his wife more or less dragged him to a symposium, where for the first time he not only saw other (perfectly normal looking) infertile people in very large numbers, but, while still retaining full anonymity, he listened to the viewpoints of a selection of experts in the fields of reproductive medicine, emotional health, adoption, etc.

"Two years later," he said, "we are the parents of a beautiful son. We owe our parenthood to what we learned that day about ourselves and about the process."

Setting Goals and Objectives

The purpose of this process is to create a plan for managing your infertility experience, a plan that will allow you to reassert control over as many aspects as possible of your family planning, a plan that will take into account your dreams and desires, while realistically addressing your limitations. Using the information you have gathered, you will make long lists, transfer them to charts (some couples have found index cards helpful), and during the course of several hours you will add options and delete options as you discuss them. For many couples, this is the heart of and the reason for a retreat weekend.

Strategic planning—for battle, for business, for personal lives—presumes the setting of goals whose success can be measured in some fashion and which will be periodically re-evaluated. Broad general **goals** (example goal: To create an exciting birthday for Belinda), are achieved through a variety of possible **objectives** (example objectives for making an exciting birthday for Belinda: Party at home on Sunday the 24th; Dinner at La Tour; friends pitch in on "the perfect gift;" etc.) Objectives are reached through the completion of highly detailed **strategies** (example strategies for the objective of Belinda's at-home party: Engage a caterer. Plan a menu. Arrange for florist to deliver flowers. Send invitations, etc.) In light of the success or failure of various objectives explored and strategies attempted, goals are evaluated and reaffirmed or restructured.

The first step in creating your personal plan for taking charge of infertility is to decide together on your major goal. You will already have begun talking and thinking about your ranking and weighting of infertility's losses, and this will lead you to the task of determining through negotiation and compromise what the two of you as lifetime partners identify as your major goal.

Do you need to regain control? Do you want a pregnancy? Do you want to parent? What is number one?

Having identified your major goal, you need to examine all of the objectives that could help you to reach that goal. Brainstorm and be as expansive as possible. You can always delete objectives at some later time.

For example, if your goal is to regain control of your lives, some of your objectives might be

1.   To become better informed about treatment alternatives.

2.   To set a time table for continuing treatment.

3.   To find other parts of our lives in which we CAN feel a full sense of control.

4.   (Continue to add your own possible objectives)

If your primary goal is to become parents, your list of objectives might include a need to list and then rank and weight several alternative methods for achieving this goal, such as

1.   Becoming pregnant with a child genetically related to both of us.

2.   Using donor insemination (or adoptive embryo transfer, or contracting with a surrogate.)

3.   Adopting.

Beneath each of these objectives, brainstorm a list of all of the strategies you can think of that would assist you in reaching this objective. During this stage you should list every imaginable strategy, even those that initially may seem unrealistic.

For example, under the goal of becoming parents, and the objective of parenting a genetically related child, you might list

1.   Continuing standard treatments with a local gynecologist/urologist.

2.   Pursuing treatment with a nearby fertility specialist (reproductive endocrinologist or andrologist).

3.   Finding the clinic or the physician most renowned in the country (or even the world) for expertise in our problem area(s) and traveling to this clinic for treatment.

4.   (Add as many others as you can possibly imagine)

If you are working on a medical treatment plan, you should know how many treatment alternatives there are for your medical problem(s) and list them all.

Beyond that, for future discussion, how many non-medical alternatives are you willing to explore? List them all in a chart or on index cards, and include there the symbols for each of your four limited resources (time, money, physical capacity, emotional reserves) so that you can begin to allocate those resources.

Having created a list of possible objectives and strategies, begin a careful list of pro's and con's for each strategy you listed under any objective. What are the advantages and disadvantages of each alternative? Do you have the resources available to pursue all of these options at once, or will your pursuit of one option use up enough of your resources to make another impossible? If so, how do you feel about that gamble?

Try to regain as much objectivity about your situation as you possibly can. Now is the time to get real. In the following paragraphs I have provided a sampling of questions to consider in formulating your discussion, but my lists are far from exhaustive. Your own lists should be!

How much physical capacity do you have? This involves first a realistic assessment of the severity of your fertility impairment. Remember that only slightly more than 50% of couples who get the most expert of care will successfully conceive and give birth to a child genetically related to them both. Is giving birth to a jointly conceived child an important enough goal and all other alternatives so painfully second rate that you are willing to risk expending all of your other resources for a very low likelihood of conceiving and carrying a pregnancy to term? Yes? Well, begin to build a plan with your resources. No? Well, how much would you risk? How high must the odds for success be in order for you to be willing to try a treatment? How many attempts are each of you willing to make?

What about your other physical abilities? How is your energy level? What about your partner's? What impact are various medications or treatments likely to have on your physical abilities to carry on in other parts of your life? Will you need and do you have available medical leave time? What reactions to medications can you expect? How do you plan to manage the physical exhaustion that might be produced by these options? What impact might each possible medical alternative have on your own future health? On the health of your future children? (For example, how carefully have you considered the risks to both yourself and your children if you experience a multiple conception and give birth to more than two children? What do you know about the odds concerning the relative health of triplets or quads? There now exist in many large cities, support groups of parents of multiples who will be more than willing to share their experiences and concerns with you before you decide to take this risk.)

What about money—your financial resources? Few of us have an unlimited source! On the other hand, it is important that you don't make assumptions based on incomplete information about how much various options will cost! The fact is that there is a great deal of myth out there concerning the costs of various alternatives. Ask many questions of your medical service providers. Make contacts with local adoption groups for realistic information about the costs of agency adoption and independent adoption and international adoption.

How is your insurance coverage? How is your savings? Can you afford to use money on a high risk, low rate of success medical option and still have reserves to spend on another option, say adoption or hiring a surrogate, if you are not medically successful? How many cycles can be attempted within your budget? Have you carefully and realistically considered the financial impact of a multiple gestation and/or a multiple birth? If traditional adoption or gamete adoption are among the options you will be exploring if treatment doesn't work, you will want to consider allocating your financial resources in such a way as to create a reserve for these, which can be expensive. What fees can you expect to pay to an agency or to the specific intermediary you have identified as able to help you? Would any costs be covered by your insurance? Can you obtain a loan for this purpose if necessary? If you pursue independent adoption, what impact would the lost expenses in a failed adoption have on your ability to pursue adoption again? Is adoption insurance available to you? Does your employer have an adoption assistance benefit?

Remember that it takes a lot of money to raise a child! Be certain to keep in mind as you budget that you will need to have money in reserve for this purpose after your child arrives.

The clock is ticking. How much <u>time</u> can be expended? You will need to look at time from more than one angle: near term and long term. This one (especially long term time consideration) is difficult for some of us. We don't like thinking about how the consequences of our decisions to delay marriage or parenting or the number of years spent in pursuing unproductive treatment have affected our future, but we must. You may need to stop for a while here and give yourselves time to recharge before seriously plunging into considerations about how to budget your time.

In the near term, how busy is your life? Both medical treatment and the various adoption and quasi-adoption options are likely to consume large amounts of time in order to be successful. In fact, one of the factors that seems to make infertility so difficult for many couples is that it does seem to take over almost every aspect of life. An important component of the stress that often accompanies infertility comes about when couples do not make a conscientious effort to preserve private spaces, pursue leisure activities, continue spontaneous love making, and in general attempt to keep infertility in some sort of perspective that will allow them to continue to enjoy one another and their lives.

Are each of you willing and able to carve out the significant amount of time that this may take? If travel is involved, can you take time from your work or are you willing to have the treatment impact negatively on your job or your long term career opportunities? For how long? In pursuing an international adoption, would one or the other of you be able to travel to and live in another country for several weeks?

How does your age affect your chances of becoming pregnant? Especially for women, the answer to this question will dramatically affect your other resources. Some medical conditions (endometriosis, for example) tend to become worse over time. Most studies show that even with increasingly successful assisted reproductive technologies, odds for success in achieving a pregnancy are lowered proportionately as one ages. While it is true that advancing technology has allowed several women to become pregnant and deliver a baby even after menopause, this remains statistically unlikely and is thus very expensive to pursue. Certainly this is an option to be pursued, but you must realize the impact that it will have on all of your resources.

What about your future? How old are each of you now? Your ages may raise ethical and moral questions related to your pursuit of parenting. In looking at your choices, you are going to need to consider whether you have passed a personal point of no return in planning to parent a child from birth. This is your own decision to make. No one can or should impose his or her values on you. However, no matter how youthful both of you feel now, be realistic about where you are likely to be in ten years, in twenty years, and think about not just your own needs, but the needs of the children you want to parent. What impact does your age have on your financial resources? For example, will you be paying for college during retirement? Will your ages have an impact on your growing children? Teenage years are particularly difficult and demand elasticity and both emotional and physical stamina. From your own observation and experience within your family (whose genes you have inherited, and to whom you are therefore likely to be similar), try to project whether it is likely that you will have these when your children are teens. What are the odds that your future children might lose a parent before adulthood? At what age might they be called upon to deal with the problems of aging parents? Are there ways that you can manage these problems in advance (e.g. being particularly well insured, committing yourselves to making plans about moving to a continuing care community while you are still healthy and independent so that your young adult children will not be faced with guilt about what to do about a "declining" parent while they are parenting their own very young family, etc.)

If you are considering adoption, you should know that some agencies do have age and length of marriage requirements, some countries impose such requirements on international adopters, and in adoptions where birthparents select adopting parents for their babies they may have strong feelings about age as well. If the answers to these questions produce a feeling that perhaps it is too late to begin with a baby, don't reject adoption before carefully examining the idea of adopting an older child. Consider as well that adopting without an agency is an alternative to agency adoption and may, if carefully explored and pursued, neutralize some of these restrictions.

Consider the <u>emotional energy</u> involved in each option being considered. Be aware of your gut level moral or ethical reactions to each option being considered. Look back at the emotional components of the questions we've already raised about your resources of time, money and physical energy. Determine how much emotional energy you are willing to spend on each alternative under consideration. Think about the emotional consequences of repeated attempts which are unsuccessful. Remember that no matter which partner is in treatment, the stress of treatment is felt by both partners, so that each of you has a right to set limits on the expenditure of this resource. No matter how physically or emotionally strong one partner feels after facing a loss of pregnancy after a GIFT cycle or a disappointing change of mind in an adoption, the other may feel depleted and unable to go on. Can you come up with a mutually agreeable level of comfort beyond which point one partner has the right to call, "Stop!"

After you have thoroughly brainstormed and created what seems like an exhaustive list of options and considered their "expense" in terms of all of your resources, you will begin to delete those strategies that simply won't work for you. For example, you may feel that some strategies are morally or religiously offensive to either or both of you. Some strategies may demand more of certain resources than you are willing or able to expend. You may be unwilling or unable to travel for treatment, unable to afford certain treatments, or constrained by time from certain alternatives.

With a more realistic list of alternatives to consider it is important to constantly evaluate your reactions and your willingness to compromise, expecting total openness and honesty from one another and considering questions such as

1. Is this decision being considered after having thoroughly dealt with the loss of our assumed child?

2. What effects will choosing this alternative have on our feelings about ourselves, on our moral or religious convictions, on our self esteem?

3. What effects will this alternative choice have on the feelings of my spouse?

4. What effects will this alternative choice have on my feelings about my spouse or his or her feelings about me? In other words, how will this affect our relationship with one another?

5.   (If the alternative under consideration is not childfree
      living) What effects will the choice of parenting by this
      alternative have on the relationship each of us will have as
      parents to the child who will join our family in this way?

6.   What effects will our choice of this alternative have on our
      relationship with family and intimate friends, and how do
      we each feel about this?

Strategizing

Your finished plan, while vastly streamlined from your
expansive brainstorming, will probably include more than one
alternative, each listed in prioritized order. Your first choice is
your first objective; your second choice becomes your second
objective, etc.

The planning process presumes that because each
objective is time consuming, you will want to accomplish some of
the tasks of each objective concurrently. For example, if adoption
is one choice, but not the first choice, you still need to begin to
explore some specifics like how long the wait is on the list of an
agency with which you would like to work. Perhaps the wait is long
enough that you feel it wise to get on the list now, while you are
still working on medical treatment.

A word of caution. Conveyor belt couples may find it
tempting to race from medical treatment directly to another
option. Deciding to end treatment is a big step. Resolve to give
yourself space for reflection and re-evaluation between the end of
treatment and the aggressive pursuit of either gamete or
traditional adoption or before taking any permanent birth control
steps toward becoming child free.

Following the Plan

After you have put in the intense effort required to build a
long term plan for taking charge of your infertility you will have a
complex document in your hands. It will take both of you to carry
it out. Your strategies will be very specific, and each of you will
want and need to take responsibility for pursuing some of them

(e.g. writing necessary letters and making phone calls, reading books and articles).

With such a plan in your hands you will likely find that you feel more like partners in dealing with infertility than ever before. Whose body is less fertile makes little difference now. You've recommited to the marriage and you are preparing to move forward to accomplish shared goals about which each of you feels excited. Still, occasionally you may find yourself led off track by others—friends or family or professionals—who have not been part of the planning process. These challenges require that you keep one another steady. Yes indeed, any good plan should be flexible enough to be changed if change is merited, and even with a plan in hand you understand that each decision to be made along the way is a new and unique decision, but with a plan in hand, you should no longer find yourself confused by the interference of others.

Barbara and Rusty spent their retreat weekend ensconced in the lake cabin of Barbara's parents. For three days they reflected, shuffled index cards, debated pros and cons, cried some in realizing that some dreams were being let go, and built a plan for themselves.

They wanted a child to parent, and they weren't getting any younger. At 33 and 38, they were beginning to watch their oldest friends emerge from the stresses of caring for very young children and find time for adult pleasures again. Their insurance plan had covered only the basic parts of their treatment. Now that they were involved in assisted reproductive technologies, they found themselves with ever mounting balances on their bank cards. Already they had had to cash in an investment bond that had been earmarked for the down payment on the larger home they would need in a few years when they did become parents. Rusty had been a loving and supportive partner of Barb's wish to become pregnant, but his patience was wearing thin. The drugs of each cycle of GIFT made Barbara moody and strident and sick. She produced eggs, all right, but only a couple each month, despite the high doses of hormones. They had never had a positive pregnancy test. Rusty was running out of energy and patience. He needed to move on. After the retreat weekend, Barbara knew that she did, too.

Their plan resulted in a decision to stop GIFT and put their energies and resources into adoption. Barbara would tell her doctor at her next appointment the following week.

The appointment went differently than she had expected. She tried to tell him about their decision to stop treatment, but her doctor had just come back from a professional meeting with exciting ideas about new things to try. The pump might be the answer: wearing a device which would constantly pump the appropriate levels of medication through a shunt in Barbara's arm might help induce better quality ovulation. He was so excited that it was hard for Barb not to get caught up in his enthusiasm. She went home having promised to talk to Rusty and get back to him.

But Rusty was full of his own enthusiasm. Part of his "homework" after the retreat weekend had been to make calls to two agencies, an adoption attorney, and a consulting service in town to gather preliminary information. On his second call, to an agency facilitating open adoptions, the workers had been excited to hear from him. Did Barbara believe that?! It seemed that they were working with a birthmother who was Jewish. Five months pregnant, she wanted her child to be placed with Jewish parents, and, frankly, they had only two resumes on file, neither of which had intrigued this birthmother. She had asked Rusty to bring Barbara in for an interview sometime in the next few days.

"Remember what we decided, Barbara? No more 'medical maybe's.' It's time to invest in a surer thing!" Rusty pleaded.

And, you know, for the first time, Barbara didn't even hesitate. Their weekend of hard work had paid off. Both of them knew where they were headed now.

Evaluation

Good planning calls for periodic evaluation. In fact, all goals and objectives should carry with them a projected completion date. Time, of course, is budgeted as a resource, built into the plan in such ways as your having decided to pursue three cycles' worth of a particular therapy before re-evaluating whether or not to continue or pursue another course of action, or your planning to place an advertisement directed at birthparents in five issues of a national newspaper before evaluating whether to renew or revise it.

Your overall plan should carry the expectation for periodic evaluation, too. I recommend that part of your commitment to one another and to your jointly made plan should include scheduled promises to meet over dinner to discuss progress at least quarterly until your goal has been reached and, in the event that your initial goals have not been met, to plan another retreat weekend to be held one year following your first. At this time you can evaluate your progress, adjust your goals and objectives if necessary, and develop new strategies.

We'll still be stuck a year from now? I hear you exclaiming. No. If your plan has been made carefully and takes into account the limitations of your resources, the odds are that you will be feeling successful and will not need to rework your plan. All good planning, however, contains a contingency measure for reevaluation and reexamination of the goals within a year or less (if needed.)

No one said that managing your fertility impairment would be easy. In making all of your decisions, setting all of your goals, following all of the strategies that will allow you to meet your objectives, be certain that the decisions you make now are made together and with enough care that you will remain comfortable with them ten, twenty, or thirty years into the future. It is always easy to look back and say "if only..." When decisions are made carefully, with complete knowledge, and with full communication between partners, they can last for a life time.

Even couples facing what seem, on the surface, to be similar fertility impairments may make entirely separate decisions about how to proceed based on their individual and jointly shared values. Let me share with you examples of couples who have already worked through the decision making process outlined in this chapter...

John and Mary consider the losses of infertility and identify what they each wanted most from their original decision to become parents. For Mary, the need was to experience a pregnancy as well as to be a parent, yet she also mourns the loss of sharing a pregnancy and then a child with John. For John, on the other hand, genetic continuity is just not important. John's dreams are of parenting—reading bedtime stories, coaching athletic teams. For this couple the carefully discussed choice to use donor insemination to circumvent the barrier to parenthood raised by John's low sperm count will be an attractive one, offering them each the opportunity to achieve their dreams and avoid infertility's most painful losses. If this option is successful for them, each of them wins what s/he wants most. Both, however, agree that their highest priority is shared parenthood, so that, should D.I. prove unsuccessful, John and Mary are ready to embrace adoption as an equally attractive way to build a family. They have begun to gather information about international adoption just in case.

Mark and Amy, on the other hand, acknowledge different needs. The grandchild of Holocaust victims and survivors, Mark mourns deeply his inability to provide another generation for his family. He is willing to go to dramatic lengths to improve his sperm count and to enhance his chances of impregnating his wife. Amy, too, wants a genetic connection, and initially sees clearly that she can have it, if only she can convince Mark to agree to D.I. Their physician, too, has endorsed this choice, reminding Mark that no one need ever know that Amy's child is not his by blood. With the help of a skilled facilitator, their communication leads each to see that for Mark to accede to such a demand from Amy would create a win-lose situation in the balance of their relationship and could impair his ability to relate positively to the child to whom Amy would give birth. The child would serve as a daily reminder that Mark had lost what both wanted most—genetic continuity—while Amy had achieved it! Additionally, for this couple, the interest in parenting is simply not strong enough in the face of their powerful interest in genetic linkage for either to consider that there could be a win-win after loss-loss in the compromise option of adoption. After careful reflection and a reaffirmation of their primary commitment to one another and to their marriage, this couple decides that their interest in a jointly conceived child is strong enough for them to spend significant amounts of time, money and energy researching and seeking out the clinics in the world with the highest rate of success in treating Mark's problem. After having pursued surgery, medications, and several courses of IVF without achieving a pregnancy, this couple chooses to embrace a child*free* lifestyle.

Carmaine and Randy have been stymied by Carmaine's premature ovarian failure. Both want desperately to parent, but Randy is finding the idea of adoption particularly difficult because of his firmly held convictions (not shared by Carmaine, who is ready to adopt!) that bonding can be achieved only through genetic connection. Since Carmaine cannot ovulate, they can see no hope, and their relationship has become increasingly pressured by their blaming of one another for their joint failure to become parents. Almost serendipitously they approach their pastor just as he has recently met just the right counselor, a woman well versed in infertility issues, who, after spending several sessions with them working through their reactions to their individual and joint losses and encouraging them to mourn those lost expectations, opens windows not even seen before: surrogacy and adoptive embryo transfer. They seriously consider both, find medical and legal advisors to answer their questions about each, and decide to pursue as first choice adoptive embryo transfer. If successful, this option will allow the two of them to experience the pregnancy and birth together. If not, and if they decide on surrogacy, Randy will have his genetic connection and Carmaine her child to love and nurture. There will be winners all around!

Sara and Matt are the owners and operators of a family farm. Together they are clear about their major interest: to become parents. They have pursued all of the least invasive medical treatments they can to try to prod Sara's stubbornly uncooperative ovaries. She responded best to a cycle of human menopausal gonadotropin. (Expensive for this uninsured couple with limited financial resources.) The reproductive endocrinologist working with them at a major medical center sees GIFT as a promising treatment and has provided them with a great deal of literature, encouraging statistics of success for couples who try three cycles at the center's clinic, and a promise to work them into the waiting list quickly. Their doctor is convincing. It's tempting, and, frankly, they are having trouble letting this very nice doctor down, but they really don't see how they can afford up to three cycles of GIFT. Sara and Matt will more or less disappear from the clinic—not formally ending treatment, but just not coming back. Through their church, they learn of a young woman in another community who is parenting one child alone and is pregnant again. Within months they are the parents of her two children, a toddler and a newborn, in an open adoption. The birthmother's employee insurance plan has covered all medical expenses of the birth, the local department of social services provided their homestudy, and their total expenses involved minimal legal fees of an attorney specializing in family law who is also a member of their congregation.

Each of these couples considers themselves successful in resolving infertility issues and making family building decisions. Their carefully considered choices were right for the two of them. Each was ultimately nurtured by a caring, helpful professional who accepted their personal needs, limitations and values and was able to feel personal success reflected in their joy. There could be more Mark and Amys, Carmaine and Randys, Sara and Matts, and John and Marys and fewer drifting, disappointed infertile people if all of the professionals working with fertility impaired people would make it a part of their practice to link services and provide a full spectrum of information and care for their patients and clients.

RESOURCES

National and Regional Organizations Offering Support and Information

RESOLVE, Inc. (1310 Broadway, Somerville MA 02144, telephone 617-623-0744) is a U.S. national nonprofit network of 54 chapters offering information, referral, support and advocacy services to infertile people. Dues of $35 annually (includes both national and local chapter membership). Their newsletters, fact sheets and symposia can be indispensable tools. Currently RESOLVE is putting a great deal of effort on a state by state basis into achieving mandated insurance coverage for infertility treatment. They have been successful already in Massachusetts, Maryland, California, and several other states.

Infertility Awareness Association of Canada (523-774 Echo Lane, Ottawa, Ontario KK1S 5N8, CANADA, telephone 613-730-1322) is a Canadian charitable organization offering assistance, support, and education to those with infertility concerns by issuance of its bilingual publication *Infertility Awareness* five times a year; establishment of chapters to provide grass roots services; a resource centre; information packages; and a network of related services. Services are bilingual (English and French.) Membership is $30 Canadian annually. A complimentary information kit will be sent to interested Canadians upon request.

Ferre Institute (258 Genesee St, Ste 302, Utica, NY 13502, 315-724-4348) is a non-profit organization dedicated to the promotion of quality services in infertility, to the education of professionals the the public about infertility and its treatment and to encouragement for research in the spychosocial as well as medical aspecis of infertility and reproductive health. Although direct services are offered only in a limited geographic region, their excellent newsletter *FerreFax*, directed primarily at professionals, is available to others.

American Fertility Society (1209 Montgomery Highway, Birmingham AL 35216-2809, 205-978-5000) is an international membership organization of professionals (predominantly doctors, but including nurses, reproductive biologists, mental health practitioners and health educators) who have a special interest in family planning and reproductive health. In addition to providing information about local members to consumers seeking a care provider, its special interest group the Society for Assisted Reproductive Technology is a membership group of IVF/GIFT clinics who have agreed to report their successes and other statistical data to AFS for dissemination through the annual SART Report. Its Psychological Special Interest Group focuses on the emotional ramifications of infertility. AFS publishes the prestigious medical journal *Fertility and Sterility* and many booklets directed toward patients concerning specific infertility problems and topics.

Endometriosis Association (8585 N. 76th Place, Milwaukee WI 53223) is a non-profit with chapters throughout the U.S. The organization publishes a newsletter and offers referrals and support for those dealing with the multiple issues related to endometriosis, only one of which is infertility.

The Organization of Parents through Surrogacy (OPTS) (7054 Quito Ct., Camarillo, CA 93012, 805-482-1566) is a national non-profit, volunteer organization with three regional chapters whose purpose is mutual support, networking, and the dissemination of information regarding surrogate parenting, egg donation, sperm donation as well as assisted reproductive technology including IVF and GIFT. OPTS publishes a quarterly newsletter, holds annual meetings, has a telephone support network, and actively lobbies for legislation concerning surrogacy. Membership is $40 annually.

The Childfree Network (7777 Sunrise Blvd #1800, Citrus Heights, CA 95610, telephone 916-773-7178) is national organization for singles and couples who have elected a childfree lifestyle. The network publishes a quarterly newsletter, *ChildFree*, containing many helpful articles on the positive aspects of life without children. Though some members made this choice after infertility, most have not experienced infertility, so that one will not necessarily find the newsletter uniformly sensitive to or informed about infertility issues. Subscriptions are $20.00 annually.

Adoption Council of Canada (P.O. Box 8442, Station T, Ottawa, Ontario K1G 3H8. Phone 613-235-1566.) This network collects and disseminates information about adoption throughout Canada, facilitating communication among groups and individuals interested in adoption and promoting understanding of the benefits and challenges of adoption.

Adoptive Families of America (3333 Hwy 100 North, Minneapolis, MN 55422. Phone 612-537-0316.) An excellent source for purchase of books and tapes and of referral to local parent groups, AFA is the largest organization for adoptive families in the world. AFA publishes *OURS: The Magazine of Adoptive Families* bimonthly and sponsors an annual national conference designed specifically to reach out to those considering adopting and adoption-expanded families. Its Annual Adoption Information and Resources packet lists several hundred agencies nationally and offers consumer advice.

General Decision Making

The 7 Habits of Highly Effective People by Stephen R Covey (New York: Simon & Schuster, 1989)

The Confident Decision Maker: How to Make the Right Business and Personal Decisions Every Time by Roger Dawson (New York: William Morrow & Co, 1993).

Yes or No: The Guide to Better Decisions by Spencer Johnston M.D. (New York: HarperCollins, 1992).

Woulda, Coulda, Shoulda: Overcoming Regrets, Mistakes, and Missed Opportunities by Dr. Arthur Freeman and Rose DeWolf (New York: HarperCollins, 1989.) cognitive therapy

Overcoming Indecisiveness by Theodore Isaac Rubin, M.D. (New York: Harper & Row, 1985).

Coping with Loss

How to Survive the Loss of a Love by Melba Colgrove Ph.D., Harold Bloomfield, M.D., and Peter McWilliams. (Los Angeles, Prelude Press and Bantam, rev. 1991) A simple yet powerful handbook for getting through loss—of a person or of a dream.

Living through Personal Crisis by Ann Kaiser Stearns (New York: Ballantine Books, 1984. A practical guide to dealing with grief.

When Bad Things Happen to Good People by Harold S. Kushner (New York: Shocken Books, 1981) A reassuring approach to understanding loss and suffering.

Chapter 4

CHOOSING SERVICE PROVIDERS

*I hold every man a debtor to his profession;
from the which as men of course do seek to receive
countenance and profit, so ought they of duty to
endeavor themselves to be a help and ornament
thereunto.*

> *Sir Francis Bacon*
> *"Preface"*
> Maxims of the Law

As you work on taking charge of your infertility by identifying and treating its causes or by defining the future for your family, you and your partner will need to make choices about several different types of professional service providers. You will choose a physician, and, in fact, you may decide to change physicians over the course of your treatment. When you select a physician, his or her practice will then dictate that you use certain other care providers—nurses, technicians, a particular hospital, etc. Some couples exploring assisted reproductive technologies select a clinic itself, and then choose a physician who practices there. You may also seek the services of a counselor or a support group. Should you explore adoption you may need to choose an agency, an attorney, a consultant or even all three.

Finding the "right" service provider, one in whom you can feel confident and with whom you can feel comfortable, is an important part of regaining some control over your reproductive life. Making good choices is dependent upon your becoming an informed and confident consumer, one who is willing to ask the right questions and evaluate the answers received. In making

96

decisions about choosing professional service providers there are several areas of concern to be addressed:

How can we obtain a reliable referral?
How do we assess a professional's qualifications?
What questions should we ask?
How will our choice affect our resources?

The Doctors

Most couples who suspect, after several months of unprotected intercourse, that they may have a fertility impairment, begin treatment with their primary care physician—the person who already knows them and has treated them for regular checkups and various illnesses. For many people this may be a family physician or an internist. Already familiar with your medical history, this doctor should be able to help to educate you about basic fertility awareness issues: how to try to read your body's symptoms (basal body temperature, condition of cervical mucus, etc.) to predict and chart ovulation, timing intercourse properly, etc. He or she will be familiar with your basic medical history and how previous surgeries or infections or illnesses and medications you are taking might affect your fertility. One advantage of beginning fertility evaluation with a general care physician is that these medical practitioners are trained to see themselves as generalists, and most assume that part of their role is to refer patients to more specialized care as appropriate.

Some patients will be referred to or will refer themselves to a "specialist" in infertility. Since in many states any physician who has completed medical school and been properly licensed to practice general medicine may self-proclaim himself as a specialist in any field, wise consumers will seek more specific information about their care provider's training, certification, and experience rather than merely accepting the description in the telephone book or the title spelled out on the letterhead or the office door.

Many women see an obstetrician/gynecologist (OB/GYN) as their primary care provider. OB/GYNs are physicians who limit their practice to women's health issues—family planning, reproductive health, delivering babies. It is possible, however, to limit one's practice to this area without having specialized training in the field.

A board-certified OB/GYN is one who has completed training beyond medical school and internship in an additional two year residency featuring study and training in women's health and reproductive issues. These physicians then take a series of tests offered in the United States by the American College of Obstetricians and Gynecologists. If they pass these tests after their residency, they can become board-certified OB/GYNs and are then indeed considered specialists in the field of women's health. OB/GYNs can and do offer extensive services in diagnosing and treating infertility, and the average infertility patient with a relatively uncomplicated fertility problem will find these services adequate, will become pregnant, and will deliver a child.

For many years OB/GYNs who had a special interest and more than average experience treating infertility were accepted as infertility specialists. But advanced research in the area of reproductive medicine has produced so much new knowledge that over the last two decades a sub-specialty of obstetrics and gynecology has developed called reproductive endocrinology and infertility (R.E.) These doctors have completed the steps for becoming board-certified as OB/GYNs and have gone further by completing a two year fellowship (beyond their OB/GYN residency) in which they have focused specifically on infertility testing and treatment, both medical and surgical, including microsurgery, hormonal manipulation and ovulation induction, and the most current diagnostic techniques and assisted reproductive technologies. Upon the successful completion of this fellowship period, a physician is considered to be board eligible as a reproductive endocrinologist and infertility specialist. To become board certified, these physicians take and pass a series of exams offered by A.C.O.G., the same professional body which certifies obstetrician/gynecologists. Most (though not all) clinics which offer assisted reproductive technologies such as *in vitro* fertilization or gamete intrafallopian transfer (GIFT) etc. are managed by reproductive endocrinologists.

Urologists are physicians who have completed a residency and become board-certified through testing by the American Urological Association to specialize in urinary tract diseases in both men and women and reproductive problems in men. Not all urologists are comfortable with infertility issues, but many have chosen to limit their practices to male infertility. In the last several years a subspecialty has developed in this field, as well. It is called andrology, and focuses exclusively on male infertility problems.

Andrologists are as relatively rare today as reproductive endocrinologists were fifteen years ago, but their numbers are growing.

Look for appropriate credentials in the certificates that adorn your doctor's office walls. If s/he is a diplomate of A.C.O.G. or A.U.A. and board certified as an OB/GYN and/ or a R.E. or as a urologist or andrologist, s/he will proudly display this information. Membership in the American Fertility Society, while, unlike A.C.O.G. or A.U.A. certification, should clearly be understood not to represent an endorsement of competence, does suggest a strong interest in keeping abreast of current research in the field of infertility.

Finding these doctors is not that difficult. Yellow Pages shopping and friend-of-a-friend referrals, however, are not the best resources. The American Fertility Society will provide you with the names of local members. RESOLVE annually surveys physicians throughout the United States and maintains a referral list. Your local infertility support group can provide you with information, including the names of patients who will be willing to speak with you about the physician's and his staff's and practice's style and manner.

Should You See a Specialist?

Many patients have medical problems which are quickly and easily identified, respond to relatively simple treatments and so can be treated by a family physician or generalist OB/GYN. But at least half of infertility patients have complex medical problems which, in order to be successfully treated, need more specialized care than the training in OB/GYN or general urology can prepare a physician to offer. These patients most certainly should see a reproductive endocrinologist or andrologist. But it is usually impossible for patients themselves to know at the outset of treatment that they fall into this category.

Most patients assume that if they need more help, their physician will refer them on. Sometimes, however, patients are not referred to subspecialists. It is not uncommon for a gynecologist or urologist, for example, to see himself as a specialist and to be far less inclined to refer beyond his office than would be a family doctor or general practitioner.

It is important, then, for patients to be aware that subspecialists exist and to be prepared, as well informed consumers, to ask for a referral to a R.E. or andrologist. Patients should be prepared to request referral or refer themselves whenever they feel that they have spent enough time (or money, or emotional energy, or physical reserves) on traditional therapy or when their physician begins to suggest surgical therapy, sophisticated hormonal therapy or assisted reproductive technology.

When is that? The decision must be yours as a patient. My own bias, as a consumer advocate who was once a too-unassertive, too-trusting patient, is that the "when" should be sooner rather than later.

The fact is that the same tests when viewed by physicians with different levels of expertise and experience may be interpreted differently. It is not uncommon that a patient who makes the switch from an OB/GYN to a reproductive endocrinologist, carrying with her written records of earlier tests, will find herself repeating those tests when the R.E. feels that earlier-done tests were poorly timed. An R.E who sees actual films from laparascopy or hysterosalpingogram or ultrasound may read them quite differently from the first doctor. Often when a specialist finds that films from such procedures are unavailable, she may feel that she must view the pelvis herself rather than rely on the written description of others.

Several factors keep people from seeing a specialist to begin with. One very large factor is denial, a fear (often unconscious) that their fertility impairment will be permanent. This very denial, however, can aggravate the fertility problem by wasting time, wasting emotional and physical energy, misidentifying (and thus complicating) some problems, and even exposing a patient to less effective treatment than he or she would receive from a more experienced and expert physician.

Another excuse is inconvenience. A decade and a half ago reproductive endocrinologists were a very small group, and their practices tended to be concentrated in major metropolitan areas and major medical centers. Here in Indiana, for example, when the first infertility symposium for consumers offered anywhere in the world was held in 1979, there were only three board certified reproductive endocrinologists in our whole state! One practiced at a well regarded diagnostic clinic outside of the state's second largest city, and the other two were on the staff at Indiana

University Medical Center in Indianapolis. At that time, when in order to be seen by a specialist many patients needed to drive several hours away to distant cities, and when patients in cities where R.E.'s practiced waited months to be seen, it made a lot of sense for patients to hesitate about seeing a reproductive endocrinologist. But R.E.s are no longer such rarities. There are over 300 board certified reproductive endocrinologists today, and half again that number who are board-eligible. In major metropolitan areas there are so many qualified physicians that they often compete aggressively with one another. Even in more isolated medium sized cities of 200,000 or so it is becoming more and more common to find at least one reproductive endocrinologist in practice and eager to see new patients.

Finally, many patients incorrectly assume that seeing a specialist is financially unfeasible. The reality is that in most instances evaluation and treatment by a specialist may involve a smaller investment of all four resources: time, money, emotional reserves, physical capacities. While their hourly rates may (or may not) be higher than obstetricians/gynecologists, most often reproductive endocrinologists offer a more streamlined approach to testing, which results in fewer visits overall, and visits which are carefully timed to allow several tests to be performed at once. Once diagnosed, any infertility problem has a much higher chance of being corrected by a physician whose specialization in a field means that not only has she had more training, but she also has developed significantly more expertise, as this is all she does, day after day.

Alternative Medicine

Those of us raised in the North American culture steeped in the mystique of "modern medicine" often know very little about alternative approaches to health care. Yet increasingly consumer newsletters are carrying articles and letters discussing how alternatives to western medicine such as acupuncture, homeopathy, or chiropractic approach and treat infertility. For some couples part of taking charge of infertility may include investigating and/or pursuing alternative treatments.

Being an informed consumer is important in making choices here, too. Practitioners in any field include both excellent caregivers and incompetent practitioners. Patients need to be prepared to read carefully, seek out and make contact with professional organizations, and speak to a variety of patients and clients before expending budgeted time, money, physical energy or emotional reserves on any treatment—medical or alternative. Ask questions and expect clear answers. Remember, you are in charge.

Mental Health Professionals

Many of us find that the stress of infertility treatment can be better managed or our communication with partners be improved after having spent several sessions with a qualified mental health professional. Those who pursue adoption will, in the majority of cases, be required to see such a person. These professionals, too, have varied credentials, qualifications, experience, and sensitivity to infertility issues.

Psychiatrists are medical doctors whose focus is mental health. They have gone through medical school, internship, have taken a medical residency in psychiatry, and are licensed by their states as physicians. They provide both individual and family therapy, and because their training is in medicine, they are qualified to prescribe medications to alleviate depression, chemical imbalance, etc.. They can be board certified in this specialty area of medicine.

Psychologists, on the other hand, are not physicians. Their training can include either a Master's in counseling (M.S. or M.A.) or a doctorate (Ph.D.) in psychology. Some states license psychologists, but others do not. It's important for you to know whether your state does.

In the United States, most of the time social workers have at a minimum a bachelor's degree, preferably in social work (a B.S.W) but often in an unrelated field. Social workers may also have a masters degree (M.S.W.) and some achieve a doctorate in the field. Some states, but far from all, require that social workers be licensed or certified, resulting in a designation such as C.S.W. (Certified Social Worker). Beyond this, some states make available an examination which offers those who pass the designation Li.C.S.W. (Licensed Certified Social Worker)—a step above C.S.W.. Some social workers acquire even more specialized professional status by working to achieve the nationally recognized designation

A.C.S.W., as fellows of the Academy of Certified Social Workers conferred by the National Association of Social Workers.

While most clergypeople do do some counseling, some members of the clergy are more specially trained to specializing in the field of pastoral counseling. This does not require certification, nor is there a cross-denominationally agreed upon set of educational criteria for such professionals.

These steps mental health professional take may seem familiar to infertility patients, who are familiar with the training and certification steps physicians take from M.D. to graduate OB/GYN to board-certified OB/GYN to Sub-specialist in Infertility/Reproductive Endocrinology to Board-eligible in Infertility and finally Board-certified Reproductive Endocrinologist/Infertility Specialist. What you will likely remember about the docs, though, is that unless you are a careful consumer, many of them will allow you to presume that they have the highest rank of training and credentialing. The same is true in the mental health fields.

It may surprise you to learn that there are very few courses in schools of social work or psychology which focus just on adoption issues, and none which focus only on infertility. Infertility and adoption issues are normally covered as small parts of larger general courses with titles such as Child Welfare Issues or Marriage and the Family. Most of what therapists learn about adoption's or infertility's issues is learned on the job or as a part of continuing education training through seminars offered by the American Fertility Society or Serono Symposia or Child Welfare League of America or North American Conference on Adoptable Children and by reading the journals of professionally related organizations and consumer advocacy groups. But seminars and journal subscriptions are both expensive and time consuming, so that many mental health professionals whose employers do not reimburse for such continuing education are able to pursue it only on a small scale or not at all. It is not unusual, then, for well prepared consumers to be better informed about adoption's or infertility's emotional issues than an inexperienced recent graduate.

Many therapists specialize in a particular form of therapy—Gestault, Freudian analysis, cognitive therapy, etc. Some specialize in group work, others with couples, still others with individuals. A few have chosen to focus their work in the areas of infertility, reproductive loss, and/or adoption.

With the exception of those who are certified as psychiatric nurse practitioners, most nurses do not have thelevel of counseling training that the other professionals discussed here have, yet some nurses do engage in what they label "infertility counseling" as opposed to patient education. Former patients, too, often set themselves up as "counselors" for those pursuing infertility and adoption options. How does one determine the level of expertise of a professional before working with him or her?

Specialists tend to work closely with the infertility advocacy and medical communities and will be well known to them. Your local infertility support group and/or your doctor are excellent referral sources. Most will have joined the American Fertility Society's Psychological Special Interest Group and other specially-focused professional organizations. To know what your therapist's qualifications, experience, and training are, you are going to have to specifically ask, and it is entirely appropriate that you do so. Before committing to working with any professional, begin with an interview.

As the medical community becomes more and more sensitive to the emotional turmoil brought about by infertility, the largest infertility practices and IVF/GIFT clinics have begun to make mental health services a part of their "packages." I see this as having both positive and negative effects.

Certainly having a therapist knowledgeable about the emotional aspects of infertility readily available to patients is a plus. Often this can relieve patients of the stresses which can come from shopping for a counselor and finding many who are unfamiliar with infertility issues. When the program is well designed, on-site (or at the very least directly associated) program-affiliated mental health professionals can fill in the glaring gaps often found for patients needing to explore their feelings about and readiness for assisted reproductive technologies with their inherent risks and third party reproductive options such as donor semen, donor eggs or embryos or gestational surrogacy. This makes the option of connected medical and mental health services much more attractive than having no services at all.

On the other hand, patients in such comprehensive programs often feel that they cannot freely share their negative feelings about certain professionals, certain procedures, or the milieu of the office as a whole without risking that their complaints will get back to the nurse or the doctor. Despite the fact that any reasonable person would understand that an ethical mental health practitioner would consider such information confidential, patients under stress find it difficult to trust this enough to freely unburden themselves. Additionally, patients often have legitimate concerns about whether clinic staff become so enthusiastic about and loyal to their clinic and its opportunities that they lose their own objectivity, not to mention having a vested interest in seeing patients continue with treatment rather than end it or move to other options.

In the best of worlds, several knowledgeable, infertility-specializing mental health providers who were independent of clinics and professionals would maintain cordial relationships with advocacy groups and all area physicians offering infertility medical services and all agencies, consultants, attorneys and other intermediaries offering adoption services, so that patients could freely shop among the groups and the individual counseling services for the best "fit." While we wait for that best of all worlds, contact your local infertility support group, or, in their absence, speak to other patients before choosing a counselor.

Adoption Professionals

Should you explore adoption, there are three kinds of professionals who are likely to play important roles in your achieving adoptive parenthood. They are adoption intermediaries, counseling professionals, and legal professionals.

Adoption intermediaries are the people who bring adopters and birthparents together to arrange an adoption, whether the two sets of parents actually meet each other or not. Intermediaries may be agency social workers, adoption attorneys, physicians, adoption consultants, or, informally, even clergypersons or family friends. Counseling professionals help those considering adoption sort through the many ramifications of this family planning alternative, pointing out options, providing information and education, and helping birthparents and adopters make careful, objective choices. The counseling role may appropriately be filled by agency social workers, independent social workers, family counselors, mental health therapists, professional mediators, pastoral counselors, or other trained counselors. Finally, since adoption involves a legal transfer of parental rights from one set of parents to another, it is impossible to complete an adoption without the assistance of at least one attorney.

Once again, in that best of all possible worlds to which we keep referring, each of these roles would be filled by separate people, each offering his or her own objective assistance to birthparents considering adoption and to prospective adopting couples. Increasingly, however, the roles have become somewhat blurred, so that, sometimes because of a lack of information, sometimes because of an effort to save money, and sometimes in an effort to retain control, both birthparents and adoptive parents are refusing, avoiding, or simply not being informed of the option of the assistance of one or more of these types of professionals—most often the counselors/educators. In my opinion leaving out the counseling is a serious mistake that may have far reaching consequences.

Successful adoption is to a large extent dependent on finding the right resources to support a growing family. Your experience with other professionals in other fields has no doubt demonstrated for you that not all professionals are good at what they do, despite education and training, despite fulfilling licensing or specialization requirements. It is important that you, as prospective adoptive parents, understand and take hold of your power and responsibility if you choose this path to parenthood. Through the national offices of Adoptive Families of America and North American Council on Adoptable Children you can locate local parent groups in the cities in which you are exploring adoption (whether that is at home or across the country from you) which will help you with accurate information about any of the service providers working in their areas.

Social Workers and Counseling Professionals

Who makes the match? In a traditional public or private agency adoption, birthparents and adoptive parents are brought together by an agency's staff—usually social workers. In independent adoption sometimes two sets of parents are brought together by an attorney or consultant or physician or other intermediary. In the hybrid called direct or identified adoption, social workers do the assessment and counseling after the two sets of parents have matched themselves to one another in some other manner. Social workers are most often the professionals employed by courts to do pre-finalization assessments to provide a recommendation to the courts in independent adoptions as well.

The social workers we described above in the section on counselors and therapists have the same training as do social workers who choose to work in adoption. The proper role of the social worker or other mental health professional is to build on a client's strengths. Not all counseling professionals are able to understand this concept and follow it, however. Finding the right social worker and/or the right agency will make an enormous difference in your ability to make the parent preparation process a positive experience and a productive one for your future family.

In the best of all possible worlds prospective adopters would shop for just the right agency and/or social worker, whose qualifications, experience, and interactive skills would be a perfect match. But in the real world of adoption, most of the time this is not an option. Because of the limited number of agencies, the size of their staffs, and the qualifications which may limit your acceptability from agency to agency, in reality, U.S adopters will probably feel that they have considerably less control over choosing their social workers than they had in selecting physicians during the treatment phase of their infertility.

Even if you are not able to apply at an agency whose policies and procedures make you feel completely enthusiastic, you can make the best of the situation by understanding what the process should be and filling in some of the gaps you find for yourself. Adoption education is available through many parent groups and through adoption consultants. Infertility advocacy organizations often offer support groups and symposia which are adoption focused. Subscribing to several adoption periodicals and reading as many books as possible will help you to move forward.

Attorneys

Attorneys practicing in this field are unprepared for adoption's intricacies when armed only with their law school training. Attorneys learn about the basics of the law and adoption in courses on family law, but most of adoption practice is learned on the job. While adoptions which are arranged by well regarded agencies usually involve fairly straightforward and simple legal work, independent adoptions are much more complicated and require specialized expertise.

Attorneys who choose to specialize in this field must truly be legal experts. In essence, adoption law is every bit as much a complicated specialty as is reproductive medicine. Of course you would not have had your brother-in-law the podiatrist perform tubal reconstruction surgery. Similarly, you will want to choose an attorney who has experience and expertise in this form of law to handle your adoption. The person who wrote your will or closed your real estate deal or defended your neighbor falsely accused of theft is probably not the person to finalize your adoption.

One of the major criticisms about attorneys who serve not just as legal advisors on adoption but act as adoption intermediaries or facilitators has been that they are not trained in counseling or mental health fields but often seem to be practicing in these fields in trying to provide counseling for birthparents and preparation for adoptive parents. For years adoption agencies have felt that the danger of exploitation and poor preparation is exceedingly high in independent adoption. Certainly the highly publicized Baby Jessica case is a prime example of such poor preparation of birth and adoptive parents.

In fairness, it must also be pointed out that as adoption in America becomes increasingly entrepreneurial, a not insignificant number of licensed agencies have begun to provide services which appear to be less than optimal. Agencies which advertise nationwide find it difficult to mandate birthparent counseling for clients who do not live in the state where the services is located, and so, increasingly, some agencies don't insist that the birthparents who plan adoptions through them receive options counseling!

Increasingly, attorneys concerned about developing a high standard of ethics in the field of adoption law are speaking out as advocates on controversial issues such as the need to refer clients to counseling services, the need for birthparents and adoptive parents to have separate attorneys each advocating for their particular rights, the need to bill for services on an hourly basis, and more.

The American Academy of Adoption Attorneys is a relatively new professional association which holds as one of its goals the establishment of guidelines and ethical standards similar to the guidelines and standards established by professional organizations in the medical field such as the American College of Obstetrics and Gynecologists for attorneys practicing in the field of adoption. Membership in this organization is one of the criteria adopters and birthparents can look for in seeking the best of legal services in the adoption field.

Adoption Consultants—an Emerging Field

If you are using an adoption consultant as your intermediary, know that this is not at this time a quantifiable professional field. Instead, people from all sorts of educational and vocational backgrounds who have a strong interest in adoption issues simply set themselves up as adoption consultants. Consultants are often people who have themselves adopted and who wish to pass on their knowledge and experience about networking to find a baby, about how to write a resume, about what books and articles will provide useful information to prospective parents.

This can be a very useful service. However, it is important for consumers to understand and be cautious concerning the entrepreneurial nature of such work. One cannot take courses to qualify for such a position. There is no degree. There is no licensing. There is no specific form of continuing education. The result of this is that there is even more variation among consultants than there is among social workers and attorneys. Consultants, however, do not run agencies and therefore don't have lists of qualifying factors for their clients, so the choice to use or not to use a specific consultant is perhaps much clearer and more easily made than the choice to use a particular agency. The entrepreneurial nature of this emerging field results in rapid changes within it.

Building Effective Relationships with Medical, Legal, and Mental Health Professionals

A recent study in Michigan of how couples in infertility treatment measured their level of satisfaction with treatment provided some interesting results and some valuable data for medical practitioners interested in improving the milieu in which their patients are treated.

L. Jill Halman, Ph.D., of the Institute for Social Research, University of Michigan; Antonia Abbey, Ph.D., of the Department of Community Medicine at Wayne State University; and Frank M.

Andrews, Ph.D., of the Department of Population Planning and International Health, School of Public Health, University of Michigan created a study of 185 husbands and wives in treatment for primary infertility in which participants were interviewed in 1988, 1989, and 1990 to measure their satisfaction with treatment. Eighty-seven percent of eligible patients elected to participate in this study, which drew participants from each of the major infertility practices in the area, as well as from several support groups. Contrary to the expectations of the authors, how long couples had been in treatment and treatment costs were not related to satisfaction with treatment. Rather, their confidence in their doctors' technical skills, whether or not their emotional needs were being well met, and whether they felt well informed and in control of their treatment were the major predictors of satisfaction with treatment.[1]

While this carefully crafted study is important in that it affirms patients' feelings for a professional audience in a highly respected medical journal (*Fertility and Sterility*, published by the American Fertility Society) and offers suggestions for improving practice, most consumer advocates might respond, "So, what else is new?" We have long realized that in a society which has been moving more and more swiftly toward embracing the concept of empowering the client and ending paternalism, medicine may have been a little behind.

In the end, it comes down to this: we are all responsible for how medical treatment or adoption works today, whether we are patients or medical practitioners, adopters or birthparents, gamete donors or surrogates, patient advocates or adoption professionals. There are good and bad individual practitioners in every field. There are good and bad organizations as well. No matter what our role, we must accept individual responsibility for trying to make the "system" better. Actively trying to build solid, trusting, and cooperative relationships with the professionals who assist us is an important part of the improvement of services.

All successful relationships—between co-workers, friends, family members, marriage partners, etc.—depend upon the development of mutual trust and admiration and a willingness to cooperate with one another. While you may feel angry about having to deal with infertility, while you may see the adoption

1.Halman, L.J.; Abbey, A.; Andrews, F.M.; "Why Are Couples Satisfied with Infertility Treatment?" *Fertility and Sterility*, Vol. 59, No. 5, May, 1993, pp. 1046-1053.

system itself as adversarial, in order for you to be successful you must come to see yourself and the professionals with whom you work as part of a team.

Recognize that the professionals with whom you will be working are human beings and they deserve your courtesy and respect, just as you deserve the same from them. All professionals are human beings who come with strengths and weaknesses and may be well informed or misinformed. As individuals, these professionals have good and bad days. In many cases these professionals are employees taking orders from a "boss" with whom they may or may not have a positive relationship. While they are paid for what they do, in some cases they are not well paid! When you are able to see these overworked professionals as individuals and to build individual relationships with them, you will be able to access their strengths to your benefit, rather than to suffer their weaknesses silently and resentfully.

Good manners are at the heart of good relationships. Not only do we expect to be treated politely, but we must do our best to treat others politely as well. Nice touches (a friendly smile, a thank-you note where appropriate, compliments about the parts of the process that you particularly enjoyed or appreciated, consideration of feelings) will go a long way to enhance relationships.

There may indeed be times when you are not treated well. Ignore those instances which do not have long term consequences if you can. Perhaps you could write a furious letter and then not mail it. Keeping a sense of humor about petty annoyances can also be helpful.

However, when problems arise that really signify a need for change either now or in the future, point them out, if you possibly can. At the very least keep a file of concerns you intend to raise and suggestions you will really make after your relationship with the institution ends, so that you can help to assure that future clients will not face similar obstacles. Never, however, under any circumstances, go along with allowing yourself or, in the case of adoption, your child's birthparent to be grossly mistreated or exploited!

Who Is in Charge Here?—An American Perspective

A Canadian friend who reviewed a draft of my last book, *Adopting after Infertility*, pointed out that she felt that "the systems"—both the medical system and the adoption system—might be perceived less adversarially by Canadians than my writing would appear that it did for Americans. It's true, the majority of Americans with whom I come in contact do experience infertility as a challenge to be met and adoption as a game to be played, or a competition to be won. Perhaps this difference in American/Canadian perception is due to the competitive nature of modern American society, and perhaps this is one of the biggest differences between these two North American sister societies.

In the U.S.'s free market society with a privately paid rather than socialized medical system, consumers are used to being able to do quite a bit of "shopping" for service, expecting that they can freely change providers if they are unhappy with results. They are rarely in a position to need to "qualify" for acceptance by a medical service provider.

This expectation is one of the things that has made revamping our medical care system so challenging for the politicians who will ultimately design any new plan. As I write, the president has just announced his new plan and opened the debate. While we cannot predict what the final plan will look like, it is discouraging to note that this first proposal does not include assisted reproductive technologies as a covered feature under pregnancy-related and family planning services. Some infertile Americans (most notably those in the several states which already mandate coverage of ARTS) may find that they are being asked to give up something they have worked very hard to gain.

In the U.S., prospective adopters have far less control and far fewer choices in terms of finding help in building a family by adoption than they did in finding medical assistance with their infertility. The media has also made most Americans very aware of some pretty scary issues for those hoping to "win" a child to parent: there are fewer and fewer healthy babies to adopt and more and more people hoping to adopt them, and among children not considered healthy babies the problems seem to be becoming more and more serious, challenging, and thus threatening and off-putting to prospective adopters. Statistically, however, for those who do decide to actively pursue adoption with the same energy and commitment that others expend on treatment, there is a much higher likelihood of "success" (as measured by having a child to parent) in adoption than there is in high tech treatment.

Canadian people deal with a different medical system. Since the system is socialized, there is much less entrepreneurialism and competitiveness, almost no financial incentive for physicians to train in highly specialized skills in the medical community in Canada, and indeed Canadian patients queue up for long waits for many specialized services. Spoiled middle class American consumers would find such waits intolerable! While there is doctor shopping in Canada, it doesn't happen to the same extent that it does in the States, and patients tend to feel much less in control of their treatment in Canada than they do in the United States—partially because of the socialization of medicine. When they then turn to adoption, and find a system of long waits and in-control professionals, Canadians may be far less surprised and off-put by this, as it is not that different from their experience with medical care.

While providing trainings in Canada I've noticed that Canadians seem to assume that all of the U.S. states are as wide-open in their approach to adoption or surrogacy as is a fabled and exaggerated place called California. In reality, of course, most Americans understand that, while the media does paint a rather strange portrait of what is going on in California, and while the California approach and experience may be slightly different from what is happening in other parts of the country, the media picture of California is far from accurate, nor is it typical of what is happening in the United States. Most of the U.S. remains rather conservative and traditional, though change is definitely occurring. The Canadian approach to infertility and adoption is probably only slightly more conservative, overall, than is the average U.S. approach to these issues. Consumers in Canada have similarly limited choices and similar "requirements" to meet.

The difference in perception concerning the adversarial relationship between consumers and professionals, then, may be in the different "conditioning" to professional intervention infertile Americans have had through the experience with an increasingly competitive infertility medical system before they move on to adoption. But in either case, what consumers look for is a way to feel re-empowered, more in control of their family planning choices—and the professionals with whom they come in contact play a major role in facilitating that empowerment.

Filling in the Gaps—Note to Advocates and Professionals

In that best of all possible worlds we dream of, infertile couples would have available to them within any major city a stepped program that would offer them information, support and assistance with medical factors of infertility and its treatment; decision making help, support, and referral to service providers in dealing with options; and well thought out services within each of those options that would mean that there was continuity in the education, decision making, and support services families need.

As an infertility and adoption advocate and educator, one of my greatest frustrations is that services for infertile people are so poorly linked with one another. This has changed very little in the past twenty years. Both the medical and social service systems seem to be so overwhelmed, understaffed and detached from one another that there tends to be quite a bit of confusion, a number of rather large holes for consumers to fall through, and little continuity. I've been looking pretty carefully over the last ten years for a model program in some community somewhere to hold up as an example of well linked services, and I haven't found one! Despite a large number of trainings I've done on this topic and the enthusiastic reception from professionals to the concept of linking services, evidently the hurdles have been too high to leap so far.

What are those hurdles? One, of course, is money. In the not-for-profit world hospitals and agencies have been cutting back on services rather than adding them. For a brief window of time in the early '80s it looked as if the competitive drive that makes a capitalistic society run might encourage the for-profit hospital system and the for-profit adoption practitioner system to lead the way in establishing new and innovative services. But in the '90s even the for-profits are cutting back.

A second hurdle is that mobility factors in modern society mean that not only are families more on the move and thus not as likely as families once were to be able to reconnect with their service providers should future problems arise, but workers are also more mobile, so that when families do recontact adoption agencies, for example, they are not likely to find a person on staff who is intimately familiar with their particular case.

A final hurdle is a credibility gap, the competitiveness that is so often perceived between consumers and professionals in fields related to infertility and adoption. I believe that the best way to eliminate this credibility gap is for professionals to begin to work more closely with the volunteer advocates in the field.

Professionals often fail to understand the importance of peer links. As a society we tend to assign much more credibility to workers who are paid and services which are purchased than we do to the work of volunteers. Yet infertility, surrogacy, and adoption oriented groups provide an amazing range of services for their members and clients using tiny budgets, kitchen table offices, and volunteer labor. Some of the best, most current, and most easily accessible information on infertility and adoption for lay people comes from the newsletters and magazines of advocacy/support groups. While professionally staffed organizations such as agencies and hospitals put on fine conferences, several of the largest and most highly regarded national and regional conferences for consumers on infertility and adoption are planned and implemented exclusively by volunteers.

Professionals must come to respect the value of the work that advocacy groups and their volunteers do, and to refer to them when appropriate rather than to compete with them by duplicating the education and support services that they provide so well. True respect means referring to them as early as possible after contact from the consumer, and consistently reminding the client of the availability of such services through their time spent with the agency or clinic rather than as a last ditch effort as the consumer departs the clinic after unsuccessful treatment or from the agency with a newborn in arms. True respect also means acknowledging and accepting the consumer group's need to maintain a certain distance and organizational separateness from service providers in order to protect their role and their reputations as consumer advocates.

But, you say, your medical practice or your adoption agency does refer families to such groups, and it isn't your fault that they choose not to take advantage of them. Perhaps you need to reevaluate your approach to referral. In what form do you present this referral? Keep in mind that people in crisis are unlikely to notice or pick up brochures lying around the waiting room and will retain less than half of what is spoken to them. In order to take seriously your referral to a peer group, clients need for a staff member they trust and respect to hand them a brochure and specifically recommend a program.

What services do you describe or emphasize? Could it perhaps be only the support offered by such groups? Please remember that there is a great deal of denial in operation in both infertility and adoption. Infertile couples tend to deny their infertility for a long time, and it is not at all uncommon for them to refuse to identify themselves as "one of them" when thinking of an infertility support group unless they have been given a clear (and rare) diagnosis of permanent sterility. Professionals who truly respect and appreciate the peer support and connections provided by groups such as RESOLVE or IAAC will be careful to endorse the education and information services and the advocacy components of such groups. These valuable programs are far less frightening and intimidating to consumers, and often provide the access to a group that can, if later needed, lead both to appropriate support and to transitional services to carry the client beyond treatment.

Beyond treatment, denial of difference is a common coping method for families new to adoption—even more so for couples who have not dealt effectively with resolving the multiple losses accompanying infertility. Being in control contributes mightily to a sense of well being. Adopters will often reject adoptive parenting groups while thinking "Those are for people with problems. We don't need help."

Support is not the issue that will "sell" group participation here, either. Nor is social interaction. If a family is denying difference or refusing to identify with others in their same situation, they will not be interested in singling themselves out by socializing with other families who are also "outside the norm." But, nearly all new parents (no matter how their children arrive) are information hungry. They want to do a good job. They want to know about parenting methods, about programs of benefit to parents, about books to read and to share. Parent groups are especially strong at gathering and disseminating such information. Emphasizing this information and education component opens the door, allowing parents to discover for themselves the benefits of peer support.

Professionals need to have flyers on hand and to feel no qualms about offering them often and repeatedly. Waiting rooms so often supplied with subscription copies of magazines should also include copies of local and national newsletters and magazines which are infertility-related and adoption-related. Professionals might even consider plugging into local groups on the couple's behalf, making a first year membership in a local infertility support group or parent group one of the perks that accompany medical or adoption services for which the consumer is paying.

If professionals would stop competing with one another and with the volunteers in these fields, it wouldn't be that difficult to link existing programs and fill in the gaps to provide a comprehensive educational and support program for infertile couples. Hospitals and clinics and doctors could and should join with local RESOLVE chapters and mental health professionals and adoption practitioners to offer periodic and regular "When to Stop," "Is Adoption for You?," "Considering the Childfree Alternative," "Exploring Assisted Reproduction with Donor Gametes" seminars that allow consumers to explore alternatives in an environment that is anonymous and noncommittal.

In such an environment where patients note that professionals are open to the talents and opinions offered outside their own office walls everybody wins. Patients win because they gain resources too difficult for just one provider to offer. Professionals win because their patients appreciate that the professionals are truly interested in meeting each patient's unique personal needs.

RESOURCES

National Organizations Offering Helpful Information and Referral for Consumers in Search of Services

RESOLVE, Inc. (1310 Broadway, Somerville MA 02144, telephone 617-623-0744) is a U.S. national nonprofit network of 54 chapters offering information, referral, support and advocacy services to infertile people. Dues of $35 annually (includes both national and local chapter membership). Their newsletters, fact sheets and symposia can be indispensable tools. Currently RESOLVE is putting a great deal of effort on a state by state basis into achieving mandated insurance coverage for infertility treatment. They have been successful already in Massachusetts, Maryland, California, and several other states.

Infertility Awareness Association of Canada (523-774 Echo Lane, Ottawa, Ontario K1S 5N8, CANADA, telephone 613-730-1322) is a Canadian charitable organization offering assistance, support, and education to those with infertility concerns through the distribution of its bilingual publication *Infertility Awareness* five times a year; establishment of chapters to provide grass roots services; a resource centre; information packages; and a network of related services. Services are bilingual (English and French.) Membership is $30 Canadian annually. A complimentary information kit will be sent to interested Canadians upon request.

American Fertility Society (1209 Montgomery Highway, Birmingham AL 35216-2809, 205-978-5000) is an international membership organization of professionals—predominantly doctors, but including nurses, reproductive biologists, mental health practitioners and health educators—who have a special interest in family planning and reproductive health. In addition to providing information about local members to consumers seeking a care provider, its special interest group the Society for Assisted Reproductive Technology is a membership group of IVF/GIFT clinics who have agreed to report their successes and other statistical data to AFS for dissemination through the annual SART Report. Its Psychological Special Interest Group focuses on the emotional ramifications of infertility. AFS publishes the prestigious medical journal *Fertility and Sterility* and many booklets directed toward patients concerning specific infertility problems and topics.

Endometriosis Association (8585 N. 76th Place, Milwaukee WI 53223) is a non-profit with chapters throughout the U.S. The organization publishes a newsletter and offers referrals and support for those dealing with the multiple issues related to endometriosis, only one of which is infertility.

The Organization of Parents through Surrogacy (OPTS) (7054 Quito Ct., Camarillo, CA 93012, 805-482-1566) is a national non-profit, volunteer organization with three regional chapters whose purpose is mutual support, networking, and the dissemination of information regarding surrogate parenting, egg donation, sperm donation as well as assisted reproductive technology including IVF and GIFT. OPTS publishes a quarterly newsletter, holds annual meetings, has a telephone support network, and actively lobbies for legislation concerning surrogacy. Membership is $40 annually.

Adoption Council of Canada (P.O. Box 8442, Station T, Ottawa, Ontario K1G 3H8. Phone 613-235-1566.) This network collects and disseminates information about adoption throughout Canada, facilitating communication among groups and individuals interested in adoption and promoting understanding of the benefits and challenges of adoption.

Adoptive Families of America (3333 Hwy 100 North, Minneapolis, MN 55422. Phone 612-537-0316.) An excellent source for purchase of books and tapes and of referral to local parent groups, AFA is the largest organization for adoptive families in the world. AFA publishes *OURS: The Magazine of Adoptive Families* bimonthly and sponsors an annual national conference designed specifically to reach out to those considering adopting and adoption-expanded families. Its Annual Adoption Information and Resources packet lists several hundred agencies nationally and offers consumer advice.

American Academy of Adoption Attorneys (P.O. Box 33053, Washington DC 20033-0053.) A national association of attorneys who handle adoption cases or otherwise have distinguished themselves in the field of adoption law. The group's work includes promoting the reform of adoption laws and disseminating information on ethical adoption practices. The Academy publishes a newsletter and holds annual meetings and continuing education seminars for attorneys.

National Council for Adoption (1930 17th St NW, Washington DC 20009, telephone 202-328-1200.) An advocacy organization promoting adoption as a positive family building option. Primarily supported by member agencies, it does also encourage individual memberships from those families who share its conservative stance on open-records/confidentiality and its wary view of open placements. If you have decided to pursue a traditional, confidential, agency adoption, call NCFA for a referral to a member agency.

North American Council on Adoptable Children (NACAC) (970 Raymond Ave. #106, St Paul, MN 55114-1149. Phone 612-644-3036.) An advocacy and education resource concerning waiting children, NACAC publishes the periodic newsletter *Adoptalk*, which reviews new books and tapes, and sponsors each August an enormous, well respected conference on special needs adoption for professionals and parent advocates. This conference rotates through five geographic areas. If you are considering a special needs adoption, call NACAC first for information about local and national resources, parent groups, and adoption exchanges.

Chapter 5

MAKING MEDICAL TREATMENT CHOICES

I began to grow skeptical about the accepted methods for infertility treatment when I realized that I wasn't meeting the needs of my patients. Although I was investing a lot of energy and emotion into their problems, I wa becoming more and more frustrated with the way they responded to my care.

Many of my patients acted a if they didn't hear my instructions. For example, every time I told Lori I'd have her test results in three days, she'd call me the next morning for the results... I couldn't understand why these intelligent and highly motivated people reacted so erratically.

The reasons became clear once I discovered how my patients blossomed <u>when they became a positive force in their infertility treatment.</u>

> Mark Perloe, M.D.
> *from* Miracle Babies and
> Other Happy Endings for
> Couples with Fertility Problems

Just one and a half generations ago the options for diagnosing and treating most conditions which produced infertility were extremely limited. Many problems could not be identified and little could be done for most problems which were identified. But the boom in research in reproductive health in the last third of the twentieth century has produced new options with dizzying speed.

On the one hand, of course, this is wonderful! Today it is generally accepted that over 50% of couples who seek specialized care and who are appropriately diagnosed can be helped to achieve a pregnancy from their own gametes and to give birth to a healthy baby.

But the menu of options also produces tremendous pressure. To begin with, the fact that a couple is seeing a specialist most often leads the medical team to presume that they intend to go "all the way", however that is defined by the limits of current technology. The fact that technology exists at all is often coercive to the extent that it seems to carry with it the presumption that of course it will be used.

Among all of the thousands of patients I have spoken with over the last fourteen years, I could count on my fingers and toes the number who have told me that their physician ever asked them if they wanted to take a break from or even to stop treatment unless they were also being told that further treatment simply did not exist. Without feeling that they have permission from the professional team to take a break, many patients report that they are afraid to talk to their physicians about such a need. Often they feel that in quitting they are "letting the medical team down." The result is that physicians and nurses in my in-service workshops always acknowledge that a significant number of patients simply "disappear" from treatment somewhere along the line.

Even worse, advancing technologies appear to have created relational problems that may not have existed a generation ago. In his 1993 book *Pursuing Parenthood: Ethical Issues in Assisted Reproduction* ethicist and infertility patient Paul Lauritzen writes

> One of the peculiar aspects of infertility is that it is typically a condition that a couple suffers. As Leon Kass has noted, infertility is as much a relationship as a condition. Yet infertility treatment, structured as it is by available technologies, leads us to view infertility individually. It is the individual who is treated, and it is the individual who must accept responsibility for childlessness, if he or she refuses treatment. From a situation in which infertility is a relational problem for which no one is to blame, infertility becomes an individual

problem for which an individual who refuses treatment is to blame."[1]

To some, this all may sound overwhelming. And it is, of course, very serious stuff. But keep in mind what we've been emphasizing all along: The two of you are partners, and this is not a conveyor belt, but a series of separate and distinct opportunities to make the decision to go on or to stop. The result of each test brings a new opportunity for evaluation. Each proposed treatment can be accepted or rejected. And, most important of all, for couples who have carefully thought through and talked with each other about their individual reactions to the potential losses of infertility and have decided to take charge of their infertility as a team, no one is "to blame" for the infertility. For couples who have taken charge there is no such thing as "refusing treatment" in the sense that Lauritzen describes. Take-charge couples may choose to end treatment or may choose not to try a particular treatment, but they do not deny one another treatment.

There are few right or wrong answers in weighing options. What seems right for one individual may be wrong for another patient with a similar diagnosis. No one can or should make these decisions for you. Partners may find it helpful to ask others for advice, but ultimately you must decide together what will work for you. The most important thing here is that you remain committed to deciding together what to do next.

Having done the work of understanding, ranking and weighting infertility's losses for each of yourselves and the two of you together and then inventorying your personal resources of time, money, physical reserves and emotional energy, you are, as a couple, in a much better position to formulate the questions that will need to be asked at each step along the way.

Couples who are attempting to make decisions must explore the immediate and future ramifications—physical, temporal, financial, emotional, ethical—of each proposed treatment on each of their own lives, on their life together, and on the lives of the children they hope to parent.

Because those children seem so distant by this time, so unreal, it is not at all uncommon for infertile couples to put their

---

1. Lauritzen, Paul; *Pursuing Parenthood: Ethical Issues in Assisted Reproduction.* (Bloomington, Indiana University Press, 1993) p. xiv

future children's best interests completely aside. In fact, infertility is such an overwhelming experience that far too often conveyor-belt couples have not thought at all beyond conception and birth to issues of parenting. But pregnancy and birth are a several month experience, while parenting requires eighteen to twenty-one years of day-to-day responsibility and a lifetime of involvement.

Making good decisions, then, means having thought carefully about the impact of those decisions on the lives of the children who may arrive as a result. How might this treatment affect their health? How might this alternative affect their psychological well being? How will our age affect our ability to be effective psychological and social parents to them? These issues which impact the future are as important, perhaps moreso, as are the technical issues relating to the immediate treatment.

Because things are changing so rapidly, this book will make no attempt to describe specific treatments exhaustively, but will instead offer you some guidance about how to go about formulating questions that need to be answered and then finding relatively objective answers to those questions.

Doing Your Homework

Being in charge requires becoming informed. Most infertility patients are not physicians or researchers (though of course one in six physicians or researchers can expect to deal with a fertility impairment, too!) and so cannot be expected to know a lot about the current state of the art of treating infertility.

But you can and should become a well informed consumer. Making appropriate choices about which of several treatment options to pursue demands that consumers be much better informed than they have ever before been expected to be. They must carefully assess the odds of a treatment's being successful, and those odds are influenced by the degree of the physical problem, their relative health, and the skill and experience of the particular physicians and other professionals involved in their care.

How does one gather the information needed to make such judgements? By reading, attending workshops, and asking as many questions as they can formulate.

Let me be blunt about my personal bias here. I believe that it makes no sense at all for the infertility patient seeking up-to-date information to rely only on his or her physician to provide that information. Physicians are human. They bring with them their own personal biases and their own values. This means that as humans they find it challenging to objectively support decisions which they themselves would not make under the same circumstances. Additionally, while the overwhelming majority of medical care providers are honest and ethical, every profession has its "bad apples" and they are very difficult to identify. Certainly you need information and advice from your physician, but you also need objective and/or corroborating information.

Infertility is awash in statistics. When it comes to using them in decision making, it's wise to be skeptical and to ask for confirming data. It's also wise to try to think about the statistics you are hearing from other angles. HMG produces a 70% pregnancy rate? Donor insemination produces a pregnancy within nine cycles for 85% of recipients? What are the medical and demographic profiles for such patients? Do you match it? When a clinic cites the (accurate) statistical probability of pregnancy in one cycle of normal sexual intercourse in a young, healthy, fertile couple as 24% and then points out that at their clinic the take home baby rate for a cycle of GIFT is also 24%, apples and oranges are being compared. The outcome (pregnancy and a baby) may be similar, but the investment doesn't compare. The healthy young couple have different eggs and sperm than does the infertile couple. The emotional investment in the 76% "failure" rate for the couple who is not infertilite is minimal compared to the emotional reaction of an infertile couple who have been through the mill. A few minutes of intimacy and pleasure in the privacy of one's bedroom doesn't compare at all to a closely monitored menstrual cycle replete with shots, blood draws, ultrasounds, multiple hovering professionals, time away from work, etc. The physical investment in intercourse is similarly different from the physical investment in a treatment cycle. The financial investment in intercourse is near zero, while a GIFT cycle will cost thousands of (possibly unreimbursable) dollars.

The consumer press regularly reports on research published in reputable medical journals and presented at medical conferences. But because medical reporters cannot be expected to have access to all of the research necessary to evaluate the innovations being reported, the daily newspaper or weekly news magazines should not be considered a primary source of accurate medical information.

To the consternation of cautious and conservative good doctors, media reports themselves often drive the use of experimental techniques and, at the opposite extreme, create unnecessary panic in patients. By making patients more broadly aware of early results of trials, the popular media send eager patients scurrying to their physicians to request the latest techniques or frighten patients with still unproven concerns.

The Summer, 1993, issue of *Fertility and Sterility* (Volume 60, Number 30) carried several articles concerning this issue. Included were an article authored by the International Federation of Infertility Societies calling for caution about a small, poorly designed, but widely reported, study which seemed to find a causative link between fertility drugs and ovarian cancer. The authors pointed out serious—perhaps even fatal—flaws in the small first study and asked for cooperation in further study by research institutions. A second article by Drs. Fluker, Zouves, and Bebbington ("A Prospective Randomized Comparison of Zygote Intrafallopian Transfer and *In Vitro* Fertilization-Embryo Transfer for Nontubal Factor Infertility") shows that ZIFT, a variation of IVF which was widely offered after early reports suggested it as promising, does not, in fact offer better results than IVF-ET, though it is more expensive.

This same issue of *Fertility and Sterility* carried an editorial by McMaster University, Canada, physician Dr. John A. Collins calling on physicians to exercise more caution in evaluating journal reporting of promising new techniques and responding to patient requests for treatment. In his article "New Treatments, Preliminary Results, and Clinical Practice" (pp. 403-405) Collins reminds physicians that they serve an important role in judging appropriateness of therapy, "The majority of infertile patients, including those who are most anxious, are likely to think twice about any treatment that is considered by their own physician to be untested or unproven."

How, then, does a consumer evaluate reported news of alarming research? *Lupus Journal* from the Lupus Foundation of America offered some helpful advice as reported in the Summer, 1993 issue of *FerreFax*. The article quoted Drs. Donald Ebersold (Director of the University of Cincinnati Family Practice Center) and Dr. Jack Kues (Director of Predoctoral Medical Education for the U.C. Department of Family Medicine) as suggesting that the source of the information is most important. It's considered more reliable if a study involves human subjects rather than animals (or is confirmed by multiple, multi-center animal studies), if it comes from a large research center or medical school or one of the federal research agencies such as the National Institutes of Health, and if it is an independent study not funded by someone with a financial interest in the outcome. Physicians consider research more reliable if it is printed in a respected peer-reviewed journal, such as *The New England Journal of Medicine*, or AFS' *Fertility and Sterility* or the *Journal of the American Medical Association* or the British journal *Lancet*. Studies done as pilots or preliminaries are usually in their earliest phases, so that it is important to watch for end-of-the-study confirmations of findings before making firm decisions. Doctors Ebersold and Kues advise that patients discount out of hand anecdotal information— anything based on something a doctor has seen in his own practice but hasn't tested and scientifically confirmed in a formal laboratory study.[2] This last advice can be particularly important to keep in mind, as, in the increasingly entrepreneurial world of reproductive medicine, private clinics are more and more often releasing their anecdotal information in a format that appears to the unwary like that of peer-reviewed research but which is actually little more than a public relations press release.

I make no attempt to hide my bias about the need for patients to be connected to the national consumer organizations: RESOLVE in the U.S., I.A.A.C. in Canada. In their newsletters you will find articles by professionals written in consumer language. Through these groups you will have access to a wide variety of specially focused fact sheets and booklets which, by the very nature of their being easily redone, are guaranteed to be more up-to-date than a book can ever be. In these groups' newsletters you will learn first about the newest and best books and the newest and best programs.

Seminars and monthly meetings held by infertility groups are another important source of information. Additionally, many groups periodically hold an infertility symposium. These are day-long events which offer a menu of presentations by medical, counseling, and social service professionals on most medical

---

2. Suthers, Derwent; "When Should You Act on the Latest Research: Advice for the Learning Consumer;" *Ferre Fax*, Volume 9, Number 1, p. 5.

issues and treatments and some lifestyle alternatives. They are sometimes singly sponsored and sometimes sponsored by these groups in conjunction with a drug manufacturer or a hospital or a college or university. Since these large meetings are often annual or biennial events, you may find that your own timing doesn't match that of the group. Don't underestimate the value of such educational opportunities. They are worth making special arrangements and taking special effort to attend. If you discover, however, that you've just missed such an opportunity, inquire as to whether the sessions were audio-taped and are available for borrowing or for purchase.

Through these national groups, their local affiliates and the independent local infertility groups in some cities, you will have access to objective referral and to other consumers who will be willing to share their own experiences.

If you are avoiding membership in such organizations, you are probably making a serious mistake! Perhaps you think that you don't want support. Fine! Don't take advantage of that opportunity! Perhaps you don't want to be involved as a volunteer. OK! Let "the other guy" do the work and you just support him or her by paying your dues and fees. Perhaps you feel you won't "need" to be a member since you're going to become pregnant quickly. Terrific, don't renew after your initial membership runs out! But right now you are not pregnant, and this is the way to get the information you need to get pregnant! Perhaps you don't agree with the group's politics. You have two choices: ignore politics and just take what other information and assistance you need from the group or get in there and change the group's focus from the inside!

Beyond consumer groups, The American Fertility Society and some drug manufacturers publish patient booklets and pamphlets on a number of topics. You should of course browse in bookstores and libraries, but be aware that neither can be depended upon to stock the newest and best of titles. Because infertile people tend to be somewhat "closeted," librarians and booksellers are often completely unaware of the size of the audience. Thus they are likely to carry only token numbers of titles in this field rather than a broad and up-to-date cross section of titles, making their purchases primarily on the recommendations of large publishers' salespeople. This often means that materials from smaller publishers (like Perspectives Press, for example) will not be on the shelf (though booksellers can and will special order them), or that the titles in stock will be older titles which have already established a sales history but may not be as up-to-date as a newer title. To find the newest and most helpful books, read reviews in consumer group newsletters and then ask your bookseller or librarian to order the books you want. You do not have to buy. For a nominal fee (and often even at no charge) your local library can obtain nearly anything they do not carry through the interlibrary loan program.

Some consumers want to read medical journals, despite the fact that these are written in academic style and language for a professional audience. Hospitals and medical schools often make their libraries open to consumers for research. Your physician may be willing to have his staff do a computer search of professional literature on a particular topic for you. This, however, is not standard practice.

Learning to do your homework properly about infertility is not too unlike those junior high research projects where you learned that the encyclopedia wasn't enough and you were taught to use interviews, the *Reader's Guide to Periodical Literature*, etc. Take-charge patients will need data from a variety of sources: the popular media, seminars, newsletters, journals and books. They must also assure themselves that they are under the care of a physician whose advice and judgement they can trust. Be cautious in accepting and evaluating all of this raw intellectual data, weigh it all against your emotional and ethical impressions, communicate effectively with your partner to seek compromise or consensus, and realize that final decisions are entirely your own.

The Basic Work-Up

Once upon a time not very long ago, couples produced a few basal body temperature graphs and found themselves plopped into Clomid™ therapy, which might or might not result in a pregnancy. If it didn't, after a few months some more tests were run.

I'd like to be able to write that this doesn't happen any more, but I can't. The truth is that it does continue to happen in very large numbers to couples who are being treated by physicians who dabble in infertility but have no specialized expertise in the field. This is why it is so important for couples who want to be in charge of their own quest for fertility to become as knowledgeable as possible about the process itself and the qualifications of the professionals with whom they intend to work.

Today those of us who have educated ourselves about infertility (both consumers and professionals) understand that in order for a couple to be successful in obtaining treatment for a fertility impairment, they and their care providers must be knowledgeable about and sensitive to the statistics: while not all infertility is curable, just 10% or less of couples have a condition which really can't be diagnosed when both partners are examined by experts; husbands are just as likely to be infertile as are wives; and a large percentage (perhaps as many as 35% or more) of couples who experience a fertility impairment have more than one fertility problem.

A basic work-up should begin with a consultation between the physician and his patients, the infertile couple. Note that I did write *couple*. Because this is a condition which directly affects two people no matter whether one or both has the medical problem, both partners should be involved in the information gathering and the decision making about testing and treatment from the very beginning.

At this consultation the physician will clarify with the couple his questions about an already submitted medical/sexual history, and will discuss with the couple a suggested approach for evaluation and treatment: which tests will be performed and at what intervals, what physical side effects can be expected from certain procedures, how much each procedure can be expected to cost and information about how best to determine what facets will be covered by insurance, how long the basic evaluation process will take, etc. Ideally, the physician will make available a written summary of this plan for the couple to take home and discuss and refer back to as needed.

A thorough basic work-up uses both detailed history-taking and the most up-to-date tests to check that general health is good and free of lifestyle concerns that could affect fertility (extreme stress, use of tobacco, alcohol or "recreational drugs", obsessive exercise, eating disorders, etc.); that sperm count, shape, and movement are adequate and that proper delivery of sperm is possible in the man; that ovulation appears to be occurring regularly and that both fallopian tubes and uterus are well formed and free of obstructions in the woman; that various hormone levels of both husband and wife are within normal ranges; and, via a post-coital test of some sort, that sperm remains viable once delivered into the wife's vagina. The usual procedure is to do the least invasive procedures first, and to recommend evaluative procedures involving surgery (laparoscopy, testicular biopsy, etc.) only after less invasive procedures have been completed or when there is a clear indication that such procedures are necessary.

The results of the battery of tests involved in a basic work-up combined with a basic understanding of the statistical realities of infertility should help in formulating questions. Without all of these most basic of tests having been accomplished it usually doesn't make sense to agree to any drug therapy, surgical intervention, or an assisted reproductive technology. For example, why would a wife be treated for anything at all before a husband had even had a semen analysis done? Perhaps the wife has a tubal obstruction in addition to ovulation problems. Perhaps both the man and the woman are slightly subfertile and each needs treatment. Why treat a partner for one problem without verifying that it is the only problem?

Treating before thoroughly testing wastes significant amounts of all resources. Money may be spent on drugs that have no hope of producing a pregnancy. Time can be wasted in months of treatments that cannot be productive. Emotional energy is expended on that monthly roller coaster ride of escalating hope and crashing despair. Physical reserves are used up and some medical conditions can even be come worse over time when left untreated.

What constitutes a basic work-up changes as newer tests are added. The very best way to determine just exactly what tests are considered part of a state-of-the-art work-up right now, today, as you are reading this book, is to phone the office of RESOLVE and order their fact sheet on the medical work-up. This fact sheet is updated frequently by medical professionals and reviewed by experts to take into account changes in research and technology, and so is able to be much more up-to-date than any book could be.

It is important to reemphasize that it is rarely in a couple's best physical, psychological, financial, or temporal interests to work with a physician who does not operate from a clear, pre-identified, step-by-step plan but instead drifts with them from test to treatment to test to treatment. Nor is it in their best interests to work with a physician who is unwilling to encourage the couple to be a part of customizing that plan. A physician who is threatened by a well informed patient's questions is not a good choice for a couple who wishes to take charge of rather than be taken charge of by their infertility.

Drug Therapies

Many conditions which cause infertility, including endometriosis, ovulation problems, retrograde ejaculation, and more, may respond to drug therapies. Additionally, many of the assisted reproductive technologies use drug therapy as a part of the protocol. Any medication, however, can be successful only when properly administered and properly monitored. The expertise of the physician and the sophistication of the laboratories used to monitor results can affect the success of therapy.

Drugs used to treat fertility problems almost all create various emotional and physical side effects. These can affect not just your fertility, but your relationship with your partner, family, friends and co-workers, and therefore your life as a whole. Some drugs may have the potential to create future health problems for the patients who ingest them as well as for the children born to these mothers. Some drugs create a higher risk for conceiving multiples, and this carries with it a greater risk for miscarriage, a greater risk for premature birth and related medical problems, not to mention the difficulties created for a lifetime in parenting more than one baby born at the same time.

As a patient you have a right to expect that your physician will advise you properly about all potential side effects of any medication she prescribes. You should read all that you can get your hands on —newsletters, fact sheets, books—and speak to several patients who have taken such drugs both successfully and unsuccessfully before saying yes to any medication.

It is also important for you to understand that even two drugs that appear from a consumer viewpoint to be used to treat the same medical symptoms can be very different in terms of their cost, their administration, their monitoring, and their physical and emotional impact on you and your partner. For example, clomiphene citrate (brand names Clomid™ and Serophene™) and human menopausal gonadotropins (hMG, marketed under the brand names Pergonal™ and Humagen™) are each used to treat patients with ovulatory dysfunctions. How they work and how they are administered and monitored, however, is very different.

Rose Kegler Hallarn described her experience with these two drugs in the November, 1984, RESOLVE of Ohio newsletter like this

> (In considering taking Pergonal) You may say "I've been though Clomid treatment for ovulation induction, so what's the big deal?" The "big deal" is that there is no comparison between clomiphene and Pergonal in terms of the emotional roller coaster ride involved. Clomiphene is the kiddie-land version and Pergonal is the King Cobra.

Drugs which are used to stimulate production of ova have two potentially serious side effects. The first is hyperstimulation of the ovaries, which, while not a common reaction, is potentially fatal when it does occur. This potential side effect is serious enough that RESOLVE, for example, recommends in its consumer fact sheets that only infertility specialists administer hMG, which demands meticulous monitoring to carefully screened patients.

The second serious side effect is the risk of a multiple pregnancy. Being realistic about this is difficult. Almost every childless infertile couple thinks that having several babies at once sounds absolutely wonderful—instant family! And besides, giving birth to several babies at once is associated with super fertility rather than with infertility, so few couples are able to imagine that such a thing could happen to them at all! But a multiple pregnancy is a high risk pregnancy which produces the possibility of major medical hazards for both mother and children, including the statistical probability of premature birth. Most commonly, multiple pregnancies do not go to term, and the babies, which are almost always of smaller birth weight than singletons, are born prematurely. Their very prematurity and resulting lack of maturity threatens their survival. Helping them to survive is extraordinarily expensive.

In order to be realistic, you need to talk to patients who have experienced such a high risk pregnancy successfully and unsuccessfully, as well as to parents of multiples, especially those parenting triplets or quadruplets.

According to their infertility support group, Anna and Trevor were incredibly lucky! Their third IVF cycle had resulted in their giving birth to four babies, two boys and two girls. How perfect! They had become almost legendary. Of course Anna and Trevor weren't active in the group anymore. They were too busy, but that was to be understood.

Truth be told, Anna and Trevor weren't such happy campers. The only place they felt comfortable these days was in a small local parents-of-multiples group where they could feel free to share their frustrations. The pregnancy had required complete bed rest for six months. Anna had been "good." Their children, now four years old, had been born prematurely, and one had cerebral palsy. Anna felt guilty that she hadn't done enough to prevent this problem.

Their medical expenses for the treatment itself and then the pregnancy and delivery and the several weeks the babies remained in the intensive care nursery were astronomical and only partially covered by their insurance. Raising four children was expensive, and the business community that had been so generous with baby food and diapers and equipment when the babies were brand new couldn't be expected to continue to support the family after the novelty wore off. Day care for four had been an impossibility, both because it was impossible to find and because it would have cost more than Anna's take home pay. So Anna had not been able to return to work. This represented a real squeeze on their budget.

Of course the babies were preschoolers now, and so mostly they slept through the night. That first year had been a bear! But it was still nearly impossible to arrange baby-sitting so that Trevor and Anna could go out. A teenager couldn't handle four kids at once, so they needed to hire two at a time. That was both expensive and difficult to arrange so that the teens didn't entertain each other and forget about the babies.

Once a month, in the multiples group, which met at a local church which provided child care for the families in another room, Trevor and Anna could let their hair down. Of the nine families in the multiples group, only one birth (of twins) had not been a result of infertility treatment. Trevor and Anna's and one other set of quads, two sets of twins and four triplets had been born after ovulation induction and/or GIFT or IVF. Of course they all loved their babies! But nobody except the group seemed to understand their frustrations. And nobody except the group understood their exhaustion. And nobody except the group understood their financial problems. Would they do it again? They weren't so sure. All of them felt that they had not been given enough information before choosing the treatment.

There is now the alternative of a pregnancy reduction, a procedure in which, via ultrasound and laparoscopy, some embryos in a multiple pregnancy are selected for termination and are aborted to allow the remaining fewer embryos a greater chance of survival. Recent follow-up with patients who have undergone such procedures demonstrate that nearly all experience strong ongoing emotional reactions to this procedure, even when it results in the successful birth of healthy babies, so that it remains best to try to avoid the need for it, it should not be considered "routine" and it must come accompanied by appropriate psychosocial support.

Asking well informed questions can help you in determining how certain medications will affect the budgeted resources which are a part of your overall plan for taking charge of infertility. Some questions to ask include these

1. Is·the purpose of the drug to cure the problem once and for all or to by-pass a problem which will remain once you are no longer taking the medication?

2. How many cycles are recommended before this medication's effectiveness in your case should be reevaluated or before this treatment protocol will be considered complete?

3.   In what form will the drug be administered and will its administration require assistance from your partner or from professionals?

4.   How, when and where will the drug's impact on your body be monitored and how will this monitoring affect your normal routine and/or your work life?

5.   What immediate side effects can be expected and how will they affect your everyday life both physically and emotionally?

6.   Are there possible long-term side effects for yourself or for future children for you to consider?

7.   What is the statistical likelihood of multiple pregnancy while using this medication? If such a pregnancy occurs, what are the risks and what are the alternatives? How can the risks of conceiving more than two children be reduced?

8.   What will be the total expense for the medication, its monitoring, and any other attendant costs per cycle or for the length of a completed treatment? Will these costs be covered by your insurance?

9.   What is the statistical likelihood of the drug's success (measured in terms of taking home a health baby) in cases just like your own?

10.   Are there alternatives?

In the U.S. the Food and Drug Administration has stringent guidelines for the development and introduction into the human population of new drugs, but even with FDA guidelines in place we know that in some cases negative side effects of drugs have appeared only after many years. It was an entire generation later, for example, before patients who took diethylstilbesterol (DES) to prevent miscarriages in the 1950s learned that this drug had caused abnormalities in the reproductive systems of the children born while they were taking the drug, resulting in significant male and female infertility in these babies in their adulthood.

While there is no reason for you to be unduly frightened that any of the infertility drugs commonly used today will create similar problems for your children, as an informed consumer you owe it to yourself to be conscientious about making choices by asking questions and being properly concerned about research you hear of that raises questions, using guidelines listed in the "Doing Your Homework" section above.

Surgery—When to Cut

From an exploratory laparoscopy to wedging ovarian cysts to removing endometriosis to repairing a varicocele to reconstructing damaged fallopian tubes, surgery is both a testing and a treatment tool in infertility. But surgery is an invasive procedure not without significant risk—from anesthesia, from infection, from error—and so it is not something into which most patients enter lightly. Furthermore, since surgery is often a one-chance option, which, if unsuccessful, may in some cases make the problem worse rather than better, it makes sense to examine carefully your surgeon's expertise in this area.

Many surgeons develop expertise with a particular style of surgery. Some are expert in microsurgery, for example, while others prefer to use the laser. Surgeons expert in either technique have reported similar success rates for treating most conditions. Overall research statistics to date do not indicate that one style of surgery is generally better than another for most infertility problems, but technique used may have a financial impact.

Some surgeons will develop expertise in a particular procedure. For example, some surgeons become known for their success in treating varicoceles or for the percentage of patients who delivery healthy babies after their repair of diseased fallopian tubes. Determining your surgeon's reputation and success rate with cases similar to yours can significantly enhance your statistical odds for success. Sometimes the investment of some of your resources of time, money, and physical and emotional energy in traveling great distances for treatment can produce the best return on the investment as measured by successful treatment.

Once again there are a number of questions to consider in determining whether a suggested surgery fits your budgeted resources and your overall plan for taking charge of your infertility.

1.   Given your diagnosis to date, are there less invasive or less expensive or statistically more successful alternatives? For example: Hysterosalpingogram as opposed to laparoscopy; drug therapy as opposed to surgery for endometriosis or for retrograde ejaculation; GIFT as opposed to IVF.

2.   What are both the long term and short term effects of the surgery on your physical health? Are you a well motivated "good healer," one who tolerates pain and discomfort well and is likely to recuperate quickly?

3.   How about your emotional well being? If the odds for success are not extraordinarily high, how well prepared are you for dealing with your disappointment? Is emotional support available through the service provider?

4.   How much will this cost, and what will be its impact upon your overall budgeted financial resources to be invested in infertility treatment and alternatives?

5.   Averaged overall statistics for success are much less important than the statistics of your own surgeon. How well qualified in terms of training and peer-judged professional accreditation is the physician who proposes to do your surgery? How experienced is he in terms of how frequently he performs this particular procedure? How successful is he as measured by the percentage of patients who have successfully given birth to a baby following his performing such a procedure? Who is more successful, and is that physician accessible to you?

6.   Will photographic surgical records be made so that the condition of the organs at the time of surgery could, if need be, later be made available to another physician for evaluation?

As an example of this kind of analysis concerning how to spend your resources consider these two couples' decision making processes.

On the surface, Jason and Hillary and Roberto and Lupe, patients of the same physician, appeared to share the same diagnosis: blocked fallopian tubes. But their cases were quite different.

The fimbriated ends of Hillary's fallopian tubes had been severely damaged by a serious Chlamydia infection and the complications of endometriosis, resulting in their total closure. Adhesions caused her tubes to adhere to bowel and bladder. At 39, Hillary was feeling the pinch of her age. Roberto and Lupe, on the other hand, were both in their early 30s. Lupe's laparoscopy showed some relatively simple adhesions in an otherwise "clean" pelvis.

For Roberto and Lupe surgery to repair her fallopian tubes (an expense covered by insurance at a financial investment equivalent to two IVF procedures not covered by insurance, physical investment in terms of pain and recuperation from a major surgery, time investment including six weeks off work to recover from surgery, etc.) produced a high statistical likelihood of a cure. The result would be that Lupe's tubes would be open and functioning and thus offer a good chance that pregnancy might occur not once but even twice or more without more intervention. Lupe was young enough that she felt that she would still have time, should she not become pregnant on her own in a couple of years, to try IVF or GIFT.

Hillary was not such a good candidate for surgical success. Because of the extent of damage in her tubes, even if she was fortunate enough to overcome the less than 20% odds that she would conceive after surgery, the possibility of an ectopic pregnancy was very high. Given the odds and their perception of the ticking biological clock, Hillary and Jason decided that it might make more sense to invest the same money, physical resources and less time in two attempts at IVF which would by-pass the damaged tubes but not cure the infertility problem.

Assisted Reproductive Technologies

Assisted Reproductive Technologies are those procedures which provide the possibility of achieving a pregnancy not through sexual intercourse, but through techniques which by-pass fertility problems. Most commonly ARTS use the gametes (sperm and ova) and body parts of just the infertile couple. The husband's sperm, for example, may be placed in his wife's vagina via catheter in a procedure known as HI (husband insemination) and earlier known by the more negative term AIH (artificial insemination with husband's sperm.) In the least complex form of *in vitro* fertilization the wife's ova are harvested via laparoscopy or transvaginal ultrasound and placed in culture with her partner's sperm in a petrie dish for a specified number of hours until the resulting embryo has divided appropriately and then the embryo is placed via catheter in the wife's uterus for gestation. A husband's sluggish or sparse sperm may be injected directly into his wife's egg's zona pellucida through several complex processes involving *in vitro* fertilization (the newest of which is called subzonal injection, or SUZI). GIFT is an even less invasive procedure developed from the IVF technology. In GIFT, a process which attempts to answer the concerns and prohibitions of the Catholic church about fertilization occurring anywhere but in the body, the aspirated ova of the wife are collected in a catheter. Her husband's sperm is put in the same catheter (but separated from the ova). The two are then placed directly into the fallopian tube (as opposed to *in vitro*) to meet and fertilize.

Assisted Reproductive Technologies, can, however, become much more complex, involving donor eggs, or donor sperm, or gestational surrogates or embryo adoption, etc. Since the alternative of third party assisted reproduction will be covered in a separate chapter, this section will look only at issues related to ARTs involving the gametes and reproductive capacities of just the infertile couple themselves.

ARTs have brought new hope to a generation of couples dealing with what once would have been hopeless infertility. Since the birth in 1978 of Louise Brown in England, thousands of babies have been born worldwide through IVF, GIFT, and their variants.

ARTs have also become big business. Over 300 clinics now offer ART services in the U.S. and they operate almost entirely in a free-market environment. There are few if any governmental regulations concerning the training and experience which qualify the staff of an ART clinic. Because the business is so competitive, most clinics market themselves aggressively and have a strong public relations component. Local newspapers and television stations often receive and use press releases which announce the availability of procedures and protocols which would appear to any but the most sophisticated reader to be examples of properly peer-reviewed, academically supervised, objective cutting edge research. Sometimes this is indeed the case. Other times it is not.

Although most physicians are ethical and honest, some clinics inflate their apparent success rate by manipulating the figures they report. Because statistics are very difficult to interpret this is easy to do. Clinical pregnancy rates, for example, are significantly higher at any clinic than is the rate of live births, and often it is this very high clinical pregnancy rate that is advertised to potential patients.

Coverage in the popular media over ten years has made ART seem almost commonplace today. And indeed with GIFT centers springing up at even very small hospitals throughout the country, ARTs can appear to be deceptively routine and commonplace. In fact, overall less than 5% of couples try ARTS. Whether that is due to lack of appropriateness, lack of access, lack of money, lack of enthusiasm, or a conservative reaction to the statistical probabilities, we don't know.

In the late 1980s and early 1990s concern about this lack of regulation and unchecked marketing resulted in Congressional hearings on the issue and some legislation. It also produced an interest among practitioners in heading off the need for government regulation by voluntary self-reporting and regulation.

Over two thirds of the clinics now in operation have agreed to report their data in a uniform format to the American Fertility Society's Society of Assisted Reproductive Technology on an annual basis. Actual membership in SART requires a willingness to follow stringent AFS guidelines for both staffing and reporting. Some non-member clinics (often those who do not meet SART's strict professional training criteria) also report using the SART's format and are part of the annual *Clinic Specific Outcome Assessment*. The system for gathering and the information itself is not perfect. AFS members continue to debate the best approach to data collection. But availability to consumers of this standardized information can help them in trying to evaluate their odds and their options with these alternatives.

Though the IVF-related procedures are no longer classified as experimental by the American Fertility Society, statistically they remain only moderately successful. According to the AFS' Society for Assisted Reproductive Technology's *Clinic-Specific Outcome Assessment for the Year 1991* (the most recent SART Report) as summarized in *Fertility and Sterility* (Vol. 59, No. 5, May 1993, pp. 956-962), the overall take-home baby rate for IVF among the 212 programs reporting was just 15.25% per egg retrieval (though the success of individual clinics varied dramatically from 0% success to over 30% success.) GIFT appeared to offer higher success rates than did IVF, with 26.5% of retrievals resulting in the delivery of a baby. From a much smaller number of ZIFT procedures reported, there were 19.7% deliveries among retrievals. Sixty-six to 70% of these births were of single babies, and 25-38% of the multiple births were twins. The report verifies a dominant effect of age and male factor diagnosis, suggesting that the younger woman in couples with no identified problem with sperm parameters has a much greater probability of delivering a baby than does the older woman or the wife in a couple with male factor infertility. Couples who make up to three attempts at ARTs are apparently statistically more successful, but after three attempts, statistical odds for success appear to decline dramatically. This is what the AFS has to say. I'd believe these numbers over those of any individual physician.

Yet, despite these somewhat discouraging odds, the average patients who enter an ART program expect to be successful and are shocked when they are not. Many patients later complain that they "might not have tried had they known more about the process, the tension and the outcome."[3]

More and more experts in the field are raising concerns that the technology is being abused. In far too many cases, say these doctors writing in consumer group newsletters and fact sheets and speaking to one another at medical conferences, patients both for whom there are less expensive and invasive alternatives just as likely to produce pregnancy or who are very unlikely candidates for success are being referred to and treated with ARTs. These doctors are vocally calling for open discussion about the development of standard criteria about patient age, response to ovulation induction and sperm capacity "challenge" tests, etc. To date, they are not being taken seriously.

---

3. Murray Nusbaum, M.D.; "Who Needs ART?"; *Ferre Fax*, Volume 9, Number 1, p. 1.

Despite odds of significantly less than 50% success, for couples hoping to avoid the losses of genetic continuity, a child conceived together, and the physical and emotional gratifications of a pregnancy experience, ARTs offer great hope and deserve careful consideration.

Such couples need not be victims of unrealistic expectations. You can and should gather all available information. Additional factors to be considered include

1. Given your diagnosis, what are the alternatives to this procedure?

2. Are you a good candidate medically for such a procedure? Your age and your diagnosis are important parts of this equation.

3. What physical impact can you expect from the protocol at this clinic? For an accurate view ask to speak to both successful and unsuccessful patients who have used this particular clinic and whose diagnosis and social profile are similar to your own.

4. How will the protocol affect you emotionally? Ask to speak to both successful and unsuccessful patients at this particular clinic for an accurate view.

5. How much time will each cycle involve? Can you manage this within your work routine or can you arrange time off?

6. What will be the cost for one complete cycle—drugs, monitoring, medical care, surgery, hospitalization, etc. What proportion of these costs will be covered by insurance?

7. How many cycles does the clinic consider necessary to ensure the best statistical odds for success? After getting a realistic picture of the process from patients who have already been through it, are you and your partner prepared emotionally, physically, financially for this many cycles? If not, how are your statistical odds affected should you elect to do fewer cycles?

8.   What is the clinic's stand on and experience with pregnancy reduction? After speaking to patients who have been through it, how do you feel emotionally and ethically about this possibility?

9.   Is the clinic a member of SART? If not, can they explain to your satisfaction why they are not?

10. If not SART members, do they participate in the SART report? If not, can they effectively explain why not?

11. Can the clinic you propose to use provide you with satisfactory proof of a high enough live birth rate per egg retrieval by this particular team and facility among patients who fit your profile (age, diagnoses, etc.) to allow you to feel that proceeding creates an acceptable emotional, physical, temporal and financial risk and meets your ethical criteria?

In addition to these questions, since most ART procedures involve ovulation stimulation both to ensure that there are ova to harvest and to help in predicting timing for the procedures, couples considering ARTs should carefully consider the questions posed earlier about medications.

Furthermore, the probability of producing multiple fertilized embryos demands that you and your partner have a serious and realistic discussion about what is to be done with them. (See section above on drug therapies.) If your ART produces multiple embryos, will all embryos be implanted, increasing the risk of a multiple pregnancy and its significant attendant dangers both to mother and children? In the event of a multiple pregnancy of more than triplets, would you be able to consider a pregnancy reduction? If all embryos are not to be implanted at once, what will you do with those in excess of the number you have chosen as optimal for implantation? Will you freeze them for your own future use? If so, for how long and at what cost? Would you ask that unused embryos be destroyed? Will you donate unused embryos to be adopted by another infertile couple? If so, under what conditions would you make such a donation?

Having gathered the answers to your own careful questions and accurate statistical information only you can determine whether the odds for success with a particular procedure at a particular clinic in the hands of a particular medical team fits within your plan and is affordable within your personal budget of time, money, emotional energy and physical capacities.

> Zeke and Bea both came from large blood-is-thicker-than-water families and wanted a large family of their own—a family that shared their genes. But their shared infertility problems had not responded to traditional therapies. When their physician suggested IVF or GIFT they were at first hesitant. They needed to ask lots of questions, and they did.
>
> Zeke and Bea were lucky. They lived in a state where coverage of this procedure was mandatory, and they worked for employers sensitive to their need for time off. After speaking with their priest about their religious and ethical questions they felt comfortable that GIFT was an acceptable procedure.
>
> Bea conceived on the first cycle and gave birth to twins. Later Zeke and Bea invested even more time and energy and emotions and money in GIFT. Several cycles were unsuccessful, and they were disappointed. But they couldn't give up. The result of their tenacity was four children in six years. Just right for them!

References: A Reasonable Request?

Each of the sections in this book which discuss how to gather information which can help you make a decision suggests that you ask your service provider for the names and phone numbers of patients/clients willing to talk to you about their successes and failures in the program. A few service providers have taken issue with this, suggesting that it violates their patients' confidentiality.

My response? Baloney! Of course a professional should not give out such information without the patients' permission, but many clients would be willing and even eager to provide this service to other potential clients.

Look at it this way: would you hire someone to do a $7500 remodeling job on your house without asking for references? Would you have your classic car refurbished at a cost of $20,000 without talking to the professional's prior clients? I didn't think so! Did you choose your hairdresser after seeing the work he did on another client? Why some of you didn't even purchase this book before having had it recommended by others in whose judgment you trust!

Clinical Trials and Research Protocols

Some patients are offered the opportunity to participate in FDA-approved clinical trials of new drugs or in the testing of new ART protocols and procedures. Participating in medical research has its own special form of stress.

Most often in a well managed study of medications the participants are divided into two groups, one of which receives the proposed new treatment and the other of which does not. Patients are not told into which group they have been placed until the trial is over. The result of this is that half of the participants have no statistical chance at all of benefitting from the new medication, since they are taking a placebo instead. Often patients are told that the placebo patients will be treated with the experimental drug after the trials if the trials prove successful.

Experimenting with new technical procedures is a similar process to testing new drugs, but such experiments do not involve FDA approval (unless a new medication is involved) and usually involve a small number of patients all of whom are receiving the new treatment rather than involving a control group and placebos. Since testing new techniques most often is a variation on an already available procedure, often patients are expected to pay the cost of the original procedure but not to absorb the added costs of the experimental process.

Some of the questions you will want answered before saying yes to such a trial include

1.   Who is conducting the trial and how is it set up? (See the section on "Doing Your Homework" above. Also consider the physicians' credentials and experience.)

2.   How long will the trial last and how much time will be involved in treatment and monitoring during each cycle?

3.   How much will it cost? (Sometimes, but not always, all or part of the treatment is free during a clinical trial.)

4.   What physical and emotional side effects can be expected during the treatment and in future?

5.   What about increased risks of birth defects or miscarriage?

6.   If you are part of a drug control group (and thus receive a placebo rather than the medication being tested) will you be offered treatment after the trial? At what cost?

Someone, somewhere, served as the "guinea pig" for all of the drug trials and protocol testing that led to the wonder drugs and the miracle procedures now available to infertility patients. Only you and your partner can know whether or not you can afford to expend your time and your physical and emotional energy and financial resources on participation in a research project.

It had taken 11 years of unsuccessful treatment and roller coaster emotions, but to the happy couple smiling out from the Sunday newspaper photo who had just become the parents of a son who was the first child born of their medical center's experimental protocol in subzonal sperm injection (SUZI), being part of an experiment appeared to have been worth it. The article went on to discuss the 40 other couples who had not yet conceived, about one fourth of whom had dropped out of the program. Evidently the statistics weren't good enough for them. But how much do you want to bet that on Monday morning the medical center's switch board was flooded with calls from couples dealing with male infertility who wanted information about becoming a part of the new protocol?

Investing in a "Sure Thing"—Considering Packaged Infertility Services

After having been whispered about among certain entrepreneurial professionals and patient advocates on both coasts for a year or more, a controversial new approach to family formation was first introduced in the spring of 1993 in Northern California. An ART clinic and an independent adoption service formed an unusual partnership, wherein, for a substantial single (but in this first case not all-inclusive) fee, they offered pre-qualified infertility patients a stepped approach to adding a child to their family. The first year would involve a specific number of tries at IVF using the couple's own gametes. If this was unsuccessful the couple would try a specific number of IVF attempts using donated ova in the second year. If that did not succeed, the program would then assist the couple in attempting to adopt independently.

An intriguing concept, to be sure, and one which will undoubtedly be followed by other possible packages which include ART treatment options, surrogacy or donor insemination options, and/or adoption. But many things in general about such an approach (not to mention some couple-specific questions we'll address next) need to be considered and/or acknowledged before "mainstream" advocates and professionals are likely to board this new train and recommend it to patients!

First, it must be clearly understood that such programs are unlikely ever to be open to the general universe of infertility patients, but will instead be offered only to those who fit a certain statistically optimistic medical and social profile: couples whose medical problems are highly likely to respond to IVF treatment and/or whose social profile will appeal to birthparents making an adoption plan. When thought about in this way, patients who are unlikely to fit such a profile and idealistic advocates may feel more than a little indignant. But, hey, this is what capitalism is all about, and such a program is built on capitalistic principles, not on charitable principles.

Any such package involves a financial gamble for both providers and participating couples. The gambles on the part of the package providers is that they can help a high enough proportion of couples achieve a pregnancy early enough and easily enough to make a substantial profit even though some participating clients will eventually exhaust their medical trials and move to adoption, where they will hopefully adopt quickly and without "failures." The gamble on the part of the patients is a more pessimistic one: that they would be unlikely to achieve a pregnancy through several attempts at more traditional ART procedures for the same amount of money as the packaged service plan. Couples who pay a large program fee and then conceive after one or two attempts at IVF would spend significantly more money than their actual costs, and so would, in essence, subsidize the less successful attempts of patients who entered phase three of the program, adoption.

If, after acknowledging these realities a couple continues to find the idea of interest, their next step is to be absolutely certain that both of them are agreed upon two things. First, is each of them comfortable enough with the life long consequences of each of the alternatives in the program's progression (conception via IVF, parenting the child of an egg or sperm donor or of a surrogate, parenting in adoption, etc.) that they feel equally enthusiastic about all of these possible parenting outcomes for their lives? Second, are they willing to change courses after having taken charge of infertility in a way that asks them to see each step as a whole new decision and instead move into a program which binds them either to follow a stepped progression of very different life choices or forfeit a substantial financial investment?

Having satisfied themselves that they can live with any and all of the possible parenting outcomes, the remaining questions couples will wish to explore involve being satisfied with the specifics of a particular program:

1.   Can the program provide satisfactory answers to all of the ART, surgery, and drug therapy questions listed in the earlier sections?

2.   What parts of drug therapy, medical procedures, and/or adoption plans and legal fees are not included in the overall program fee? Ask for estimates of costs of any pieces of the process not included in the program fee.

3.   What proportion of program costs (if any) are likely to be covered by existing insurance?

4.   What mental health and social services are available as a part of the program fee (e.g. support groups, individual or

couples counseling, donor/surrogate screening, donor/surrogate/birthparent counseling, parent preparation for adopters, post adoption support)? Are any of the above services which aren't included in the program fee available at an additional fee?

5. What approach(es) are available regarding surrogacy or donor gametes (known donor or anonymous, confidentiality or ongoing openness, etc.)

6. What style(s) of adoption are offered (e.g. agency or independent, confidential or open, domestic or international)?

On the Horizon

Hours before this book was to be sent to the indexer the press headlined one more new option: researchers at George Washington University's In Vitro Fertlization and Andrology Laboratory had managed to clone human embryos. The research had been conducted on flawed embryos already identified as inappropriate for transfer with no plans to implant them and they had been discarded after about six days. The experiment had followed the voluntary guidelines set forth by the AFS, but reaction was swift. Ethicists cried out for immediate ethical review and instantly pointed out that the control of research which is on the slippery slope of human experimentation today is in the hands not of academics or the government but of entrepreneurs, who in their view evidently can't be expected to make decisions which are moral. The researchers vollied back that such discussion is exactly what they hoped to promote. The Vatican issued a statement calling the research perverse.

This is what's new today, at the beginning of 1994. Different? Yes. Controversial? Absolutely. But then, who would have thought in 1960 that IVF would be readily available now? Who would have believed in 1970 that adoptions would frequently involve open communication between birth and adoptive parents? Who would have believed in 1980 that genetic grandparents would gestate and give birth to their own grandchildren, or that women over 50 would give birth—even after menopause?

This situation simply serves to highlight the most complex issue surrounding infertility treatment today: the research and the options are so complex and carry with them such significant possibilities beyond providing a baby for one infertile couple to love that society is not about to ignore us. The spotlight shines on infertile couples and the decisions they make today in ways that it has never shone before.

RESOURCES

National or Regional Organizations

RESOLVE, Inc. (1310 Broadway, Somerville MA 02144, telephone 617-623-0744) Their newsletters, fact sheets and symposia can be indispensable tools, especially for keeping up to date on the newest in treatment protocols.

Infertility Awareness Association of Canada (523-774 Echo Lane, Ottawa, Ontario K1S 5N8, CANADA, telephone 613-730-1322) See earlier RESOURCE sections for detail.

American Fertility Society (1209 Montgomery Highway, Birmingham AL 35216-2809, 205-978-5000) See earlier RESOURCES for more detail.

Ferre Institute (258 Genesee St, Ste 302, Utica, NY 13502, 315-724-4348) See earlier RESOURCES for more detail.

Endometriosis Association (8585 N. 76th Place, Milwaukee WI 53223) is a non-profit with chapters throughout the U.S. The organization publishes a newsletter and offers referrals and support for those dealing with the multiple issues related to endometriosis, only one of which is infertility.

Written Materials

The newsletters and journal articles, fact sheets and consumer booklets from RESOLVE, from IAAC, and from the American Fertility Society will be more up-to-date than any book can be in a rapidly changing field. (See addresses/phones above. Order by phone with your credit card in most cases.) Books mentioned here are current now, but may not stay current long. They are listed as examples of types of books that can be helpful.

Clinic Specific Outcome Report for the Year____ from the American Fertility Society and Society for Assisted Reproductive Technology (Birmingham: American Fertility Society, annual) The annual collection of success data on reporting ART clinics from thoughout the U.S. Participation is voluntary, but widespread. Organized by regions, each section may be ordered separately.

Overcoming Endometriosis by Mary Lou Ballweg (New York: Condon and Weed, Inc., 1987.) By the founder of the Endometriosis Association.

Beyond Infertility: Understanding the New Reproductive Technology by Susan Cooper and Ellen Glazer (Boston: Lexington Books, 1994) A thorough guide to the complex practical, ethical and emotional issues surrounding ARTS and quasi adoption options.

The Infertility Book: A Comprehensive Medical and Emotional Guide by Carla Harkness (second edition, Berkeley: Celestial Arts, 1992) This carefully crafted blend of emotional and medical information is liberally sprinkled with anecdotal information.

Pursuing Parenthood: Ethical Issues in Assisted Reproductive Technology by Paul Lauritzen (Bloomington: Indiana University Press, 1993) A carefully reasoned exploration of the ethics of assisted reproductive technology and other family building options and of the professionals who offer them to the infertile written by one who has himself dealt with infertility.

Overcoming Infertility: A Practical Strategy for Navigating the Emotional, Medical & Financial Minefields of Trying to Have a Baby by Robert Nachtigal M.D.& Elizabeth Mehren (New York: Doubleday, 1991)

Miracle Babies and Other Happy Endings for Couples with Fertility Problems by Mark Perloe M.D. and Linda Gail Christie (New York: Rawson Associates, 1986) though technologically dated is an example of the kind of physician-written book that is patient-sensitive.

How to Be a Successful Fertility Patient by Peggy Robin (New York: William Morrow & Co., 1993) A well thought out consumer guide to getting the best medical help to have a baby.

From Infertility To I.V.F.. by Geoffrey Sher, M.D. (New York: McGraw Hill, 1988). A practical discussion of the risks and benefits of ARTs.

Chapter 6

BEYOND
FINDING THE CURE

*The treatment process has its own momentum.
The sense of inadequacy that makes the medical route
appealing in the first place is reinforced by every
failure. The fear that you may have wasted yourself and
your life becomes greater as the investment becomes
greater, and feeds the compulsion to keep going.*
Elizabeth Bartholet
from Family Bonds: Adoption
and the Politics of Parenting

Deciding to end treatment is not a decision to become
childfree. Deciding to end treatment is not a decision to try third
party reproduction. Deciding to end treatment is not a decision to
pursue adoption.

Instead, deciding to end treatment is its own decision, and
before partners can truly decide to be childfree or to adopt or to
parent a child genetically related to only one of them, they really
must decide first to end treatment.

Yet, without a clear diagnosis, without a complete failure to
respond in any hopeful way to treatment, without a complete
absence of new and promising treatments just over the horizon,
how do couples decide to stop trying to fix their fertility
impairments? A generation ago lots of couples got such final
answers. But not today.

With each year that goes by a cadre of new treatments is
introduced. While to date nearly all of them have produced results
so limited that fewer than one third of the couples who use them
become pregnant, their very existence makes it difficult not to at

least try them. And next month there will be one more, and the next month another, and another, and another.

Any hint of success is tantalizing. For couples who have had one or more positive clinical pregnancy tests within ARTs, for those whose medical problems involve repeated miscarriages rather than an inability to conceive, recognizing that the time has come to end treatment can be even more difficult. In the absence of a clear-cut and final answer deciding to end treatment is very likely the most difficult choice of all.

Nearly all couples eventually reach the point where they realize that taking charge of infertility may include a decision to stop treatment. Some couples are able to move beyond treatment with relative ease, while others find it nearly impossible. The difference between these couples is in their differing reactions to infertility's six losses—losses which now appear to have moved beyond the theoretical, beyond the potential, to the real—and in their perception of what ending treatment means.

Despite having done a wonderful job during a weekend retreat of talking through one's feelings about this possibility in the abstract, facing the reality of loss is something quite different. It hurts.

And so couples who have researched well, budgeted wisely, examined the risks of various treatments and reached the place they hoped never to reach in their plan, the spot where they must evaluate treatment and give up on it, still find it difficult. Suggesting the need for a serious decision about whether to try donor insemination or whether to place an adoption ad in the personals column carries with it much more significance than trying to decide whether to try hMG after clomiphene citrate.

You may need more time between steps than was written into your plan. You will need to think through and then talk through all over again an alternative that you thought you'd discussed to death. This is as it should be.

Even in having taken charge of your infertility you still could not control it. That hurts.

Losing the dream of a jointly conceived child hurts.

Losing genetic continuity hurts.

Giving up on the desire to experience being or making pregnant hurts.

Facing the idea of choosing an alternative route to parenthood hurts.

Childfree living, third party reproduction, adoption. Are these really options? In choosing these are we moving on, or are we giving up, and how do we know the difference?

The pain of grief deserves its own time and space. The disappointment of loss deserves a full stop and a new decision. Don't push or pull one another to the next step. Each of you must be ready to choose to take it. Keep in mind that you may want help in making this transition. But now you know how to find it.

What It Means To End Treatment

Take-charge people will recognize that broaching the idea of ending treatment involves some emotional risk, but will understand that the risk is important. Take-charge partners will be willing to respond to a spouse's need to consider this option. One couple attending my decision making workshop described the day as having brought into sharp focus the very thing they had been trying to deny.

> "Right in the middle of the workshop each of us realized separately that we'd been compelled to throw good money after bad," wrote Lew, "because we didn't want to face the reality: we are among the 50% of couples for whom treatment isn't going to work. Writing that down hurts a little, even now that we've moved on and found the place we want to be. But the great thing was that when we came home that night we each knew we had some things we needed to talk about, and we were incredibly relieved to learn that we both felt that need to talk."

For take-charge couples, ending treatment is an active process rather than a passive one. It involves the same careful reflection and discussion that every other decision has required.

To the take-charge person, ending treatment does not mean just not getting the prescription filled or "forgetting" to chart one's cycle. It does not mean calling to cancel an appointment and allowing the medical office or one's partner to assume that it will be rescheduled.

Deciding to end treatment does not have to be permanent, but it should be clearly defined by the partners. Together you should agree on a time frame for taking a next step, whether that next step under consideration will be reentering treatment or exploring new lifestyle options. Perhaps you will take two months off, perhaps six, perhaps twelve. Your ages, your emotional state, your finances will all contribute to this decision.

Some couples will end treatment temporarily in order to regroup and revitalize. They will find that giving themselves a break from treatment allows them to replenish some of their resources: to give themselves time to catch their breaths while off the emotional roller coaster, to recover from a physically draining regimen, to save money, to invest time and energy in their personal relationship before making the next decision. These couples end treatment fully expecting to come back to it.

Other couples will end treatment already ready to consider other choices. They will begin the process of deciding to be childfree. They will begin to explore more actively their feelings about quasi adoption and traditional adoption options very soon after treatment.

How do you know when it's time? It's time to talk about ending treatment

1. When either of you has become more pessimistic than optimistic about the outcome of your treatment regimen

2. When one or the other of you has come to dread or resent the process of the treatment protocol

3. When any one of your resources—time, money, physical capacity, emotional energy—has reached a critical low that is affecting your ability to function well in your relationship with your partner

4. When your ability to function effectively with family and friends or in your job has been impaired

5. When any one of your resources—time, money, physical capacity, emotional energy—has reached a critical low that could impair your ability to successfully pursue a parenting option that you and your partner have already discussed as a positive alternative

6.   When either of you finds that he or she has been has been spending more and more time thinking about one or more options other than treatment

Ending treatment will allow the two of you the space that is required to deal with loss if necessary and to make effective new decisions.

"It is not possible to get beyond the loss and suffering if you are still fixated on undoing the loss." [1]

Is It Forever?

When I'm doing workshops for people who are trying to make infertility or adoption related decisions I drill on one issue over and over and over. It is this

Every child deserves to be wanted for who he is and not as a substitute for the child who might have been or the child who might arrive.

What I'm trying to help listeners do when I make a statement like this is to refocus. Because of that conveyor belt syndrome, many infertile couples reach a point where they are focusing on regaining control, focusing on a positive pregnancy test and have thought very little beyond that point. They are unable to focus on the realities of parenting and its impact upon each of them and on the two of them together.

For children to become healthy adults, they must attach emotionally to their parents. Attachment occurs when a cycle of trust is built, that is, when a needy human (in this case a child) comes to understand that when he expresses his needs, someone (in this case his parent) will always try to meet them. Nature has certainly made the attachment cycle easier in humans by making babies so irresistibly beautiful, cuddly, and charming. An emotionally healthy adult who has responsibility for a healthy baby will have a difficult time not participating in the attachment cycle:

1. Bartholet, Elizabeth. Family Bonds: Adoption and the Politics of Parenting (Boston: Houghton Mifflin, 1993) p. 37

listening to the baby cry, responding to that cry with food or dry diapers or a good cuddle, and experiencing the warmth and trust and satisfaction expressed in a baby's coo or smile. When a routine like this is repeated over and over attachment grows between parent and child.

We've known for years that attachment very often begins while parents are waiting for their child's arrival. The physical changes of pregnancy provide the natural opportunity to slow down and begin to fantasize about the child to be, creating an image of how he will look or feel, giving him a name, preparing a nursery, etc. Those who have done research on the bonding experience have noted a specific series of necessary steps toward attachment that pregnant mothers and fathers take during their nine month wait.

Those who have observed couples waiting to adopt a child have noticed a parallel series of steps. When a couple has completed a parent preparation process or been selected by a birthfamily and know that an adoption really is likely, they go through a series of psychological steps very much like those taken by pregnant couples.

Now of course some things can get in the way of attachment and bonding, but these are not the focus of our discussion here. I bring up bonding and attachment here in order to help you understand the importance of couples giving themselves the opportunity to anticipate a particular child's arrival. To think about him, fantasize about him, yearn for him, prepare for him. This child deserves to be wanted not as a prize for having beaten the game, not as a symbol of regained control, not as a second-best adopted stopgap while you continue treatment so that you can have the real thing, but as long-awaited, much loved answer to the dream of becoming parents.

Every child deserves to be wanted for who he is. And so every attempt at pregnancy needs to be rooted in the dream of parenting a particular fantasized child. Every step toward adopting needs to be rooted in the dream of parenting a particular fantasized child. When preparing to love a particular child, how he arrives—by birth, with third party assistance, by adoption—will no longer be the issue. Instead, wanting him and making him a part of your life will be the issue.

Am I saying that having ended treatment one can never go back? No. Am I saying that once one has chosen an alternative route to parenthood, treatment is a "wrong" choice for a subsequent child? No. The fact is that changing circumstances in both treatment and adoption often mean that the best routes to parenthood change for an infertile couple over time.

What I am saying is that as you pursue parenthood, what you should be focused on is the arrival of a particular child and allow both yourselves and that child to bask in the glow of his arrival. Let me share two stories with you...

Tammy and Scott worked through the issues and decided that parenting, by whatever means, was their most important need. Since treatment wasn't working and Tammy was feeling anxious about the ticking clock, they decided to explore adoption more thoroughly. Rather quickly they determined that they could adopt a baby just a few months old from outside the U.S. in less than a year. They explored all of their feelings about this. Did adoption seem like a positive way to form a family? What would their families say about adopting a child ethnically different from themselves? Could they afford it? The answers were all reassuring. They decided to go for it. Eight months later Eduardo arrived and filled their lives with pure joy.

Two years later Tammy and Scott were so thrilled with their son that they were ready to expand their family. They were shocked to find that Eddie's homeland had closed its adoption program and that international adoption was looking much more difficult and expensive than it had been before. They decided to look once more at treatment options and discovered that a new protocol was being used, one which offered much promise for their infertility problem. Most of the costs would be covered by their insurance (adoption would not be.) They decided to go for it. Fifteen months later, Eddie's sister Marisa was born, filling three lives with joy.

Every child deserves to be wanted for who he is.

Sybil and Frank were a go-get-'em couple. They knew what they wanted and they went for it. Five cycles of Pergonal™ and two attempts at GIFT had been unsuccessful. They decided that the way to get a baby was to adopt. They plunged full steam ahead into a program of advertising while continuing in treatment and within five months heard from a birthmother who was impressed with their profile: professional couple, great house, two luxury cars, a boat, and a dog. Tina asked them to parent her child, who would be born in May.

Great! They were set! But they decided to continue treatment, and the next month they conceived.

Two babies four months apart! How wonderful! Of course Sybil knew better than to tell Tina about her pregnancy. After all, Sybil could miscarry or Tina could change her mind. They waited, sure that they would be parents in just a few months.

In late May Tina's baby was born a little late. Sybil and Frank were delighted! They arranged for their attorney to pick up the baby, and so Tina never saw them.

They plunged into parenting and were surprised at how hard it was, but, hey, it would all be worth it. Two months later Sybil went into labor early, and a daughter was born. She remained in the hospital for three weeks.

The caseworker from the county was definitely not pleased when asked by the court to do a report on this family who had petitioned to adopt a baby and discovered that they also had given birth. And when she contacted Tina to verify that her consent had been freely given Tina was shocked by the news that her baby was not the center of Sybil and Frank's existence. She felt betrayed, but, hey, what could she do about it? The adoption went through. Sybil and Frank moved to a new city.

"The twins" started school together. By adolescence they were resentful of one another as

AMAZING FINDS on **Black Friday!**

On Friday, November 26, Goodwill Store & Donation Centers are your location for great 2010 holiday values and savings!

Truckloads of items are just arriving:

- TOYS from a national retailer

- NATIONAL BRAND new digital LCD TVs (7-inch and 10-inch models) priced right at $29.99 and $39.99

Quantities are limited.
Customer may purchase a maximum of two 7 inch TVs and two 10 inch TVs.
For store locations and hours visit amazinggoodwill.com

facebook

twitter

You Tube

Follow AmazingGoodwill

well as their parents because of the attention they received which made them constantly have to explain their arrivals. One girl (the daughter who had been adopted) was an athlete and the other a scholar, like Sybil and Frank, her birthparents. This was always so funny to teachers, who delighted in pointing out how different the girls were. But it is no fun for adolescents who want to be just like everyone else.

One day, the knock on the door was Tina, interested in meeting her daughter. Imagine that teen's reaction when she learned that her birthmother felt she had been duped.

Parenthood is an experience replete with challenges no matter how one becomes a parent. And being a kid in any family has its ups and downs, too. But forging good relationships between parents and children begins with a child's understanding of how much he was wanted and loved just for being himself. As Mr. Rogers says, "You're special because you're you."

The Dilemma of Unexplained Infertility

Couples who have not been given a specific diagnosis may find it particularly hard to stop treatment. Without a named reason, couples with unexplained infertility may waver between everpresent hope and the depression of feeling that they are being punished. As these couples continue to beat their heads against the wall of infertility, they need to know that, according to work done by Machelle M. Seibel, M.D. of the Faulkner Center for Reproductive Medicine in Boston, at least 50% of their number who have never before conceived are statistically likely to conceive without any treatment at all within 5.7 years. Women who have been given no explanation for why they are experiencing secondary infertility can expect a 50% pregnancy rate within 2.7 years without any medical intervention. In an article in Serono's Insights into Infertility newsletter (Winter, 1992) Dr. Seibel notes that studies performed by the Infertility and Behavioral Medicine Department at Deaconess Hospital, Boston, found a 30% pregnancy rate among couples with unexplained infertility during the six month period following their having received ten months of relaxation training... success rates comparable to those achieved with assisted reproductive technologies.

One way to look at statistics like these is to note that the significant investment of time, money, emotional and physical energy in treatment may produce no better results for those with unexplained infertility than will doing nothing.

The Value of Rituals

Many significant beginnings and endings in our lives are marked by rituals that publicly mark the transition and invite the support—either in celebration or in mourning— of others. Weddings, funerals, christenings, baby showers, bar mitzvahs, graduations, going-away parties are examples of transitional rituals. Psychologists and sociologists are increasingly noting that transitions which are not accompanied by ritual—divorce, loss of a job, miscarriage, private changes of direction—are often harder to make, since they lack support.

Many infertile couples are finding it important to create and participate in private or public rituals which acknowledge the progress of their lives. Several RESOLVE chapters have put together periodically repeated mourning ceremonies for miscarried or unborn children. Such ceremonies offer the opportunity for couples and their supportive family and friends to experience a release similar to that in a traditional funeral service.

Bonnie and Lawrence Baron of San Diego personally composed a ceremony in which they formally ended treatment and moved on to adoption. Their ceremony was firmly rooted in their Judaic tradition and included elements of several ceremonies and prayers as well as including some nonreligious readings and music.

Mike and Jean Carter of North Carolina, authors of *Sweet Grapes: How to Stop Being Infertile and Start Living Again*, note in their book and in their presentations the formal way in which they marked their choice to live a childfree lifestyle.

Wendy and Rob Williams of Ontario, Canada, created a poignant and very personal ceremony for saying goodbye to the child whose adoption was not completed because his birthmother changed her mind several weeks after placement.

In many ways the structure of the decision making format here encourages the opportunity for using or developing rituals whether formal or informal. You may wish to explore with your partner the idea of participating in appropriate transitional rituals yourselves as you mark your journey.

In "The Picnic," one of the wonderful short stories in her collection *The Miracle Seekers: An Anthology of Infertility*,[2] Mary Martin Mason tells the story of Jill and Dan, frozen in time and unable to move beyond the miscarriage of Gerald, the baby they had waited for so long. In an awkward attempt to help, Dan takes Jill on a picnic along the raw Rhode Island shore. With her sketch pads and charcoal in hand, Jill makes her way to an ancient cemetery to do some rubbings. Dan finds her later, weeping over a one hundred year old tombstone that bears the names of a couple and their five sons—each of whom was named Josephus, each of whom died in infancy.

Here Jill comes to see that what is preventing her from moving on is the fact that no one—not her mother-in-law, not her friends, not her husband—has allowed her to experience her grief openly, to mourn the loss of her son, to say goodbye in a formal way to the baby who was not to be. And so, together, Dan and Jill say goodbye to Gerald by burying a baby rattle which Jill has brought with them in the earth above the babies Josephus.

RESOURCES

For a referral to formal support group sessions, counseling, or mediation, call your local infertility advocacy organization (RESOLVE, IAAC, etc.) or ask your physician.

Healing the Infertile Family: Strengthening Your Relationship in the Search for Parenthood by Gay Becker, Ph.D. (New York: Bantam Books,

2. Mason, Mary Martin. *The Miracle Seekers: An Anthology of Infertility*, can be ordered for $14.95 from Adoptapes, 4012 Lynn Ave., Edina MN 55416.

1990.) Based on a series of interviews with infertile couples, Dr. Becker presents suggestions for coping and moving on.

Sweet Grapes: How to Stop Being Infertile and Start Living Again by Michael and Jean Carter (Indianapolis: Perspectives Press, 1989). An excellent discussion of how to make good decisions about ending treatment and moving on.

Woulda, Coulda, Shoulda: Overcoming Regrets, Mistakes, and Missed Opportunities by Dr. Arthur Freeman and Rose DeWolf (New York: HarperCollins, 1989.) A cognitive therapy approach to making long lasting decisions.

Without Child: Experiencing and Resolving Infertility by Ellen Glazer and Susan Cooper (Boston: Lexington Books, 1988). A collection of carefully linked personal experiences from infertile couples who have pursued the full spectrum of options and experienced a variety of outcomes.

Surviving Infertility: A Compassionate Guide through the Emotional Crisis of Infertility by Linda P. Salzer (New York: HarperCollins, rev. 1991). A well regarded handbook dealing with the psychological and social aspects of infertility, its treatment and options.

Wanting Another Child: Coping with Secondary Infertility by Harriet Fishman Simons (New York: Lexington Books, 1995). Support and answers for unique problems and concerns of those who find themselves unable to conceive or carry to live birth after having done so before.

Living through Personal Crisis by Ann Kaiser Stearns (New York: Ballantine Books, 1984). A practical guide to dealing with grief and loss.

Chapter 7

EMBRACING A LIFE WITHOUT CHILDREN

*Childfree means turning involuntary
childlessness into voluntary childlessness. And we
would rather live our lives in the achievement of a
major life goal than in the constant reminder of the
frustration of one.*

Jean and Mike Carter,
Sweet Grapes

Even looking at the possibility of creating a life without
children seems to be very difficult for infertile couples to try to do.
Of course this is understandable. Having once made the decision
that you do want to have children, and having devoted
considerable resources to becoming pregnant, the idea that you
could actively decide to become a couple who consider themselves
child*free* rather than child*less* is confusing and challenging. But
before you can decide for or against pursuing a third party assisted
route to parenthood or adopting, you must first decide just how
important parenting is to you, given the reality of infertility. In
exploring this question many couples find that reexamining the
option of living childfree gives them a feeling of peace that they
had not expected to find.

The terminology itself has generated much debate. In the
universe of people (of which the infertile are only one segment)
some who have chosen a life without children and labeled.
themselves *childfree* really don't like children (anybody's) and do
not wish for children to be a part of their lives. Few of these people
ever wanted children. As a result they are often insensitive to
infertility issues. This strident group of anti-child people, however,
are not typical of those who choose a childfree lifestyle.

The Impact of Language

The word *childless* is an old word, around a long time, which until rather recently has been commonly used with little controversy to describe the group of adults in society who do not parent children. Some people who are childless are so by temporary circumstance. They may not even have thought yet about becoming parents. Some people who are childless are so by chance. They may have wanted to parent, but have not yet found themselves able to do so, whether because of infertility, the absence of a parenting partner, etc. A third group of childless people have no children by choice. They have made a deliberate decision not to become parents.

It is only this last group, those who are without children by choice, who have given themselves the label *childfree*. You can't appropriately be labeled by someone else as childfree. You have to apply the label to yourself, because you believe it applies to you.

I'm a language person. I suppose my original interest in words is part of what led me to a degree in English. This continuing interest in words has colored my current profession in significant ways, too. I have been one of several people who have taken Minnesota social worker Marietta Spencer's concept of the need to use what she called "positive adoption language" and run with it, carrying on a real campaign for reform of adoption-related language and imagery because I think that negative language is offensive to adoption-expanded families and confusing to children who call such families their own. In adoption we now refer to *birthparents* as opposed to *real parents*, and to *making an adoption plan* instead of *giving up a baby*.

We do this because language can be manipulated to create propaganda which affects opinions. Successful advertising is built on such manipulation. Ford sells New Yorkers rather than Podunkers. Buick sells Park Avenues rather than Back Streets. Jeans are Chic rather than Cruddy. Elizabeth Taylor calls her perfume *White Diamonds*, not *Cubic Zirconia*. Political agendas are furthered by language manipulation. In the 1960s Americans of African descent asked that the preferred words to describe them become *black* or *Afro-American* and that *Negro* be dropped, not to mention *colored people*. Recently the modification has been *African-American*. *Native Americans* seem to prefer that term to *Indians*. And *Inuit* people don't care to be called *Eskimos*. We go to war over words.

Mental health professionals have been encouraging doctors to look carefully at the self-esteem damaging negative terminology which is a part of obstetrics and gynecology. *Incompetent cervix, habitual aborter, failed IVF cycle...* and the list of words and terms that contribute to negative feelings about and reactions to a fertility impairment goes on.

Within the infertility community the discussion about language has been around as long as RESOLVE, the oldest infertility advocacy group, has been around. Certainly you rarely see people dealing with infertility referred to as *sterile* or *barren* anymore, though these were common terms before the 1970s. When my friend Carol Hallenbeck and I were working on starting a RESOLVE chapter, our medical partner, reproductive endocrinologist William R. Keye, Jr. (then of Caylor Nickel Clinic in Indiana, later of the University of Utah Medical Center, and now at William Beaumont Hospital in Detroit), first introduced us to the idea that *impaired fertility* more positively portrays a statistically probable cure for the medical problem. You may have noticed that I use that term often as an alternative to *infertility*.

You will also notice that I argue strongly for the term *donor insemination* as opposed to *artificial insemination* or *therapeutic donor insemination*. Those who choose this alternative are looking for an even better term, as are those who have chosen the third party reproduction option now called *surrogacy*.

When one recognizes the importance of language, one is better able to understand the need for people who are trying to be either objective or supportive to allow the people who fit the label to create the label. That's why, in discussion about abortion issues, for example, it seems to me only fair to use the terms *pro life* rather than *anti abortion* and *pro choice* rather than *pro abortion*, since these are the terms chosen by the people who hold these views. Similarly, people whose sexual orientation is to same-gendered people prefer to be called *gay* and *lesbian*. We rarely any longer see the term *deaf-mute* to describe people who are hearing impaired and non-speaking. When one chooses to change old habits and use the words selected by those personally living the issues involved, one demonstrates respect for those people.

And so it is with the idea of being childfree. If you have no children and you don't feel childfree you aren't childfree. Period. But if someone else feels childfree, who are you to be angry with how they choose to describe their life's orientation?

Denying the Loss by Tuning Out

You will have noticed by now that throughout this book I've suggested that one of the most valuable tools to use in trying to make decisions is to talk to people who have already made those decisions. These valuable resources are more difficult to find in the area of childfree living than in any other arena. You'll find folks who've adopted and are willing to talk to you about it and folks who've chosen not to adopt and will talk about it. You'll find people who have chosen surrogacy or embryo adoption or donor insemination and couples who've been both successful and unsuccessful with GIFT and are willing to talk about it.

Infertile couples who have embraced a childfree lifestyle are harder to find to talk to not because there aren't many, but because they, more than any other segment of the infertility community, often feel criticized and even ostracized by the very people they consider their peers: the infertile. When an article written by a childfree person appears in a consumer group newsletter the next issue often contains a rebuttal of some sort from a member who is angry about the term *childfree* and argues that he or she is not childfree but is childless. When childfree couples agree to speak at a monthly meeting or a symposium, their audiences are most often very small and their listerns' body language is often negative.

For a long time it was difficult for me to understand how otherwise intelligent, sensitive people could so miss the point and could become so irrational and judgmental about the lifestyle choices of others. But I've come to believe that what makes many people resistant to both the term and the topic of childfree living is panic, pure and simple.

It is possible to develop sophisticated rationalizations about most of the losses of infertility and to come to see some of them as transient—Control can be regained in other areas of life; the loss of genetic continuity can seem to be made up for by genetic connections to other family members; the loss of the dreams we had about the physical and emotional factors in a pregnancy and birth experience can be explained away as "only" nine months when compared to a lifetime; and one can argue that parenting a child together provides as important a connection as does the blending of genes to make a baby together. And the loss of the opportunity to parent can be avoided by choosing adoption or third party reproductive options.

But if treatment isn't successful and the adoption options either aren't available or are unacceptable, the loss of the opportunity to parent will affect a lifetime of expectations and plans made since childhood. Realizing the finality of such a loss can result in panic. The prospect of such a totally life altering loss may be so frightening that some infertile people can't bear even to listen to the possibility. And so they shut down. They don't listen.

Most professionals in the field never utter the words *childfree living* at all and too many couples dismiss the option of living a childfree life out-of-hand. But if the issue is taking charge of infertility, consider this: You are not in charge if you are continuing to dismiss the reality of losses and refusing to explore your feelings about them. The best way to do this is to listen carefully to all of the voices around you and to explore without fear all of the options open to you. This includes the option of a childfree lifestyle.

Getting There

Infertile couples fairly often drift into a child*less* future by abdicating their ability to make decisions about furthering treatment, exploring third party reproductive options, or pursuing adoption, but you don't drift into being childfree. You choose it, and you do so knowing that you won't turn back.

The difference between being childless and being childfree is a profound one. It's similar to the difference between being ready and being prepared. Pat Riley, an astoundingly successful basketball coach (L.A. Lakers, New York Knicks) and highly regarded motivational speaker, recently wrote about this difference in a new book, *The Winner Within: A Life Plan for Team Players* (G. P. Putnam's Sons, 1993). It's a great source of inspiration, interspersed with "Rile's Rules." I especially liked Rile's Rule of Total Preparation:

> "Being ready isn't enough. You have to be prepared
> for a promotion or any other significant change.
> Preparation demands mental and physical
> conditioning and conscious planning. A player who
> is just ready and not totally prepared simply
> increases risk and is a liability to the team."

People who really are childfree see their lives as being full and complete, exciting and satisfying without their having the parenting experience. You can be childless for a while and then later decide to become parents. But choosing to be childfree is a permanent choice, just as permanent as adoption or surrogacy or donor insemination. If you are really childfree, you see it as a forever option. People get to be childfree actively, not passively, whether or not infertility has been a part of their life's experience.

Couples who choose childfree living after infertility have carefully considered infertility's losses and laid them to rest. They understand and feel sad about the fact that they won't blend their genes to make a baby together and they won't carry forward their families' blood lines. They know that they won't experience either the emotional or the physical gratifications of pregnancy and are ready to accept that. The childfree couple recognizes that becoming parents in an alternative way (through adoption, through surrogacy, through gamete adoption) isn't what they most want. It just doesn't feel right.

In choosing a childfree lifestyle, couples reestablish themselves as in control of their family planning. They will have examined all of their limited resources. They will have talked about time. They will have discussed their emotional investment. They will have considered their physical limitations. They will have analyzed their finances.

They will come to see that what they want most is one another and a good life together. They will be prepared to invest their time and energy and emotions into other nurturing projects (gardening, friends and family and nieces and nephews, teaching, etc.) that will build creative extended family networks. They will use their financial reserves both to treat themselves to opportunities many parents can't afford and to prepare themselves for an independent old age.

The childfree couple comes to see their life as more rather than less. The couple who is truly childfree will, after time, very likely take the ultimate step toward taking charge of infertility: they will opt for a permanent form of birth control.

Trying It On

Dave and I have not chosen a childfree lifestyle, but we did give it serious thought. I had an aunt and uncle who had made this choice after infertility, and they had had a wonderful life. They fit none of the stereotypes that are insensitively assumed about the childfree. Through the years I've come to know several more couples who have actively chosen a childfree lifestyle and not one who has done so has reached middle age feeling regretful.

Most of them say that they came to this decision rather slowly. First they decided to end treatment and give themselves a complete break. Sometimes they refer to this step as "trying it on." It was after several months, perhaps even more than a year, that these couples felt that it was time to really talk it over and come to a decision about whether they saw themselves as "on a break" from treatment, or "resting before moving to a form of adoption" or as ready to seriously examine moving beyond infertility to embrace a childfree lifestyle.

I believe that every infertile couple should strongly consider trying this lifestyle on. But if you won't go so far as to actually try it on, then you must, simply must, read about it. <u>The</u> book on the topic is *Sweet Grapes: How to Stop Being Infertile and Start Living Again* by Jean and Michael Carter. Jean is an obstetrician/gynecologist. Mike is college professor. The Carters were an infertile couple. Note that I put that in the past tense. Jean and Mike <u>were</u> infertile. They don't see themselves as infertile anymore. Their book, like this one, is strong on effective communication and regaining control. In fact, the Carters are often asked to speak on decision making rather than on their childfree lifestyle, and when they do, they are a powerful team! For those who haven't thought about childfree living objectively before, I particularly recommend Chapters Five, Six and Seven, "Choosing to Live Childfree," "But What About...?," and "The Future."

Because the Carters are my good friends, and because Perspectives Press is their book's publisher, I freely admit to bias. But as an advocate and as an educator I really mean it when I say that *Sweet Grapes*, the winner of a Benjamin Franklin Award in 1990 as the best new book in the field of Psychology and Self Help, is a must-read for infertile couples.

RESOURCES

The Childfree Network (7777 Sunrise Blvd #1800, Citrus Heights, CA 95610, telephone 916-773-7178) is a national organization for singles and couples who have elected a childfree lifestyle. The network publishes a quarterly newsletter, *ChildFree*, containing many helpful articles on the positive aspects of life without children. Though some members made this choice after infertility, most have not experienced infertility, so that one will not necessarily find the newsletter uniformly sensitive to or informed about infertility issues. Subscriptions are $20.00 annually.

Sweet Grapes: How to Stop Being Infertile and Start Living Again by Michael and Jean Carter (Indianapolis: Perspectives Press, 1989). Provides information and advocacy for the infertility option of childfree living (chosen by its authors), as well, its excellent discussion of how to make good decisions makes it a good choice for all infertile couples and professionals working with them.

Never to Be a Mother by Linda Hunt Anton (San Francisco, HarperSanFrancisco, 1992)

Women without Children by Susan Lang (New York, Pharos Books, 1991)

To Love a Child: A Complete Guide to Adoption, Foster Parenting, and Other Ways to Share Your Life with Children by Marianne Takas and Edward Warner (Reading, MA: Addison-Wesley, 1992. A wonderful exploration of alternative ways to add children to one's own life and make a difference in theirs. The only title to realistically explore fostering, big brothering and other non-permanent nurturing relationships as viable alternatives to full time parenting.

appropriate fact sheets from RESOLVE (Order by phone with your credit card)

Chapter 8

COLLABORATIVE REPRODUCTION

Your children are not your children.
They are the sons and daughters of Life's longing for
itself.
They come through you but not from you.
And though they are with you, yet they belong not to you
Kahlil Gibran
excerpted from "On Children"
from The Prophet

Almost nothing about parenting is as we expect it to be before we are parents. And many of our expectations about how "like us" our children are going to be just because they are "ours" never comes to pass. Yet genetic connection and the pregnancy experience remain terribly important goals for some, so that parenting a child who is not genetically "our own" is a scary thought to many.

In exploring third party assisted options for parenthood, what we're talking about is a medically assisted form of adoption. I've sometimes called these alternatives *quasi adoptions*. Some writers have called them *partial adoptions*. Elizabeth Noble, author of *Having Your Baby by Donor Insemination*, has called these forms of family building *collaborative reproduction*. Each of these terms refers to the conception of a child using the genetic material or reproductive capacities of someone from outside the marriage. The infertile partner adopts the child psychologically and socially, even if not legally. It's important that we get that out and accept it as a reality right at the beginning of our discussion of third party reproduction.

These alternatives may mean using the sperm of a more fertile male either known or unknown to you in the process referred to as donor insemination. It may mean taking advantage of advancing technology which allows for the harvesting of ova from a more fertile woman, fertilizing them *in vitro* with the sperm of the husband in the infertile couple and implanting resulting embryos in the infertile wife in a process most often called egg donation. Some programs offer the service of combining donor insemination and egg donation by borrowing the genetic material of both another man and another woman and having the resulting *in vitro* fertilized embryo transferred to the infertile wife for gestation and delivery, a process called *embryo adoption*.

In the original form of twentieth century surrogacy a woman agreed to be artificially inseminated with the sperm of the husband of an infertile woman (using her own ova) and to give the baby subsequently born to its biological father, to be formally adopted by his infertile wife. Now, less than a decade and a half later, surrogacy could mean arranging to have another woman carry and give birth to an embryo conceived *in vitro* from the infertile couple's own sperm and egg in a process commonly called gestational surrogacy but more recently (and I believe more appropriately) labeled *gestational care* by Susan Cooper and Ellen Glazer in their spring, 1994 book *Beyond Infertility: Understanding the New Reproductive Options*. (Gestational care can be arranged using donor eggs or donor sperm or both, also.)

This all may sound quite complicated. And legally and ethically it can be! In the most complex of situations a married surrogate may carry and deliver an embryo conceived *in vitro* from donor ova and donor sperm who is then legally adopted and parented by still another couple, resulting in a child who technically has six different parents—genetic (the donors), legal (the husband of the surrogate is presumed by law to be his wife's children's father until he voluntarily terminates those rights), gestational (the surrogate), and psychological/social (adoptive.) The overwhelming majority of cases, however, involve the assistance of a single third party—donor or surrogate.

The resource section at the end of this chapter refers couples considering quasi-adoption options to several organizations, and only a handful of books and fact sheets which can help in making the decision. Though as I write even galleys were not yet available, so that I've not seen it yet, my familiarity with the authors leads me to feel confident that Susan Cooper and

Ellen Glazer's forthcoming book *Beyond Infertility* (Lexington Books, 1994) will help to fill what has been a significant gap.

Decision making resources for couples considering this group of alternatives is limited primarily because these options remain shrouded in secrecy and shame, in myth and misconception. Even the majority of physicians practicing in this field continue to deny the important reality that these alternatives are not medicines that cure infertility, but are alternative choices in family building that result in forms of adoption. This is, however, changing, as empowered consumers educate themselves as well as others.

General Issues

In making choices about using any kind of third party assistance, keep in mind that in choosing to bring a child into your family who shares a genetic connection with only one of his social parents, you are making a choice with the potential to throw the relationship into disequilibrium. Make sure that you and your partner have discussed and made decisions about these factors

1. Each partner and the two of you as a couple must deal with the loss of your jointly conceived child. This needs specific acknowledgment and discussion. Make no decisions until you have had time to mourn the loss of the child you would have liked to create together.

2. Have you both acknowledged this as an alternative choice rather than as a medical treatment? This does not cure the infertility of the partner not genetically related to the child, though it does end the childlessness.

3. Have you discussed the ongoing impact of the fertile partner's gain in choosing this option (genetic connection) on the self esteem of the infertile partner (who experiences the permanent loss of genetic continuity and connection to this child)? How might this affect the balance in the parenting relationship? Have you agreed on how to deal with this both now and in the future?

4.   Are you certain that the decision has been made positively, rather than conceded to by a guilty-feeling infertile partner?

5.   Is this a morally acceptable choice to both of you? Some religions, including Roman Catholicism and Orthodox Judaism have specific prohibitions against collaborative reproduction. Often these prohibitions are related to beliefs about what constitutes adultery. Our personal ethics have been established over many years, and it is important that each partner feels equally comfortable with the ethics of the family building choice selected.

6.   Will you tell others? Will you tell the child? If yes, have you discussed how and when? If no, have you thoroughly examined the ongoing burden on relationships of maintaining such a weighty secret? (See Chapter 12.)

While it is possible to pursue most of these options without being "approved" or being required to see a counselor, please don't shortchange yourselves or your growing family by skipping this step. Choosing a third party option has long term consequences for both parenting partners and for the children so conceived and so deserves especially careful examination and preparation. In many cities, RESOLVE support groups or a well qualified mental health professional running private groups or doing one-on-one counseling can be helpful resources for couples examining collaborative reproduction options.

Donor Insemination

When freely and positively chosen, expanding a family through donor insemination offers several exciting possibilities not otherwise available to couples where the husband cannot impregnate his wife. It offers the wife the opportunity to become pregnant and deliver her own genetic child, preventing her loss of genetic continuity (though her husband will experience this loss.) In not losing the physical gratifications of the pregnancy experience, the child's mother also allows herself to control the environment of the pregnancy—what the mother eats and drinks, her health regimen, her prenatal care, etc. While the husband will not have the opportunity to impregnate, he will have an impact on other physical aspects of the pregnancy as well as retaining other kinds of control. A donor-conceived pregnancy also allows a husband and wife to experience <u>together</u> the emotional preparations for parenthood that a pregnancy brings, not to mention the opportunity to share the birth experience itself. Most obviously, conceiving through donor insemination allows both partners to become parents.

What donor insemination cannot do is give the infertile husband genetic connection to the child he will parent, prevent his loss of the physical and emotional experiences of impregnating his wife, or provide a jointly conceived child. Couples considering this option, then, must be prepared to deal with the imbalance it creates in the parenting partnership and to make a commitment to eliminating the imbalance.

Though often lumped together with newer reproductive options and ARTs, the technique often called artificial insemination has been practiced in livestock in some parts of the world for centuries. The technology is simple and straightforward: semen is introduced into the vagina of a recipient female in hopes that a pregnancy will result. The process does not require the services of a physician. Semen collected from a willing known donor via masturbation can be collected in so simple a device as a clean turkey baster and injected by a woman herself or by a partner into the entrance to her vagina. This ease of accomplishment allows for such privacy that, while various literature claims that 10,000-30,000 children a year are conceived by donor insemination, we really have no idea at all how many children are conceived via donor insemination each year. Most infertile couples, however, do opt to use the services of a physician in trying this alternative.

In the past donors were recruited directly by physicians from among medical students, business and social acquaintance and the husbands of obstetrical patients. They always remained anonymous to the recipient couple. Sperm supplied was fresh, collected at or delivered to the doctor's office a short time before the scheduled insemination. Donors were screened only by the doctor, who usually took an extensive medical history and asked for a few routine blood tests. Because donors were few, they were often used many times. This led to concerns about the possibility of genetic half siblings meeting one another and marrying, unaware that they were related. Consumers and practitioners always worried about the transmission of sexually transmitted disease through fresh sperm, however, and the appearance of AIDS produced even more anxiety about the use of fresh semen.

When research produced the possibility of cryopreserving semen, sperm banking became a reality and businesses appeared offering to transport frozen semen collected from a much wider variety of donors who had been much more intensively screened and were located many miles away from the consumers using the sperm. This produced the added benefit of protecting against siblings inadvertently marrying. It also became possible for couples to select donors from catalogs listing physical and intellectual attributes, interests, talents, etc.

Though the freezing and thawing process does result in a slightly lower success rate with frozen sperm than does the use of fresh semen, because of the other protections it offers, most physicians offering donor insemination services today obtain semen from several commercial sperm banks located throughout the country. The American Fertility Society's standards for practice in the area of donor insemination, in fact, mandate the use of frozen semen. While there is currently no federal mandate that sperm banks be regulated, they can be accredited by following the strict standards of the American Tissue Bank Association, and if you choose to use frozen semen, you may wish to ascertain whether the bank is accredited, and if not, why not. If you choose a program which uses fresh sperm, then, you would be wise to question very carefully how this may effect your own health or the health of your hoped for child.

The impact of donor insemination on the resource budget of an infertile couple may be much lower than many other options. Because the procedure is so low tech, expenses are relatively modest. For couples who need no stimulation of ovulation, the procedure involves several office calls and the cost of semen. The investment of time and physical energy is similar to that of conceiving naturally. Most normally-fertile women will conceive within six to twelve cycles. Couples with combined fertility problems, of course, will need to factor in the complications of the wife's fertility impairment on the chances of conception with donor semen, but overall success rates in achieving a pregnancy and delivering a baby are in the range of 60-80%. The emotional expenditure is perhaps the most variable from couple to couple.

The Closeted Option

Considering how frequently donor insemination has been used to expand families over many years, it is surprising that it remains so shrouded in secrecy. Only in the last decade has there been any concerted effort to bring this family-building option out of the closet. Before that time most couples did not tell even their closest friends and relatives that they had built their family in this way. Until recently the overwhelming majority of families did not plan to tell their children that they were conceived with donor sperm. Why such emphasis on confidentiality? There have been two common arguments for maintaining the status quo:

1.   Confidentiality maintains couples' personal privacy.

2.   Confidentiality insures a ready pool of prospective donors.

The medical establishment itself, rather than the consumer population, has been and continues to be the primary proponent of secrecy about donor insemination. The argument most often put forth is that loosening policies of confidentiality at all might lead to the development of a slippery slope resulting in large numbers of donor-conceived children wanting to have more information about or even to meet their genetic fathers. The presumption behind this argument is that prospective donors would be put off by this possibility, resulting in difficulty in recruiting donors. But it is important to remember that donors are recruited and selected by administrators of banks or insemination programs, so that it is logical to assume that the donors selected would share the values of those recruiting them. It's reasonable to wonder if part of the medical establishment's rationale for supporting secrecy is that so many of past donors were the very same young medical students (or their friends) who offer D.I. services to patients today.

Several recent surveys of donors and prospective donors have indicated that a significant proportion of donors at some programs are willing to provide an anonymous letter to the children conceived using their sperm or even to be contacted by the children once grown, so that they do not see more openness as a barrier. What this may mean, then, is that were openness to become the norm we would not necessarily have fewer donors, but we would likely have different donors.

178

Some wonder if the real agenda in the fight to preserve confidentiality is to protect the ego of the infertile male from exposure, an issue that seems to imply that infertility is something about which to feel shame. Even the terminology surrounding this option seems to reinforce this concern. Once commonly referred to as *artificial insemination by donor* (abbreviated as *AID*), the confusion with *AIDS*, the abbreviation for *acquired immune deficiency syndrome*, led to the need for new terminology. (Besides, part of the old terminology, *artificial*, was seen as inaccurate and offensive by many.) *Donor insemination* (*DI*) was the logical choice for a new term, since it had been used interchangeably with *AID* for years. But the medical community quickly introduced a third term, *therapeutic donor insemination* (*TDI*), and within less than three years this became the preferred term among many professional societies, journal editors and medical textbook publishers.

The term *therapeutic donor insemination* clearly seems to be a euphemism. According to the *American Heritage Dictionary of the English Language* the definition of the word *therapeutic* is "having healing or curative powers." Surgery is a therapy. Medications are therapies. But insemination with the sperm of a donor is not therapeutic! Donor insemination creates a pregnancy in an already fertile female, but it offers no possibility for healing or curing the infertility of her partner, who remains infertile.

A few have offered a feminist argument against what they perceive as sexism, pointing out that there has been no similar attempt by the medical establishment to create a way to avoid exposure of female infertility—no call for the return to the 19th century practice of wearing padded clothing to simulate a pregnancy while waiting for an adoption (or, today, a birth via surrogate.) But I see no reason to argue this as an issue of sexism. As an advocate for infertile people, I find that a more broadly important issue is how infertile people themselves see both male and female infertility and how they allow the world to view it.

Nothing to Be Ashamed Of

Infertility is a medical condition. Like diabetes or heart disease or neuromuscular disorders, it happens. Infertility is nothing about which one should feel shame. In an increasingly enlightened society where the medical establishment has been among the forerunners in the fight to end shame as an excuse for not seeking appropriate treatment for substance abuse or epilepsy or cancer or STDs, where they have led the campaign to end the use of euphemistic terms in sex education (e.g. *peepee* for *penis*, *tummy* for *uterus*, etc.) medical professionals should be among the first to want to bring infertility out of the closet!

Yet, only in the last half decade has the issue of secrecy as policy surrounding donor insemination been opened for any debate at all, and getting the floor to introduce such debate has been difficult. Those who have called for discussion are the professionals most likely to deal with the emotional issues of patients—nurses, therapists, counselors. Taking their cues from what has been learned about more traditional forms of adoption in the last half century, and with the added credence of having heard from many DI-built families over the years, these mental health professionals have been concerned about the effects of closely-held secrets on family systems.

Secrets, these therapists maintain, are nearly always based in shame. Shame-based secrets are so closely held that they often lead to the development of elaborate systems of avoidance and layer upon layer of lies within families. While the secret itself may not be revealed, the presence of a secret is nearly always felt by those within and close to the family, and the maintenance of the secret can become toxic to relationships and to the family system.

Yet it is understandable that families do not consider such an intimacy appropriate for general distribution. In our society sexual intercourse is a private act, so most couples do not share the intimacies of their sex and reproductive lives casually. It is possible to conceive a child via donor insemination in complete privacy and most couples feel it is appropriate to do so.

The decision to maintain complete privacy may, however, have certain immediate consequences. For example, excuses will have to be made for leaving work to visit the doctor several times at mid-cycle. The cycle of hope and despair which is part of any attempt to achieve pregnancy may be heightened for women who feel that they cannot talk freely to a friend or a counselor or a support group about their concerns. Once pregnant, women often experience some anxiety about the child they are carrying, about the donor, about their own and their partner's future relationship with their child. Husbands have reported feeling left out of the experience. The sense of isolation that total secrecy imposes can make pregnancy very difficult. Secrecy often impairs one's sense of dignity.

Those who argue against secrecy in donor insemination, however, rarely discourage privacy. Few of them are calling for the use only of identified donors or fully open quasi-adoptions. These advocates are completely aware that within society at large male infertility and donor insemination both continue to carry a significant element of social stigma.

These moderate advocates (I count myself among them) respect and support family privacy. What they are encouraging is that families retain their dignity as well as their privacy by being honest and open in communicating with one another, by recognizing that it is important for the children conceived by donor insemination to know the facts about their conception and their genetic heritage, and by determining together appropriate and very personal boundaries within their immediate circle for sharing this private information with others in their system of friends and family. (In a later chapter we will discuss issues relating to talking with children about their conception by donor insemination.)

Choosing the Donor

Another issue to be decided in advance is whether to use a known or an unknown donor. Though anonymous donation is chosen by most couples, there have always been some who have chosen to use semen from known donors. In these cases often the brothers or father or cousins of the infertile husband are approached about contributing their sperm in the hope of producing a child who is genetically as similar as possible to the man who will be his social father.

Using a known donor will allow you to have more specific control about the characteristics that the child's biological father may offer to his genetic pool. In choosing a relative of the husband, couples presume (not necessarily accurately) that the closer genetic match may also produce the possibility for a better psychological fit between father and child.

But when the chosen donor is one known to and/or part of the family, everyone involved must factor in how this ongoing connection might color the future. What will be the relationship between the donor and the child? Will the child know? If so, when?

Will others within the family? These issues must be thoroughly discussed in advance (preferably with an objective facilitator) and, if a decision is made to use a known donor, it is wise to establish some procedure for mediation should disagreements later arise.

You should know that some physicians will refuse to work with couples using a known donor, but this need not be an insurmountable barrier. RESOLVE can refer you to a physician who will work with you. The simplicity of the procedure even makes it possible to accomplish the process without the help of a physician if you wish.

RESOLVE has both a booklet and an excellent fact sheet on donor insemination as well as offering a list of questions to ask about sperm banks. These materials and additional reading material listed in the resource section at the chapter's end will provide excellent practical information. A support group or a well informed counselor can provide the added expertise that can help couples decide about this option.

Partners who can accept the infertility-related losses which will remain despite the arrival of a child conceived by donor insemination, who find the gains available through donor insemination more important than the losses it cannot prevent, and who expect to see one another as full and equal partners in any parenting relationship will find donor insemination an exciting alternative to childlessness.

Jared and Serena felt they had done absolutely everything. Serena tested as normally fertile. Jared's low sperm count had not improved after surgery to repair a varicocele. An attempt at GIFT had resulted in only one fertilized egg and no pregnancy, despite the fact that Serena had responded very well to ovulation induction therapy and produced several ova. The GIFT had been expensive and exhausting, both physically and emotionally. Neither partner was prepared to try again. But Jared was not enthused about the prospect of opening their private lives to an adoption agency or proving himself to a set of birthparents. He wanted a child, but not if it involved institutional adoption. Cautiously Serena introduced the idea of a try at donor insemination.

At first indignant, Jared needed time to think. Several months later he had read, he had asked questions, and he was ready. Serena conceived on the third cycle, gave birth to a healthy child nine months later, and these enthusiastic parents are now, three years later, hoping to use the same donor to conceive a second child.

Egg Donation and Embryo Adoption

It's been just ten years since 1984, when the first egg and embryo donations were successful in humans, and the option has become so popular and so successful that in terms of numbers, it has almost caught up with the numbers on donor insemination. While the technology was first developed as an alternative for women who did not have functioning ovaries (due to a variety of factors including premature ovarian failure) but who did have a uterus in which to carry a pregnancy, the technique has proven promising as well for the increasing numbers of women who do ovulate, but who are attempting to become pregnant later in their reproductive lives and even for women who have already experienced natural age-related menopause. Research seems to show that in women with no eggs or with older eggs the endometrium retains its implantation capacity. Many of the patients pursuing egg or embryo adoption are women who have unsuccessfully tried IVF-related procedures using their own ova and are aware that the statistical odds of their achieving a viable pregnancy are greatly enhanced when using the eggs of a younger, known-fertile donor.

Early egg donation/embryo adoption programs used excess eggs or embryos from patients undergoing ARTs. When all eggs could not be used, this seemed to many couples to be a much more positive way to deal with excess eggs than to dispose of them. But cryopreservation techniques now allow these patients to freeze fertilized embryos and try to implant them in their own bodies later, so that the availability of embryos for donation through such sources has been diminished. Some programs today recruit anonymous egg providers from among women who are compensated for their time and effort or those who are preparing for tubal ligation.

According to a survey of donor egg clinics conducted by Andrea Mechanick Braverman, Ph.D. and reported in the June, 1993 (Vol. 59. No. 6) issue of Fertility and Sterility, most programs began with the use of known donors and continue with this method today. Women receive eggs from sisters, cousins, or close friends who wish to help them in their quest for pregnancy and parenthood.

This form of collaborative reproduction has often been referred to as the female alternative to donor insemination. It has in common with donor insemination the fact that it involves the use of reproductive gametes, in this case ova as opposed to sperm. Additionally, the use of donor eggs and embryos requires screening donors for diseases and potential genetic problems in ways very similar to the screening of semen donors. As with donor insemination, couples need to consider whether to use a known or unknown donor and all of the issues related to this as discussed in the previous section. As in considering donor insemination, couples must consider whether they will tell others (including the child) about the use of donor gametes. Also similar is the need to understand that this is an alternative rather than a therapy. It does not make the egg recipient fertile.

But the similarity to donor insemination ends here. Unlike donating semen, which involves a few minutes of masturbation into a clean jar, ovum donation and embryo adoption are invasive procedures with accompanying physical risks to both donor and recipient. Further, it is interesting to note that the medical community has been supportive of the use of known egg donors while being less supportive of the use of known semen donors.

While we can expect the technology to change, at present eggs do not survive the freezing process as well as does sperm, and so eggs cannot be banked in the same way that sperm now is. Interestingly, embryos survive the freezing process much better than do eggs, though not as successfully as sperm is frozen and thawed. In general, however, ovum and embryo donation procedures, while more successful than traditional IVF, do not result in as high a percentage of successful births as does the process of donor insemination.

The ovum donation process involves a cycle of IVF: drug-induced ovulation induction, careful monitoring of ova development, followed by aspiration of eggs via transvaginal ultrasound or laparascopy. Ova are then fertilized *in vitro* and the resulting embryos either frozen for later use or transferred directly into the uterus of the recipient, whose hormone cycle has been carefully synchronized with that of the donor. This option offers an infertile couple the opportunity to conceive a child from the husband's sperm and a donor's ovum so that the infertile wife may experience pregnancy and give birth to her husband's child.

Embryo adoption is the implantation of an embryo created from the sperm and ovum of a donor couple (for example an "extra" embryo from an IVF cycle) in an infertile woman. The baby then born is not genetically related to either of it social parents.

Because the procedures are riskier and involve a greater investment of time, physical capabilities, and emotional energy than does donor insemination, egg and embryo donors are more difficult to recruit than are sperm donors. Additionally, because they involve IVF, both procedures are considerably more expensive than is donor insemination. Because they involve the monitoring of two females, they are usually more expensive than standard IVF.

Couples considering these options should reconsider all of the questions suggested in the earlier chapter for those considering assisted reproductive technology; should be assured that proper screening has been done of the donor and that they will have access to medical history; should be convinced that the donor has had appropriate counseling and is aware of the risks to her health; should be properly informed about the status of this technique under their state's laws (if written contracts are involved, have them reviewed by well informed legal counsel); should determine how costs will be assessed and which, if any, costs will be covered by insurance.

Additionally, couples should be certain to ask prospective service providers questions to clarify that their odds for success are as high as possible, including verifying that the husband's semen analysis makes a pregnancy likely, that the donor's fertility history is positive, and that the clinic's own take-home-baby rate with this protocol is a good one.

When successful, egg or embryo adoption allow an otherwise infertile woman and her partner to experience both the physical and the emotional aspects of a fully shared pregnancy and birth and to share the parenting experience. Still lost, of course, are genetic connection to the child to whom this mother gives birth, and the experience of jointly conceiving a child with her partner (a loss which many say is eased by the fact that this gestating mother has given birth to her partner's genetic child.)

Surrogacy

Traditionally (and the practice goes back to Biblical times) a surrogate has become pregnant via the sperm of the husband in an infertile couple and has then given birth to a baby which she agrees to allow the infertile wife to adopt. Today it is also medically possible for a surrogate to carry and deliver an embryo genetically unrelated to her—conceived *in vitro* from the ova and sperm of an infertile couple in which the women ovulate but are unable to carry a pregnancy.

Surrogacy has become its own industry today, an option rarely offered as an extension of medical services or allied with an adoption agency, yet with ties to both of these options and their related professionals. Unlike the other third party assisted options, which in most states do not require a legal procedure, surrogacy involves the legal adoption of the child by the wife of the baby's genetic father. In states where surrogacy has legal status, this is usually a fairly straightforward procedure very similar to a step-parent adoption.

When "modern surrogacy" with its psychological and medical screening, legal contracts, and spousal adoptions was first introduced by the Michigan attorney Noel Keane in the early 1980s, its supporters described it as the female equivalent to donor insemination (egg donation wasn't medically possible yet.) Even then, because of the mystique that surrounds the pregnancy and birth experience and the widely held belief that a primal bond exists between mother and child that does not exist between a father and child, this analogy didn't fly. As a society we have had a difficult time carving out a niche for surrogacy both legally and ethically.

Since most surrogacy arrangements involve commercial agreements between previously unconnected people rather than generous assistance of one friend or relative to another, one area of concern seems to be the exchange of money. Many people have problems with the perception of women "selling" their babies.

Unfortunately, the careful attempt by supporters of surrogacy to reeducate the public to see payment as a fair exchange of a proportionately low sum of money for the service of nine months spent gestating a pregnancy and giving birth rather than as the selling of parental rights to a child seems not to be working. The closest experience most people have to this idea is adoption, and in adoptions payment of money for "services" is strictly forbidden throughout all of North America. In adoptions in most states, birthparents can only be reimbursed for medical and counseling expenses. In only a few states can prospective adopters even help a birthmother with living expenses. A result of this concern has been that in some of the states which have passed surrogacy legislation, only non-commercial surrogacy (usually involving friends or relatives) is legal.

The second widely-held concern about surrogacy regards whether or not it is in the best interests of a child to be deliberately created by its mother in order to be given to another woman. Once again, the closest analogy most people can see is traditional adoption, where children are conceived by accident and adoption is accepted as a second best alternative for everyone involved, acceptable only because it solves the major problems of everyone in the triad: the child, who needs parents; the birthparents, who have erred and are unprepared to parent; the adopters, who can have no "children of their own." Since most people know that children who were adopted nearly always struggle at some point with trying to understand why their birthparents "gave them away," critics of surrogacy are concerned about how parents could ever satisfactorily explain to a child that he was conceived for the purpose of being given away and that money changed hands in the process.

I raise these thorny issues not as an indictment of surrogacy but in order to help couples exploring this option understand the resistance they and their children will face. These widely held ethical concerns have continued to make surrogacy the least societally accepted parenting option for infertile couples. In fact, when chosen by stable and well informed couples and surrogates, surrogacy is a healthy choice. For those who choose it after exploring all of its issues carefully, it can prove to be a near miracle!

Even the most "infamous" of surrogacy cases, Baby M, should not serve to condemn the practice as a whole. Indeed, the Sterns obviously explored their losses and their needs carefully. The decision to use a surrogate meant that Betsy's greatest need, to parent, was met while she avoided the complications to her multiple sclerosis if she became pregnant. With surrogacy as an option, Bill's needs for genetic continuity (as a grandchild

of the Holocaust) could still be met. The problems
in this case came as a result of poor practice in
screening and preparing a potential surrogate and
in the Sterns' not having investigated their program
and the surrogate offered to them closely enough.

Public perception of surrogacy as being likely to produce
trouble when the surrogate changes her mind is rooted in myth
rather than reality. Only a handful of surrogacy arrangements have
resulted in dispute. Though the problems always catch the
headlines, over 95% of the thousands of surrogate births arranged
in the last ten years have been seen as successful by all of the
adults involved (the word isn't in yet on how children will perceive
their conception and birth by surrogacy.)

For couples considering a surrogacy arrangement selecting
a competent program is vital. The choice of a program which
provides psychological preparation, counseling and screening for
both the recipient family and prospective surrogates and ongoing
support for the birthmother after the adoption results in the
greatest likelihood of a problem-free outcome. Read their
information thoroughly, ask as many questions as you can about
every aspect of the program—medical, legal, emotional—and ask
to speak with earlier clients before agreeing to participate in any
program.

The Donor's Place: Business Transaction or Extension of Family?

As one whose family has been expanded after two
generations of infertility by two generations of adoption, I know
well how very much those of us parenting children not genetically
related to us love our children and consider them "our own." Few
of us would wish for different children, though most of us very
much wish that these very children could have been born to us.
This is one of the losses that remains with us after our choosing to
avoid the loss of the parenting experience by adopting children or
using third party assistance to create a quasi adoption.

For much of this century adoption was practiced in total
confidentiality not so much to benefit the children, but to protect
the parents: birthparents from the "shame" of out-of-wedlock
pregnancy, adopters from the "shame" of infertility and from the
fear that without confidentiality the birthparents might "intrude"

on their lives (for, after all, how could anyone give up their own
flesh and blood?)

But things are changing in adoption, resulting in more
information shared and more communication between birth and
adoptive parents (even when their actual identities remains
confidential) and the children to whom both sets of parents are
forever attached in significant and unavoidable ways.

When surrogacy arrangements between women previously
unknown to one another first began to be part of the menu of
parenting options, most couples seeking a surrogate expected that
their relationship would be one that was strictly business. The
surrogate would be paid what felt to the contracting couple a
substantial sum of money to be inseminated, gestate, and give
birth to a child who would then be given over to his birthfather
and his wife. End of transaction.

In the early '80s I attended a multi-disciplinary symposium
at Wayne State University which tried to examine the medical,
legal, psychological and ethical issues surrounding surrogacy. After
the academic and clinical "experts" debated, a panel of real
experts—pioneer surrogates—were asked to describe their
experiences. Universally they expressed surprise that the couples
for whom they had given birth had little interest in maintaining
contact with them or sharing information about the children to
whom they had given birth. The surrogates, nearly all of whom had
considered that altruism was their highest motivating factor,
despite the fact that they had received money, were hurt and
confused by the contracting couples' perception of the
arrangement as a business deal that was over and done with. The
exchange of money seemed to be "the problem."

One audience participant, a business man considering the
option of surrogacy, rose in response to the panel presentation
and offered this view

"When I buy a diamond from a good jeweler
as a gift for my wife, what is the relationship
between the three of us? The jeweler has sold me
something, not given me a gift. I have paid for his
professional services. My wife is grateful to me, who
has given her a gift, and may feel obligated to me for
the gift. But does she have any feelings of gratitude
or obligation toward the jeweler, who simply did his
job and was paid for it? Similarly, if we were to hire

a surrogate rather than find a friend or family member willing to do this for us out of the goodness of her heart, I don't see how we could be expected to feel a sense of ongoing emotional obligation toward the surrogate. After all, she sets the terms and the price and we pay for the services, which she willingly provides. This isn't even like adoption, where a woman becomes pregnant by accident and has a problem she needs to have solved. She may wish that she had the resources and the ability to parent her child. The agency or the lawyer is the broker here, and receives the money. End of transaction. But the birthmother receives no fee from the adopting couple, and so each is grateful to the other: the adopters that the birthmother is willing to give them the gift of her child and the birthmother that the adopters are helping her to solve her and her baby's problem!"

The panel of surrogates and the mental health professionals and the ethicists in attendance were horrified by this reaction. Many of the consumers understood it and agreed with it.

Recognition of this and other perceptual problems between surrogates or donors and recipient infertile couples has led to significant changes as third party reproductive options have matured. Psycho-social screening, preparation, and support are built-in parts of the most reputable collaborative reproduction services. Fewer and fewer recipient couples harbor thoughts like the would-be father at the Wayne State conference. As in more traditional adoption, well prepared couples who choose quasi adoption options understand that the third parties who allow us to use their genes or their bodies to create our families are a respected and valued part of our families forever, even when they remain unknown to us. Daily we will see these people reflected in our children's eyes, and be grateful to them for the gift of family.

Should Age Be a Factor?

Finally, and far from incidentally, couples who are trying to become parents past the woman's age of natural fertility should carefully explore the ramifications this may have on the parent/child relationship over time. Some IVF clinics set maximum age requirements for their prospective patients. Usually such standards reflect the medical team's understanding that conception is far less likely with older patients and concerns about the risks of a "late" pregnancy to both mother and baby.

Clinics which offer egg donation and embryo adoption, however, sometimes do not have such age limitations, or they may lift age restrictions for women who have younger parenting partners. Supporters of this stance argue that women have the same rights to become parents as do men, who are far less restricted by age. An understandable philosophical stance, this.

But those who are exploring ethical issues might question it. Is it in a child's best interest to be born to (or for that matter adopted by) a mother beyond the normal age of menopause? (Actuarial tables provide the resource for finding decision making data here!) Of course we can deal with the practical problems presented by the distinct possibility that a child might lose his mother before reaching adulthood. A combination of good life insurance and careful estate planning, including naming guardians if necessary, "solves" this problem on a practical level.

But parenting is far more an emotional and a social experience than it is a financial one. That's why you wanted it in the first place—for the experience of parenting a child, not for the experience of paying for his care by others. Besides, you aren't as likely to die as you are simply to be dealing with the issues of aging. Look around at your older relatives. As much as you would like not to have it be so, you are statistically likely to age similarly to those to whom you are genetically related. If you are 47 and your own mother is 70, you have a good idea of how healthy and active you are likely to be when your child graduates from college. Remember your mother a dozen years ago. Would she have been ready to run after a ten year old, to participate in school activities? A mother who is 47 when her child is born faces the fluctuating hormones and volatile seeking-of-self of a 15 year old when she herself is 62. Both she and he will have been subject throughout his school years to the assumption from the public that she is his grandmother. While she herself may see the stability and maturity of her age as an asset, her child will definitely find it an embarrassment at times throughout growing up years. She will be 65 and retiring when her child graduates from high school. Will she also be widowed and going it alone? Will her children as young adults have her as a resource? Will their children have grandparents? Will they need to deal with the issues of aging parents in need of their care and attention at the same time as they are beginning to care for their own children? These are the things you don't want to think about, but must address.

Before you decide that it is really a baby you should parent (remember, that you can also choose, through adoption, to parent an older child), you need to speak to the real experts in the field: people who are doing it. Find someone who is ten years older than you are right now and who is parenting a nine year old. Locate someone who is 20 years older than are you and has just put a teenager in college. Ask them to give it to you straight.

Since collaborative reproduction is a variation on adoption, much of what is psychologically true for adoption is also true for those who parent through surrogacy, through donor insemination, or through embryo or egg donation. If you are seriously considering a third party option to family building, you will find much of the next chapter of interest as well.

RESOURCES

Organizations

RESOLVE, Inc. (1310 Broadway, Somerville MA 02144, telephone 617-623-0744) offers several helpful fact sheets

Infertility Awareness Association of Canada (523-774 Echo Lane, Ottawa, Ontario K1S 5N8, CANADA, telephone 613-730-1322)

The Organization of Parents through Surrogacy (OPTS) (7054 Quito Ct., Camarillo, CA 93012, 805-482-1566) is a national non-profit whose purpose is mutual support, networking, and the dissemination of information regarding surrogate parenting, egg and/or sperm donation and ARTs including IVF and GIFT. OPTS publishes a quarterly newsletter, holds meetings, has a telephone support network, and actively lobbies for legislation concerning surrogacy. Membership is $40 annually.

Reading Material

Between Strangers: Surrogate Mothers, Expectant Fathers & Brave New Babies by Lori B. Andrews, J.D. (New York: Harper & Row, 1989). An attorney specializing in reproductive law and ethics looks at surrogacy and offers consumers issues to consider in their decision making.

New Conceptions: A Consumer's Guide to the Newest Infertility Treatments by Lori B. Andrews, J.D. (New York: St Martin's Press, 1984). An attorney specializing in reproductive law and ethics looks at new technology and offers consumers issues to consider in decision making.

Beyond Infertility: Understanding the New Reproductive Technology by Susan Cooper and Ellen Glazer (Boston: Lexington Books, 1994) A thorough guide to the complex practical, ethical and emotional issues surrounding ARTS and quasi adoption options.

Pursuing Parenthood: Ethical Issues in Assisted Reproductive Technology by Paul Lauritzen (Bloomington: Indiana University Press, 1993) A carefully reasoned but complex and academic in tone exploration of the ethics of assisted reproductive technology and other family building options and of the professionals who offer them.

Is Donor Egg for You? by Steve Litt (Reseda, CA: American Troublebusters, 1993.) This 32 page self-published booklet by a "satisfied customer" of egg donation services, while lacking in depth in dealing with pre- and ongoing-emotional issues, raises good questions about practical issues couples considering this option should consider.

Having Your Baby by Donor Insemination by Elizabeth Noble (Boston: Houghton Mifflin, 1988) An exhaustive handbook, this book takes a decidedly pro-openness view toward the issue of whether D.I. should remain anonymous.

Surrogate Parenting. by Amy Zuckerman Overvold. (New York: Pharos Books, 1988.) An in depth look at the many issues which arise in choosing to use a surrogate to achieve parenthood.

Understanding Artificial Insemination: A Guide For Patients by William Schlaff MD and Carol Frost Vercollone LICSW (Boston. RESOLVE, 1989). A helpful booklet introducing the most important issues.

Lethal Secrets: The Shocking Consequences and Unsolved Problems of Artificial Insemination by Annette Baran and Reuben Pannor (New York: Warner Books, 1989). Long-time adoption reformers (*The Adoption Triangle*) look critically at traditional practice in donor insemination.

Chapter 9

ADOPTING

*One of my favorite columnists, Ellen Goodman
(distributed by the Washington Post Writer's Group),
wrote a beautiful piece appearing August 31, 1993,
about some friends who had adopted a child. In
watching this couple whose "parenting had come
without a full genetic set of assumptions" Goodman
came to realize something important about all
parenting, but less obvious to those who parent children
genetically related to them both: that "They didn't
assume that their own strengths and weaknesses had
traveled along the DNA to their offspring... So they set
out to know him as himself. And in the process let him
be himself."*

Perhaps because it begets so many mixed messages from
the rest of the world, adoption can be a difficult and confusing
choice for infertile couples to make. On the one hand, we have
been frequently told by others all throughout our infertility
experience, "Well, you can always adopt," or "Why don't you just
adopt?" statements which seem to imply support for adoption as a
positive option in family building. On the other hand we overhear
comments to those who already have adopted such as "It's too bad
you have no children of your own. How much do you know about
his real parents?" or "How could anyone ever give up their own
flesh and blood?" or "Now that you've adopted, you'll have a child
of your own. It always happens," that make it clear that most of
society sees adoption as a second best alternative for all involved.

In adoption, the larger social and economic world
challenges the parity of our parenthood. Only recently has the U.S.

Family and Medical Leave Act created the possibility of parenting leaves (without pay) for those whose new children will arrive by adoption rather than by birth. Frequently we must argue with our employers or insurance companies about coverage for the child being adopted. Because the Fairness to Adopting Families Act, which would mandate this, has not been passed (AFA and NCFA have put full advocacy forces behind it, but RESOLVE has endorsed it in name only) adoption expenses, which are usually significant, are not tax-deductible as would be the uninsured medical expenses surrounding a birth. In many states our children are not defined as the legal grandchildren of our parents for inheritance purposes, complicating how they must be referred to in wills. The list could go on.

Even within the infertility community those who choose to parent by adoption are frequently seen as having "settled." While it is uncommon and to a large extent unexpected for those who have given birth to children to retain their memberships or continue to volunteer for infertility support groups for long after their infertility is "solved," commonly long term leadership comes from among those whose families have been formed by adoption. Even here, where we should feel safe and supported, often we find that the group expects a pregnant or newly delivered officer to take a leave of absence or resign, but becomes irritated and impatient with the "unreliability" or "poor task performance" of the officer who has just adopted a newborn.

And with all of this surrounding us, they wonder... why don't we just adopt?

Bonding: The BIG Question

The most pressing question those who explore adoption ask themselves (though rarely do they voice the question to professionals and sometimes not even to partner) is this, "Will I be able to love a child not genetically related to me?"

The answer is really pretty simple. Very likely you will.

How can I be so sure? Because you've already done it. You have fallen in love with and formed an attachment to your partner, and this person shares no genetic connection to you.

A great deal of mythology surrounds the concept of bonding and attachment, and the research in the area is riddled with controversy. Despite the advertisements and the schlocky television movies, bonding is not a one-shot experience that happens in a delivery room. It is not a kind of super glue that holds a family together. Humans don't imprint as geese do.

The reality is that both human adult pairs and human caregiving adults and their children form attachments to one another based on their learning to trust and depend on one another. One human expresses a need— for food, for warmth, for comfort, for affection—and another human meets it. Then a need is felt and expressed again, and it is met by the same human. Over time, as our expressed needs are dependably met by the same person over and over, we come to trust that that person will always meet our needs, and so we begin to form a close attachment with them.

Yes, it's true that similarities between us often enhance our ability to attach. In many cases we are drawn to the comfortable familiarity of others who are physically or psychologically "like" us. But when we are motivated to form relationships, those similarities tend to grow.

Babies are amazing creatures. They are warm and soft and cuddly and they seem to mold quite comfortably against adult bodies. They smell good. Their eyes are large and moist. They are curious and responsive. They are helpless and their need for adult help is flattering. It's very difficult for a psychologically healthy adult not to try hard to respond to the needs of a baby in his care. And when he does, that baby will attach to him and he will attach to that baby.

It is certainly true that some of the things that promote attachment between parent and newborn are different in adoption. You've not been pregnant and had nine months in which a changing body forces you to give a great deal of your conscious and unconscious attention to the pending arrival of a particular child. It's true that during a pregnancy both parents tend to move through a series of psychological stages that prepare them for parenthood.

But it is possible, and in fact it is recommended, that those preparing to adopt give themselves the opportunity to experience what is called a psychological pregnancy—giving themselves the opportunity to fantasize about a particular child, thinking about names, furnishing a nursery, allowing friends and family to give them a shower or in other culturally accepted ways treat them as expectant parents.

It is also true that attachment between parent and newborn is often easier than attachment between an adult and a child who has already experienced parenting by someone else. While this presents an extra challenge to those who adopt a child who is several weeks or more old, it is absolutely accomplishable in almost all cases— particularly with very young children.

How Do We Know If Adoption Is for Us?

Couples who choose to adopt do so because they experience a kind of paradigm shift. In examining their infertility they come to understand that of its six potential losses, the most important to them and the one they most want to avoid experiencing is the loss of the opportunity to parent.

They understand that in adoption their loss of control may, for a time, be magnified as they give over control to an adoption intermediary or cast their lot to young birthparents to choose them. They allow themselves to feel some anger about this and then to accept it as a necessary loss. They recognize that they will not have a genetic connection to their child and will not continue their family bloodlines. But, over what for many is a significant amount of time, they come to feel that in parenting a child by adoption they will extend themselves and their family into the future in profound social and emotional ways. While they will lose the opportunity to create a child conceived by the blending of their own genes with those of their much loved partner, they are pleased that the two of them will parent together, and they like the equal footing that adoption allows them as parents. They have thought about the two losses—emotional and physical—attached to the expectations they had about the pregnancy and birth experience and have come to believe that the nine months of pregnancy is not particularly significant compared to a lifetime of active parenting.

They realize, bottom line, that what they want most is to be parents. Adoption will give them that opportunity. Not only that, but, if they can be flexible about the choices they make, the odds are nearly 100% that they will be successful in becoming parents. When couples realize that what they want more than anything is to become parents and compare that very high statistical probability with the much lower odds of success with almost all treatments and ARTS, adoption suddenly seems a much more positive opportunity in which to invest their time, their emotional and physical energy, and their money.

Social worker and adoptive parent Jerome Smith, in his book *You're Our Child*, talks about the process of building a sense of entitlement between parent and child. When, over time, parents develop a healthy sense of entitlement to their children by adoption, they become comfortable and confident in their role as **real** parents. The process involves three steps. First adopters need to deal with and accept their infertility and its losses. We've been working on that throughout this book. Then they need to acknowledge that adoption is indeed different from parenting by birth in ways that are significant and unavoidable. In being open with themselves and with their children about the fact that adoption involves a blend of gain and loss for all whom it touches, they will establish a healthy style of communication with their children. Finally, they must be prepared to cope themselves, and to help their children cope, with society's negative biases about adoption: negative adoption language (e.g. "Your real mother gave you away" rather than "Your birthmother made an adoption plan"), exploitive gimmicks (Cabbage Patch dolls, adopt-a-redwood fundraisers, "Problem Child" type movies, etc.) Those who decide to adopt are prepared to work on building this sense of entitlement, and they understand that it is a life long process.

A blunt word of caution: Adoption involves a leap of faith. It can happen if you make it happen. But since every child deserves to be wanted for who he is, that leap of faith needs to be a total one. You may explore adoption options and gather information while you are still actively pursuing treatment, but if you reach a point where you have been told by an agency that they are ready to do a homestudy or if you are actively involved in a specific prospective adoption because you have been chosen by and committed yourselves to a birthparent, you must decide to leap or not to leap.

If you are ready to leap, you will be ready to end treatment right now, mid cycle, until after this child is born (remember, treatment will always be there to consider for a subsequent child.) If, despite the fact that a probable adoption is imminent, you or your partner are unable to pull yourself away from treatment until after this child is born, you are not ready to embrace this particular child as the child you are ready to parent right now. Please don't adopt him. He deserves to be cherished for who he is rather than as a substitute for the child you really want.

Adoption's Choices

Once you have decided to pursue adoption, you will have many other choices to make. What makes many of these choices difficult is that none of them are inherently bad choices, and what makes them the right choices for some couples and the wrong choices for others is often a matter of timing and circumstances as well as whether the couple has accurate information and advice.

Dave and I, for example, have adopted three times. The first time we had waited a long time approved on an agency's list but making very little progress toward a placement when an opportunity to adopt independently arrived. Our son was a newborn, and the adoption would be confidential (because nearly all adoptions were confidential 18 years ago.) We had very little specific information about his birthparents, and were a little anxious about the fact that adoption professionals weren't handling this case. Yet we felt reassured when we spoke to our agency's social worker and she told us first that she felt that we ourselves were well prepared and that the OB/GYN who had delivered this baby had a fine reputation for seeing to it that birthparents had options counseling. The second time was also independent of an agency. We knew more by now, and we sent a clear message to our daughter's birthparents that we would be happy to pay for counseling and that we were interested in openness. They said no to both options. The third adoption was through an agency. It was both transracial and open.

I think that the most important piece of information I can offer you about our experience with adoption is that despite the many differences in the style of their adoptions, all three of our children (at ages 9, 12 and 18) are happy and well adjusted people. Contrary to what the myths would have you believe, they are not jealous of one another's access to information or lack of it. I believe that the key to this is that we really do feel a sense of entitlement to our children and they to us.

We are open with our children about adoption
issues, respectful of their birthfamilies and their
genetic heritage, and have consistently
acknowledged that sometimes adoption issues are
no fun, while at the same time trying to maintain
that delicate balance between acknowledging
difference and overemphasizing it. We see our
selves as a "normal" family. We have made the
commitment to always keep each individual child's
needs uppermost and to help him or her get those
needs met. This has meant keeping ourselves both
well connected to the adoption community (which
really does in some ways have a culture of its own)
and keeping ourselves well informed.

You don't have to work in the adoption
field, as I do, to do this. But you do need to make a
commitment to doing it.

You will need to explore <u>how</u> you will adopt
(agency/independent, domestic/international, open/confidential)
and <u>who</u> you will adopt (infant/older child, boy/girl,
inracial/transracial, relative health, singleton/sibling group.) You
can explore these options, as well as the many parenting issues
that are a part of adoption in much more depth by reading my
book *Adopting after Infertility*. This chapter, though, can provide
you with a thumbnail sketch of what you will need to consider.

The resources you've budgeted all along will influence
your decisions about adoption as well. Having explored your
resources, you can then consider how to spend them in various
approaches to adoption.

* Time, for example, may be a pressing issue. The wait for a
healthy white newborn through an agency can be up to ten
years in some parts of the country. This leads some
couples to explore nonagency adoption, or noninfant
adoption, or transracial or international adoption, or
adopting a child with some special health or emotional
needs. Your own advancing age may influence the options
open to you in adoption. As you explore this issue, refer
back to the section titled "Should Age be A Factor?" on
pages 184-85.

* Money may be a factor. Some agencies assess adopters a flat fee and some charge using a sliding scale. Some independent adoptions can involve relatively minimal legal costs and modest medical expenses not covered by a birthparent's insurance and others can involve living expenses, psychological counseling, legal advice in two states, travel, etc. The same is true with international adoptions.

* Emotional reserves may lead some couples to decide that they want the "protection" afforded by a traditional, confidential agency adoption, while others are interested in risking some emotional pain in order to have more control or to save time, etc.

* Your physical resources may influence the age and the relative health and the number of children you are prepared to parent at once.

Agency/Independent: Adoption can happen through agencies or independent of agencies. There are pros and cons to each approach. Some people like the built in counseling services and the fact that agency adoption offers them a kind of buffer to disappointment, since sometimes they will not even be told about a particular child until the birthparents' rights have been completely terminated. Agency adoption offers a higher probability that birthparents have been formally counseled about their rights and options, about loss issues for themselves, and that post placement counseling will be available if needed for both birthfamily and adoptive family. Others feel that independent adoption offers them the opportunity to speed up the process by taking them out of a waiting line and putting them in a position to "market" themselves to prospective birthparents. Age and religious beliefs can be a factor with some agencies, so that some "older" parents or non-Christian couples will find that independent adoption is a more hopeful route to parenting an infant by adoption. It is a myth that private adoption always costs more than agency adoption. In fact, the opposite is often the case, depending on the specific circumstances. You need to think carefully about these and many other pros and cons and decide whether to adopt through an agency or independently.

Domestic/International: You can adopt in your own country or internationally. Often couples pursue international adoption because, whether they choose to do so through an agency or independently, it can sometimes move faster than the domestic adoption of an infant. It can, however, prove to be significantly more expensive than domestic adoption, as it often involves the same kinds of homestudy, agency and legal expenses, plus the additional expenses of translations and travel. With rare exceptions, international adoption involves a transracial or transethnic placement. You need to explore what this means and ask yourselves some pointed questions about racism and about transethnic placement before seriously pursuing international adoption. Several books and several organizations can help you explore this question thoroughly.

Confidential/Open: Adoptions today can be either fully confidential or involve various degrees of openness between birth and adoptive families. Despite the myths spread by the media, there are birthparents seeking both styles of adoption, just as there are prospective adopters interested in both approaches. Some agencies or intermediaries practice only one style of adoption, and this will limit your opportunities once you have made your own choice. Other agencies believe that their clients must be empowered to make their own choices, and remain open to the needs for confidentiality or openness of each set of parents. Academic research on both styles of adoption has not provided us with any clear data indicating that one style of adoption is better than the other for either set of parents or for the child who was adopted. Furthermore, children raised in realistic acknowledgement-of-difference adoptive homes practicing both styles of adoption seem to be growing up psychologically healthy. If you do choose openness in adoption, it is important that you feel able to embrace your child's birthfamily fully and honestly. Agree to nothing that you feel you may want to change later. There is much to read and learn about this choice before making it.

Having once decided to adopt and how, the who must be decided upon. Most couples initially think about adopting a healthy newborn child of their own ethnic background as the ideal. This is logical and natural. After all, had you given birth, this very likely would have been the kind of child you would parent. But after exploring all of their options thoroughly, some couples find that they are open to other options.

Infant/Older Child: Perhaps in exploring your feelings about what it would be like to parent you realized that infancy was not that attractive to you. If so, the passage of time in your own life may lead you to consider an older child. Myth gets in the way again. Of course it is true that a child who is not a newborn comes with a short lifetime of experiences that may influence his behavior and his psychological well being, but many adopters are shocked to find out that even young babies can experience trauma in being moved from a foster caregiver. There is help in both instances.

Inracial/Transcultural: Transethnic or transracial adoptions change the complexion of a family forever. You will never again "blend in" as just like everybody else. Those who choose to adopt transethnically must be realistic about the racism that is a part of the society in which they live and they must be prepared to live in such a way that their children can develop a sense of pride in their heritage and a sense that they are not alone in the world. This involves an honest evaluation of where it is you live. Are the neighborhood and the schools and the house of worship where you live "colorful"? If not, you risk raising a lonely and isolated child who may find adolescence particularly difficult. You must be prepared for a variety of reactions from the public at large ranging from the Aren't-you-people-wonderful experiences to accusations that you are guilty of cultural genocide. You must consider how your family will react and be prepared to help them come to embrace this new family member or to lose you.

The keys to success in adopting a child who is older or racially different than his parents or who has special needs are flexibility and information (full information about the child's background and your own research about the resources available to you to handle any special needs). Those who adopt older children or children with special physical, emotional or intellectual needs will find that it is even more important to make a connection with adoption-related consumer groups such as Adoptive Families of America, Adoption Council of Canada and North American Council on Adoptable Children, who can provide them with referrals to helpful professionals, advocacy services, and access to books, tapes, games and toys that can be of use to both parents and children.

Getting Ready for Adoption

In the old days, everyone who adopted had to go through what was routinely called a homestudy. The image people had of this was that it involved a prim and proper social worker who not only intruded on your personal lives but also did a white glove inspection of your home. That same old social worker was the one who advised birthmothers, made them see the hopelessness of their situation, and convinced them to surrender their babies for adoption.

The specter of such a disempowering experience causes many people even today—both birthparents and prospective adopters—to decide either that adoption is not for them or that they should avoid an agency at all costs and just do the adoption themselves.

Vestiges of this old system remain, but today most agencies offer very different services. They offer parent preparation to prospective adopters and they offer birthparent counseling to young people dealing with an untimely pregnancy. The difference in both approach and outcome between the old system and today's is worth our spending some time discussing.

Adoption is different from parenting by birth. That fact isn't a myth and it isn't going to go away. The idea of being different is uncomfortable for many people, and they tend to cope with difference in one of two ways: they either deny the difference or they accept it and look for ways to deal with it. Avoiding a parent preparation process is a denial of difference behavior.

Rita and Seymour figured that they knew all they needed to know about adoption. You take home a new baby and you love him. So what's the big deal? They were offended to find that several of the agencies in town wouldn't work with them because they were Jewish, and the nonsectarian agencies had long lists. They didn't want to wait.

They read some how-to books and the placed an ad in a weekly shopper newspaper. A birthmother called. It was all so easy! She had

insurance but would need some help with her
medical deductible. She didn't want to see a
counselor, because she knew what she was doing.
The birthfather didn't even know she was pregnant
and he was long gone. She herself just wanted this
to be over and to get on with her life. She didn't
want to think about this baby anymore once it was
born.

She was ready. They were ready. They called
their lawyer. He'd not done an adoption before, but
it looked pretty cut and dried, so he felt ready, too.

Looks good, huh? Get real! Rita and Seymour's adoption is
a disaster waiting to happen. They've read little, talked about little,
considered nothing about how they will deal with adoption as a
facet of their lives with their child-to-be. Their child's birthmother
seems to believe that once the baby is born the whole bad
experience will be past. She has heard nothing about grief and loss
and is unprepared to deal with a rush of emotions that could and
likely will overwhelm her once the baby is born. She doesn't
understand that the birthfather has legal rights that must be dealt
with and neither do Rita and Seymour. Their lawyer may not
understand this either!

You think this couldn't be you? Perhaps you didn't notice
the huge adoption-related story that fascinated the media and the
country during much of 1992 and 1993. A couple in one of the five
U.S. states that make private adoption illegal decided to
circumvent the long wait on agency lists and their state's ban on
private adoption by adopting in another midwestern state. They
made contact with a birthmother and a local attorney and
everything looked swell.

Soon after the birth the adoption began to unravel. The
birthmother, without any pre-adoption counseling, was overcome
by the loss reaction she felt after her child was placed and she went
to a local meeting of birthparents who feel ripped off by the
adoption process. The members of the group learned that this
birthmother had two things going for her in trying to undo the
adoption: the attorney had taken her consent to the adoption
earlier than the state law allowed, and she had lied about who the
birthfather was, so that the actual birthfather had not consented to
the adoption. Within days of the birth she told the actual
birthfather the truth and the two of them asked for the baby back.

The prospective adopters were poorly counseled too. Despite the fact that legal precedent was not in their favor, they refused to give the baby back and took off for their home state. When, months later, the courts in the baby's birth state ruled against them, the prospective adopters still refused to give her birthfather the custody that was his right by law, and asked their state to intervene. Many months and several judgments later, right up to the U.S. Supreme Court, which refused to hear the case, the child, by then over two and a half years old, was ripped from the only home she had ever known and returned to the birthparents, who had never met her but who had subsequently married and had another child, with no arrangements having been made to provide either them or the child with counseling.

What went wrong here was a string of things: poor emotional and legal counseling of the birthparents, poor emotional preparation and legal counseling of the prospective adopters, attorneys not experienced in adoption, no information on either side about bonding and attachment issues for this child. All of it could have been avoided.

Adoption is different than parenting by birth. It is different psychologically; it is different socially; it is different legally. Both you and your child's birthfamily should recognize this and be willing to do what is best for the child you share. This means preparing yourselves for the realities of gain and loss, happiness and pain that accompany adoption. It means talking with counselors, reading appropriate books, attending classes or workshops.

I don't intend to imply that all adoptions should be handled by agencies. People planning independent adoptions can be well prepared, and there are bad agencies out there as well. But I do mean to strongly endorse availing yourselves of expert professional advice—and insisting on providing it for your child's birthparents as well—from mental health professionals experienced in the field, from educators experienced in the field, from attorneys experienced in the field.

Bringing Your Family Aboard

Some couples who choose to adopt are shocked to find that when they announce their plans their family responds with stunned silence or even rejection. They shouldn't be shocked.

What they have often failed to realize is that their family is several steps behind them in dealing with the impact of infertility on their lives together. They need time to catch up.

Family members have most often not been a part of the reading and thinking and talking the two of you have done over many months before deciding to pursue adoption. Just as you were relatively uninformed about adoption and accepted as truth many of the pieces of misinformation that you now know to be false, your family members and friends need education.

Family members experience losses in infertility too. They had expected a grandchild who had the family nose or a long, lean, red-headed nephew. That child is not to be, and they must let him go. In exchange, they will need time to think about how interesting it will be to grandparent a child with dark, curly hair, to watch genetically unconnected cousins form close family connections with one another.

If they live nearby, you might consider inviting family or close friends to go to a symposium or to a parent group picnic with you. If they are more distant, you should consider sending them things to read. Start out with articles or newsletters. *OURS: The Magazine of Adoptive Families* can be a good choice. It comes bimonthly and covers a wide range of adoption-related issues (not to mention a long list of adoption-appropriate and ethnically-inclusive toys and games that prospective grandparents or aunts and uncles might want to stock up on.) Other newsletters caring others may find of interest include *Adopted Child, Roots & Wings*, or *Adoptnet*. Send them a copy of Pat Holmes' *Supporting an Adoption* or Linda Bothun's *When Friends Ask about Adoption*. Progress to longer books you've read and think they may enjoy, or send them tapes from your favorite speakers to listen to in the car or as they walk or garden or clean. Suggest they become involved in preparing the nursery or gathering garage sale bargains for the nursery and the layette.

Talk to your family and friends about using positive adoption language (send them copies of the free fact sheet from Perspectives Press) and about helping to educate others about adoption. Help them to understand that adoption is not a handicap, but a way that families come together, just as is birth or marriage. Before they have a chance to blow it, help them to learn that it is just as inappropriate to announce, "This is my new adopted granddaughter, Samantha" as it would be to offer, "This is my birth control failure grandson, Marcus."

Practice together!

I don't want to oversimplify this choice. Adoption can be a difficult life experience, especially for those who choose to deny that it is different. Reading only this chapter is not adequate preparation for deciding to adopt. Please use the resources listed here to research the areas about which you are concerned.

RESOURCES

National Organizations Offering Information and Support to Adoptive Families and Prospective Adopters

Adoption Council of Canada (P.O. Box 8442, Station T, Ottawa, Ontario K1G 3H8. Phone 613-235-1566.) This network collects and disseminates information about adoption throughout Canada, facilitating communication among groups and individuals interested in adoption and promoting understanding of the benefits and challenges of adoption.

Adoptive Families of America (3333 Hwy 100 North, Minneapolis, MN 55422. Phone 612-537-0316.) An excellent source for purchase of books and tapes and of referral to local parent groups, AFA is the largest organization for adoptive families in the world. AFA publishes *OURS: The Magazine of Adoptive Families* bimonthly and sponsors an annual national conference designed specifically to reach out to those considering adopting and adoption-expanded families. Its Annual Adoption Information and Resources packet lists several hundred agencies nationally and offers consumer advice.

American Academy of Adoption Attorneys (P.O. Box 33053, Washington DC 20033-0053.) A national association of attorneys who handle adoption cases or otherwise have distinguished themselves in the field of adoption law. The group's work includes promoting the reform of adoption laws and disseminating information on ethical adoption practices. The Academy publishes a newsletter and holds annual meetings and continuing education seminars for attorneys.

Infertility Awareness Association of Canada (523-774 Echo Lane, Ottawa, Ontario K1S 5N8, CANADA, telephone 613-720-1322) A Canadian charitable organization offering assistance, support, and education to those with infertility concerns by the distribution of its

its bilingual publication *Infertility Awareness* five times a year; establishment of chapters to provide grass roots services; a resource centre; information packages; and a network of related services. Services are bilingual (English and French.) A complimentary information kit will be sent to interested Canadians upon request.

National Council for Adoption (1930 17th St NW, Washington DC 20009, telephone 202-328-1200.) An advocacy organization promoting adoption as a positive family building option. Primarily supported by member agencies, it does also encourage individual memberships from those families who share its conservative stance on open-records/confidentiality and its wary view of open placements. If you have decided to pursue a traditional, confidential, agency adoption, call NCFA for a referral to a member agency.

North American Council on Adoptable Children (NACAC) (970 Raymond Ave. #106, St Paul, MN 55114-1149. Phone 612-644-3036.) An advocacy and education resource concerning waiting children, NACAC publishes the periodic newsletter *Adoptalk*, which reviews new books and tapes, and sponsors each August an enormous, well respected conference on special needs adoption for professionals and parent advocates. This conference rotates through five geographic areas. If you are considering a special needs adoption, call NACAC first for information about local and national resources, parent groups, and adoption exchanges.

RESOLVE, Inc. (1310 Broadway, Somerville, MA 02144. Phone 617-623-0744.) RESOLVE and its over 50 local chapters maintain current references on all infertility and adoption issues. In addition to publishing both national and local newsletters which print book reviews, the national office develops and keeps updated fact sheets on a variety of issues of interest to its membership. Several of these deal carefully with adoption subjects. Locally, chapters periodically offer, in addition to monthly meetings, day long seminars on both infertility and adoption issues. Several chapters periodically survey their geographic service area's adoption agencies and publish a resource guide.

von Ende Communications (3211 St Margaret Dr., Golden Valley, MN 55422. Phone 612-529-4493.) This audio service catalogs the sessions from numerous large national and regional adoption and child welfare conferences. An excellent source for up-to-date information from the trainers who have not written consumer books and for narrowly focused subject information for those who do not have the opportunity to attend large conferences.

Books/Tapes/Videos: General Adoption and Readiness Issues

Adopting after Infertility by Patricia Irwin Johnston (Indianapolis: Perspectives Press, 1992). An extensive three part handbook for couples considering or pursuing adoption. Readers of this book can skip section one (which examines infertility and making all kinds of related decisions) and go straight to Section Two, which explores in some detail all of the issues to be decided in adoption--agency or independent, infant or older child, international or domestic, open or confidential-- and includes guidance on choosing professionals and services which meet your needs. Section three explores life after adoption in a manner important for pre-adopters to explore: talking to kids, dealing with school and the world at large, infertility revisited, etc. This comprehensive decision-making guide also fits in each of the resource categories which follow, but will not be listed there.

Deciding on Adoption with Pat Johnston (Indianapolis: Perspectives Press, 1993) A series of three audio tapes on decision making regarding making adoption a first choice rather than second best.

Parenting in Adoption with Pat Johnston (Indianapolis: Perspectives Press, 1993) A series of three audio tapes on parenting issues in adoption, including what children understand when, embracing difference, choosing books for children.

The Encyclopedia of Adoption by Christine Adamec and William Pierce (New York: Facts on File, 1991). The title tells you exactly what this is--a collections of essays on nearly every adoption related topic you could imagine, arranged in alphabetical order. Includes hundreds of references to books, articles, studies, etc.

Family Bonds: Adoption and the Politics of Parenting by Elizabeth Bartholet (New York: Houghton Mifflin, 1993.) A provocative look at how and why genetic connection is promoted to (in the author's view) the detriment of infertility patients and adoptive relationships stigmatized except when they are quasi or partial adoptions. A powerful argument for revamping the system and society's view of adoption.

Our Child: Preparation for Parenting in Adoption--Instructor's Guide by Carol Hallenbeck, R.N.. (Wayne, PA: Our Child Press, rev 1989) is a fully scripted and wonderfully resourced curriculum guide to be used in offering a four to six week "Lamaze" course for adopting couples. (Even better: take the course! Often offered by local parent groups, a hospital, or the Red Cross.)

You're Our Child: The Adoption Experience by Jerome Smith and Franklin I. Miroff (Lanham, MD: Madison Books, rev 1987). An introduction to the idea of building a sense of entitlement between parents and children.

Books: What Type of Child?

Adoption and Disruption: Rates, Risks and Responses by Richard Barth and Marianne Berry (New York: Aldine De Gruyter, 1988). There is a great deal of mythology about what causes disruptions or failures in adoption. This book looks at the factors which contribute to an outcome of disruption and offers valuable suggestions for preventing them.

Gift Children: A Story of Race, Family and Adoption in a Divided America by J. Douglas Bates (New York: Ticknor & Fields, 1993). The memoir of a family who adopted two pre-school aged bi-racial daughters in the early 1970s. This book is not a love-conquers-all our-story, but the honest revelations of a loving family as their children grew to adulthood in a middle class primarily white small city and beyond idealism to the realities of racism in America.

Self Awareness, Self-Selection, and Success: A Parent Preparation Guidebook for Special Needs Adoption by Wilfred Hamm, T Morton and L Flynn (Washington: NACAC, 1985). A workbookish series of questionnaires and exercises for people considering special needs adoption. Order from AFA.

Adopting the Older Child by Claudia Jewett (now Jarratt) (Boston: Harvard Common Press, 1978). Though older, this is a classic resource for those considering this option, written in a totally accessible style.

Helping Children Cope with Separation and Loss by Claudia Jewett (now Jarratt) (Boston: Harvard Common Press, 1978). Another valuable resource for those considering an older child.

Transracial Adoption: Children and Parents Speak Out by Constance Pohl and Kathy Harris (New York: Franklin Watts, 1992) while not an in depth resource, offers the kind of helpful introductory overview of nearly all of the issues people ned to consider in order to make a good decision about whether or not to adopt outside their own ethnicity.

Are Those Kids Yours? American Families with Children Adopted from Other Countries by Cheri Register (New York: The Free Press, 1991). A thorough, practical, down to earth discussion about the realities of and guide to parenting a child born outside the U.S.

To Love a Child: A Complete Guide to Adoption, Foster Parenting, and Other Ways to Share Your Life with Children by Marianne Takas and Edward Warner (Reading, MA: Addison-Wesley, 1992. A wonderful exploration of alternative ways to add children to one's own life and make a difference in theirs. The only title to realistically explore fostering, big brothering and other non-permanent nurturing relationships as viable alternatives.

Books/Videos: How-to Adopt

There Are Babies to Adopt by Christine Adamec (Boston: Mills and Sanderson, 1989). An exploration of various options in and routes to adopting an infant.

A Canadian Guide to International Adoptions by John Bowen (Toronto: Self Counsel Press, 1992).

The Adoption Resource Book by Lois Gilman (New York: HarperCollins, rev. 1992). This is the most authoritative adoption how-to available and has been updated several times. Journalist and adoptive parent Gilman carefully explores all types and styles of adoption and provides excellent resources for pursuing specific strategies.

Winning at Adoption by Sharon Kaplan (now Roszia) (Studio City, CA: The Family Network, 1991). A multimedia approach to making decisions about adoption style, this well put together package includes videotapes, audiotapes and workbooks.

Beating the Adoption Game by Cynthia Martin (New York: Harcourt Brace, Jovanovich, 1988). A classic how-to with valuable insights which will help you to weigh alternative styles.

The Private Adoption Handbook by Stanley B. Michelman and Meg Schneider (New York: Villard Books, 1989). A guide to independent adoption written by an attorney specializing in the field.

The Adoption Directory by Ellen Paul (Detroit: Gale Research, 1989) A director of adoption agencies and groups state-by-state (rapidly outdated, but basic info is useful. Use a library copy.)

CWLA's Guide to Adoption Agencies by Julia Posner (Washington: Child Welfare League of America, 1989) A more comprehensive, but still easily outdated state-by-state reference book. Use a library copy.

Adopting Your Child: Options, Answers, Actions by Nancy Thalia Reynolds (Bellingham, WA: Self-Counsel Press, 1993). Guide to making decisions about types of adoption and to resources for facilitating adoptions by singles and couples, heterosexual and gay. Unique in that it includes strategy building, step parent adoptions and extended family adoptions, is more specifically helpful to minority adopters than many how-tos, and covers material for Canadians as well as U.S. citizens.

Adopt the Baby You Want by Michael R. Sullivan and Susan Shultz. An attorney specializing in independent adoption shows you the ropes. This includes a good set of cautionary guidelines.

Loving Journeys Guide to Adoption by Elaine L. Walker (Peterborough NH: Loving Journeys, 1992). A how-to with extensive decision-making guidance as well as a state-by-state and country-by-country guide that was comprehensive when new.

Books: Openness in Adoption

Adoption: A Handful of Hope. by Suzanne Arms (Berkeley, CA: Celestial Arts, 1990). A revised edition of the earlier *To Love and Let Go*, this book revisits, ten years later, several birthparents and adopting families who have chosen open adoption.

An Open Adoption by Lincoln Caplan (New York: Farrar, Strauss, Giraux, 1990). After extensive fascinating interviews with professionals on both sides of the controversy surrounding open adoption, journalist Caplan attempts to present objectively the intimate details of one particular open adoption in which both birth and adoptive parents allowed him to follow their progress from before the birth through a year following the placement, including a disturbing conclusion. The result is a book which is fascinating, and which neither pro-open or pro-confidential advocates find satisfying.

Adoption without Fear edited by James. L. Gritter (San Antonio: Corona Publishing, 1989). A series of essays written by birth and adoptive parents who participated in open adoptions through the same Michigan agency.

Open Adoption: A Caring Option by Jean Warren Lindsay (Buena Park, CA: Morning Glory Press, 1987). Though more specifically written for pregnant teens, the audience to whom teen-parent educator Lindsay most often reaches out, this book offers interviews with nearly all of the well known professionals who have an opinion on the relatives merits of openness in adoption and as well offers prospective adopters insight into the thinking of prospective birthparents.

The Open Adoption Book: A Guide to Adoption Without Tears by Bruce Rappaport, Ph.D. (New York: MacMillan, 1992) The director of the Independent Adoption Center and founder of the National Federation for Open Adoption Education's guide for consumers.

The Open Adoption Experience: A Complete Guide for Adoptive and Birth Families by Sharon Kaplan Roszia and Lois Melina (New York: HarperCollins, 1993). A practical guide to making decisions about openness adoption, living with openness over time, adapting to changing needs and relationships, this resource is unique in that it speaks to birth and adoptive families <u>together</u>.

A Letter to Adoptive Parents: on Open Adoption by Randolph W. Severson (Dallas, TX: House of Tomorrow Productions, 1991). A warm and encouraging booklet for families considering open adoption.

Dear Birthmother: Thank you for Our Baby by Kathleen Silber and Phylis Speedlin (San Antonio: Corona, 1982). This is the book that started the discussion of openness in adoption. Startlingly controversial when new, the form of open adoption it then promoted was the exchange of anonymous letters through an intermediary!

Children of Open Adoption by Kathleen Silber and Patricia Martinez Dorner (San Antonio: Corona, 1989). Nearly ten years after the practice began, Silber follows up on the growing children of some of the families with whom she began practicing openness in adoption.

"Open Adoptions: The Experts Speak Out" from Children's Services Ctr in Pacific Grove, CA features interviews with and conversations between Carol Bishop, Barb Tremitiere, Kathleen Silber, Sharon Kaplan, Patricia Martinez Dorner, Annette Baran, Jeanne Etter, Jim Gritter, Joyce Maguire Pavao and Carol Biddle.

"Our Child" from Hope Adoption Service in Canada follows one set of birthparents and one set of adoptive parents in their decision to plan an open adoption with one another.

Books: Understanding and Enhancing Adoptive Family Relationships

Adoption: The Lifelong Search for Self by David M. Brodzinsky and Marshall Schechter and Robin Marantz Henig. (New York: Doubleday, 1992). Integrating both psychological and educational theory, the authors offer a model of normal development in adoptees.

A Child's Journey through Placement by Vera I. Fahlberg, M.D. (Indianapolis: Perspectives Press, 1991). A careful look at how transferring a child from a known environment to any long term new placement--hospitalization, interim care, etc.--affects attachment, with specific suggestions for avoiding unnecessary moves and facilitating those which are unavoidable.

Perspectives on a Grafted Tree: Thoughts for Those Touched by Adoption edited by Patricia Irwin Johnston (Indianapolis: Perspectives Press, 1983). A collection of poems written by birthparents, adoptive parents, adoptees, and professionals in the field in an effort to demonstrate the gain and loss, happiness and pain that are part of the adoption experience for all involved.

The Adoption Life Cycle: The Children and their Families through the Years by Elinor B. Rosenberg (New York: The Free Press, 1992). Psychiatry professor and adoptive parent Rosenberg presents a view of the challenges of successfully integrating adoption and the changes it continuously brings into the lives of those whom it touches--adoptees, birthparents, adoptive parents.

Chapter 10

PREGNANCY

I had this dream about how it would be. He'd come home from work and I'd have a special dinner prepared, with candlelight and our wedding china. I'd be radiant. And I'd whisper, "Honey, we're going to have a baby."

Then he'd sweep me into his arms and cover me with kisses. We'd call our parents, who'd be ecstatic.

The next nine months would be perfect. We'd take a picture of me naked once a week to chart how big I got. I'd wear these wonderful maternity clothes to work. We'd shop for the perfect furniture and paint the nursery a special shade of yellow. I'd take prenatal aerobics classes and we'd go to prepared childbirth classes together.

We'd have practiced breathing so well that I'd have a quick and easy labor with him coaching me every step of the way, and then our baby would be born perfect and I'd breast feed him right there on the delivery table.

Sound familiar? Most couples have similar expectations, and in fact many of them carry these dreams with them right through all of the treatment. For many couples this dreamed-of scene can become a reality. Just because getting pregnant was hard doesn't mean that the pregnancy has to be different too.

If you are among the 50% or more of couples who will experience a pregnancy and you can allow yourself to enjoy it, please do! Buy the clothes, take the classes, read the books, decorate the nursery. Do it all. You deserve it!

But sometimes pregnancy after infertility isn't what you expected. This chapter cannot begin to cover all of the issues, but it can serve both as an overview of some of the things that could come up so that you won't be surprised or feel alone should you experience them and provide suggestions for finding more appropriate reading materials.

The most important piece of advice I can give is that if your find yourself beseiged by any of the concerns mentioned here, make contact with a local infertility support group or with the physician you treated your infertility and ask for a referral to a competent, well-informed, infertility-sensitive mental health professional.

Where Do We Fit?

The most common reaction to pregnancy after infertility reported is that couples don't feel they have a place to belong. Whether their still-unpregnant infertile friends mean for it to happen or not, often newly pregnant infertiles feel uncomfortable with their prior support system. Remembering what it was like to be jealous of someone who got pregnant, they don't want to make their infertile friends uncomfortable, so they tend to distance themselves.

But where do they belong? The couples in the typical childbirth preparation classes take their pregnancies so completely for granted that they seem to have no idea of how very special or tenuous this pregnancy feels. Couples report that they often feel out of place in their classes and even angry with their classmates' casual attitude about pregnancy.

After having spent months or years being treated by a "specialist" medical team, becoming the patient of an obstetrician/gynecologist who sees primarily normal, healthy pregnant women can result in a women's feeling that even her medical team doesn't value this pregnancy to the extent that she and her partner do.

It can be pretty lonely if you don't have a place to belong.

Who's in There?

Women who have achieved a pregnancy after taking medications, using an ART procedure, or with the assistance of donor gametes commonly spend some time worrying that their baby won't be normal.

> Peggy, who had spontaneously become pregnant after many years of unsuccessful treatment and then maintained it by taking progesterone, reported that she was besieged throughout her pregnancy with nightmares in which she gave birth to a lizard. Because she was seeing a doctor who was unfamiliar (her fertility specialist didn't do obstetrics) the staff didn't take her concerns seriously.
>
> "Normal!" they laughed. "Lots of gals have dreams like that. Don't worry about it. You'll be fine." Peggy was a healthy pregnant lady, so they saw no need for any special monitoring, let alone special support.
>
> But as Peggy saw it, her body's reproductive system had never done anything else right, so how could she expect this to work. She hadn't gotten pregnant in spite of invasive treatment. Then she did get pregnant when she was not expecting to. Then she stayed pregnant by taking medication.
>
> Her pregnancy was a miserable experience. She felt "weird" in her prenatal classes. Her husband, who was beside himself with delight at their success, wasn't a lot of help. He wanted Peggy to bask in their good fortune.
>
> They delivered a healthy, full term boy. It took right through his first six months (when Peggy felt the danger of a SIDS death was safely past) for Peggy to feel confident that this was all real and wasn't going to be snatched away.

Couples who have used donor gametes or ARTs or AIH frequently worry that the vials or the dishes have gotten mixed up and that they will deliver a child obviously not there own--perhaps of a different race, even. Not that it couldn't happen, but the odds are so low as to be nearly insignificant. But does hearing that make the fear go away if you have it? Probably not.

The High-Risk Pregnancy

Some pregnancies after infertility really do fit the medical definition of a problem pregnancy, one which needs more careful monitoring than average. Certainly women who have experienced an ectopic pregnancy or several miscarriages fit this category, as do those who are carrying a multiple pregnancy, those at risk for premature labor and those who develop complications unrelated to the infertility, such as gestational diabetes, placenta previa, toxemia, etc.

Additionally, "older" mothers have a higher rate of complications in pregnancy and delivery. According to a 1990 study in the New England Journal of Medicine, these complications may in part attributed to the fact that older women are more likely to have developed chronic health problems. But older mothers are also more likely to have multiple gestations, to miscarry, and to have babies with chromosomal abnormalities. As a result, they are also more likely to need to deliver their babies by Cesarean section.

Sometimes the issue of risk is brought about by the possibility of a health problem with the developing baby. Physicians may suggest more frequent ultrasounds, maternal serum alpha fetoprotein tests (MFAFP), chorionic vilus sampling (CVS) or amniocentesis.

If your pregnancy falls into one of these categories and you find yourself subjected to exceptionally close monitoring or confined to bed or to quarters, don't be surprised if you find yourself feeling that your body has failed you...again. Even if you are confined to bedrest, the phone can link you to needed the support you will need.

Multiples

Multiple pregnancies are more common today than they've ever been due both to the use of drugs which hyperstimulate the ovaries to achieve a pregnancy via intercourse or artificial insemination, and as a result of the number of eggs or fertilized embryos introduced into the body in GIFT or IVF. But even though the rate of multiples has increased, a pregnancy of what are called grand multiples—triplets, quadruplets, or quintuplets— remains rare.

A multiple pregnancy is almost always labeled high risk, because carrying multiples is dangerous to both mother and children. These children are at risk for low birth weight and premature delivery. As a result, a multiple pregnancy, while seen as a novelty to be joked about by nearly everyone else, is often accompanied by fear and even dread on the part of the parents-in-waiting.

Will all of the babies survive? Will they all be healthy? Can we afford this? Can we manage their care? A myriad of questions swirl through the minds of these parents, who are sometimes unable to share their anxieties—especially their feelings of ambivalence— even with one another.

Perhaps more than any other group of couples who achieve pregnancy after infertility, those who are pregnant with multiples feel isolated. Though you may need to be particularly aggressive in order to find others who have shared this experience, you need their support. If your own obstetrician's office cannot put you in touch with local couples who have gone through this, call other medical offices, childbirth preparation programs, hospital social service departments or the National Office of the Mothers of Twins Clubs until you find a resource.

Abortion and Pregnancy Reduction

Increasingly commonly physicians are offering patients carrying grand multiples (three or more babies) the option of pregnancy reduction. With this procedure one or more of the fetuses is aborted, most often using transvaginal ultrasound and a saline injection. Since the risk of miscarriage is increased by this procedure, this is a difficult decision even for those who have less difficulty with the general idea of pregnancy termination.

With this procedure, using ultrasound and laparoscopy, some embryos in a multiple pregnancy are selected for termination and are aborted to allow the remaining fewer embryos a greater chance of survival. Recent follow-up with patients who have undergone such procedures demonstrate that nearly all experience strong ongoing emotional reactions to this procedure, even when it results in the successful birth of healthy babies, so that it remains best to try to avoid the need for it, it should not be considered "routine" and it must come accompanied by appropriate psychosocial support.

Miscarriage

About 40% of all pregnancies end in miscarriage. Most of them occur in the first couple of weeks of pregnancy, before most women (except the infertile) would be likely to know they were pregnant. Fourteen to 20% more occur within the first trimester, and only three percent of pregnancies are lost after that. Losing a wanted pregnancy is always difficult, but it can be devastating for the couple who has waited so long and worked so hard to achieve a pregnancy.

Though much of society at large remains insensitive about pregnancy loss ("It was probably for the best"... "You'll have another"... "At least you didn't know him"...) it is the rare hospital which does not have a pregnancy/infant loss support system with counselors or groups training to provide assistance to the grieving family (including siblings). If your physician does not see to it that you receive this information, contact the pastoral care or social services offices in your hospital. See also several important helpful groups in this chapter's resource section.

This is a situation which cannot be realistically dealt with in a single section of a chapter in a book or even in a full chapter. Several books have been recommended here, and the recommended pregnancy loss support groups will be able to refer you to even better information, including helpful booklets to sensitize family and friends.

The Baby Blues

At least half of all new mothers experience postpartum blues. The symptoms include feeling agitated and exhausted and crying a lot. Most cases of baby blues disappear within one or two weeks. But according to a 1993 study in the journal *Pediatrics* (as reported in the October, 1993 issue of *American Baby*) women with pregnancy complications such as gestational diabetes, placenta previa, premature labor, as well as other conditions putting the pregnancy at risk, are more than three times as likely to experience postnatal blues.

Post baby blues are not confined to those who give birth to babies. Those who adopt have also been observed to exhibit some of the signs of postnatal depression.

Plenty of support and assistance after the birth can help mothers prone to the blues, so if you feel that you may be at risk, consider making advance preparations for a family member to come to stay for a while or hire a professional doula for this purpose. The helper's role should be in relieving the new parents not of baby care, but of other pressing household needs.

RESOURCES

Organizations

RESOLVE (see prior information) publishes several excellent fact sheets, and, for assistance and support when complications occur...

Center for Loss in Multiple Birth (CLIMB), Inc. (P.O. Box 1064, Palmer AK 99645) provides support by and for parents of twins, triplets or higher multiple birth children who have experienced the death of one or more or all of them during pregnancy, at birth or during childhood. A quarterly newsletter is published ($8 U.S., $12 Canadian.)

The Centering Corporation (Box 3367, Omaha, NE 68103) offers books, articles, and a newsletter focusing on issues of grief and loss. The Centering staff also does training for professionals.

Compassionate Friends (P.O. Box 1347, Oak Brook, IL 60521) is the national office of a network of local support groups for those who have experienced neonatal death or pregnancy loss.

Depression after Delivery (P.O. Box 1282, Morrisville, PA 19067) is a national self-help organization providing support, education and information for families coping with blues, anxiety, depression or psychosis associated with the arrival of a child.

National Organization of Mothers of Twins Clubs Inc. (P.O. Box 23188, Albuquerque, NM 87192-1188) can put you in touch with local chapters of parents of multiples with whom you can share concerns.

PenParents (P.O. Box 8738, Reno NV 89507) is a group offering support and information to those dealing with loss in pregnancy after infertility. The bimonthly newsletter is *Pails of Hope* ($10 annually.)

Pregnancy and Infant Loss Center (1415 E. Wayzata Blvd #22, Wayzata, MN 55391) publishes a newsletters and pamphlets for professionals and families who have experienced the loss of a child.

Books

What to Expect When You're Expecting by Arlene Eisenberg, Heidi Murkoff and Sandee Hathaway (Workman, 1992) is the best selling pregnancy book with the general public. Read this to feel "normal". Don't expect it to be especially informed or sensitive to infertility issues.

As a supplement to *What to Expect*, several of the better and more recent books on infertility have good chapters on pregnancy after infertility. In particular I recommend Carla Harkness' *The Infertility Book* (see resource section on medical treatment for this and other recommended titles.) The following books deal with special issues of pregnancy.

Infertility and Pregnancy Loss: A Guide for Helping Professionals by Constance Hoenk Shapiro (San Francisco: Jossey-Bass Publishers, 1988.) Don't be misled by the title to assume this book is mostly about pregnancy loss. Though aimed first at professionals (nurses and counselors) consumers, too, will find this insightful book of help in dealing with issues of pregnancy after infertility.

When Pregnancy Isn't Perfect: A Lay Person's Guide to Complications in Pregnancy by Laurie Rich (New York: Dutton, 1991.)

Difficult Decisions: For Families Whose Unborn Baby has a Serious Problem by Patricia Fertel (Centering Corporation, above)

When Pregnancy Fails: Families Coping with Miscarriage, Stillbirth and Infant Death by Susan Borg and Judith Lasker (Boston: Beacon Press, 1981.)

Chapter 11

PARENTING
AFTER INFERTILITY

Little Spirit to a Childless Couple

Just helping you, Mom and Dad, to develop
a trait you'll need to survive:
Patience--I guarantee you'll need it
Once I arrive

> *Carol Lynn Pearson*
> *from* The Search *1970*

Hardly any of our fantasies about parenting turn out to be realistic. And, for most people, parenting turns out to be a genuine paradox: it will be, at the same time, the most difficult thing you have ever done and the most wonderful experience you will have in life.

Because a full-blown infertility experience has created such a difficult road to parenthood, it would be unrealistic to say that it doesn't have any effect on how you parent. Of course it does. Because of infertility you have faced a major life crisis, often much earlier than others of your peers. Infertility has tested your relationship with your partner and very likely affected your style of communication and the level of your intimacy. Because of infertility you have had to examine your motivations for parenthood upside down and inside out in order to justify spending enormous amounts of time and money and physical capacity and emotional energy in a quest either to conceive or to adopt. Infertility has very likely changed you in significant ways.

But, I've known hundreds of infertile people throughout the last twenty years, and unlike some of my fellow writers on the infertility experience, I have not found that the majority of people who have overcome a fertility impairment make pathological parents. In fact, I find that the overwhelming majority of people who have directly faced their infertility and all of its medical as well as its emotional ramifications and who have worked through the loss issues which accompany a fertility impairment to the extent that they understand how those losses can continue to play a role in their lives are among the best parents I know.

Whether they have ultimately given birth, have achieved parenthood through collaborative reproduction or have adopted, parents who have confronted their infertility head on are well motivated. They tend to immerse themselves more thoroughly in the parenting experience and they don't take it for granted. They tend to have become more realistic about what can and cannot be controlled in life. Their parenting partnerships are often better balanced than those of their peers, even now, in a generation of parents who see parenting more as something that both moms and dads do.

Despite the many special issues that families built by adoption (either traditional or through collaborative reproduction) must face, these parents can rest assured that their experience will have much more in common with traditional parenting than it will have differences.

Having said this, I must acknowledge that there are certainly some exceptions to the rule of infertile parents as normal parents and parenting after infertility as a positive experience. And in an attempt to help you take charge of these possibilities, and head them off, I'll identify some of the concerns and issues that may trigger an infertility-related parenting problem.

The Invisibly Infertile—Secondary Infertility

My friend and colleague Harriet (Holly) Simons, a Boston based therapist and infertile woman, wrote a whole book, *Wanting Another Child: Coping with Secondary Infertility* (New York: Lexington Books, 1995) just for the special "invisible" population who find themselves with a fertility impairment after having given birth. These are couples who don't know where they fit. Are they fertile or are they infertile?

Like those with unexplained infertility, it is often difficult for those dealing with secondary infertility to accept that the infertility is real. Denial is a common coping mechanism, and the couple may wait much longer to seek medical help than would a couple dealing with primary infertility. (After all, they got pregnant once and delivered a child!)

The secondarily infertile are subjected to a special kind of insensitivity. Those who don't know may view a one child family and make the assumption that it is by choice. They may jokingly suggest that "You'd better get busy" or judge you as selfish. Similarly to those who have chosen a childfree lifestyle after infertility, secondarily infertile people often find that even other infertile people are insensitive, offering comments such as "Well, at least you have one." As a result, those dealing with secondary infertility are even more likely to suffer alone than are those whose infertility is a primary condition.

Infertility hurts no matter when you experience it. If you have no children and want them and are having difficulty conceiving, you are infertile. If you have six children and would like another but can't seem to become pregnant, you are infertile.

One of the issues that worries the secondarily infertile is how their children will perceive their attempts at fertility and the emotional consequences which are a nearly unavoidable part of the process of being in treatment or pursuing an adoption. We'll talk more in the next chapter about how to address this issue with children, but if you are finding that your feelings about your infertility are affecting your ability to parent your existing child, reach out to an infertility-sensitive counselor for help.

Entitlement

I first learned about the issue of parents and children building a sense of entitlement to one another in the first edition of adoption professional Jerome Smith's *You're Our Child*. Reading this was one of the milestones of my education about infertility and adoption. Dr. Smith spoke of and to only parents by adoption as he described the need for parents and children to come to believe that they are entitled to and deserving of one another and that they belong together.

Over the years I've come to believe that entitlement is an issue for all parents, but particularly for parents who have experienced infertility. Before we talk about how building a sense of entitlement works, perhaps it will be helpful to talk about what can happen when parents do not feel a healthy sense of entitlement to their children.

For those who do not feel a healthy sense of entitlement as parents discipline can be a problem. The inability to be gently but firmly consistent and to follow through with logical consequences, an unwillingness to be seen as a "bad guy" for fear of losing the love of a child, or (in any variety of adoption) an unexpressed feeling that a genetic parent somewhere is more "real" than are you and might not approve of your parenting, are all signs of an incomplete sense of entitlement.

Insistent denial of differences results in parents who are unable to talk to their children about the children's loss issues. In adoption or quasi-adoption, nearly obsessive fears about the genetic parents can prevent the parents from establishing open communication with their children. The result of such denial is a family which is unable to share with one another and operate as a family unit but instead moves as separate individuals occupying the same space.

In adoption, Dr. Smith describes building a sense of entitlement as involving three steps: recognizing and dealing with feelings about infertility, recognizing and accepting the differences which are a part of adoption, and learning to handle reflections of the societal view that adoption is a second best alternative for all involved. Once pointed out, these issues for adoption built families are obvious, and it isn't too difficult for most to see how this particular aspect of adoption applies to those who have built quasi-adoptive families with the assistance of third parties. It's a little less clear why those who have given birth to a child genetically related to both of its social parents might feel less entitled to their children than do parents who have not gone through infertility.

Self esteem issues are most often the root cause of lingering pain which contributes to an incomplete sense of entitlement.

> "When Robbie was little and he wouldn't
> mind I got so frustrated," reported Mimi. "Obviously
> I wasn't doing a very good job of being a parent,
> and I sometimes thought, well, maybe God was

trying to tell me something when he made me
infertile, and maybe I should have let things alone."

Whether negative self esteem made infertility worse or infertility
damaged self esteem, the result is the same: a person who doesn't
feel adequate, who doesn't feel normal, who can't feel confident...
who doesn't feel entitled.

Sometimes that sense of being out of control of our lives
that was so much a part of infertility comes back again with a
vengeance during a child's adolescence. Since parenting is about
nurturing in anticipation of letting go, and since it all really does
go by so fast, adolescence can be difficult. Because adolescence
really is all about finding out who we are and snatching our
independence. Adolescents distance themselves from their parents
in every conceivable way, under the best of circumstances. They
also spend a great deal of their time exploring their sense of
sexuality. If their parents' infertility has been a part of their
growing up, kids can find it a pretty scary thing as they hit
adolescence. Difficulty dealing with an adolescent's emerging
sexuality may be a lingering side effect of one's unhappy feelings
about infertility. As we will discuss in the next chapter, the two
separate, yet linked needs to talk to children about their genetic
origins and to help them learn about infertility can be a challenge
for parents still licking the wounds inflicted by infertility.

These are not minor issues! A healthy sense of entitlement
(or the lack of it) is intertwined with building an attachment to
one another. And entitlement is really at the root of many of the
other issues which will follow in this chapter. Confidence is an
important part of effective parenting. If a lack of confidence
contributes to feelings of inadequacy as a parent, talk to someone.

Unrealistic Expectations

Remember when you were a little kid and
you were waiting for your birthday party to come?
You built up all these fantasies about how fun the
games would be, and what wonderful presents
you'd get, and how great the cake and ice cream
would taste. Then the day came and it rained, and
some of the kids were late and missed the surprise
at the beginning and the toys weren't what you

really wanted, and at the end you just cried. And
your mother didn't understand.

That little kid still lives inside all of us, and sometimes
when we yearn for something for a long time it just doesn't live up
to our expectations. Maybe the birth won't be as wonderful as we
thought it would be and we'll feel disappointed in our
"performance." Or maybe the baby won't be a perfect angel but
will cry a lot and be collicky and we'll feel pretty guilty about our
irritation. Or maybe your family or your friends or your partner
won't be quite as enthralled with the baby as you expected that
they would.

Maybe, whether you birthed or adopted your child, you'll
find yourself with a case of post-baby blues. They happen to the
best of us, and often completely unexpectedly. Yes, they can be
hormonally triggered, but they are also caused by a combination of
the complete exhaustion which is standard to being a new parent
and the crush of unrealistic expectations for both ourselves and
our children.

These kinds of problems are almost predictable, and, with
support and time, they pass. But sometimes unrealistic
expectations get the better of us, and when they do, they can
damage our sense of entitlement to our children.

Sometimes, for example, the need for genetic connection
which leads a couple to stretch all of their resources to the limit in
a quest for a jointly conceived child genetically related to both of
his parents produces a different child than the one they dreamed
of, a child who is born with a physical problem, a child who is not
quite as smart as they had expected, a child who is obstinate or
who doesn't really share the psychological fit one would expect
from one's own flesh and blood. Sometimes, for example, a couple
who figured that at the very least in adopting they would get to
request a healthy child discovers in toddlerhood that the child is
hyperactive, or has a learning disability.

Sometimes a dad may find that he isn't as patient as he'd
just known he'd be, or that his son doesn't like sports as much as
he does and so isn't interested in throwing around that football. A
mom who fantasized about sewing dresses for her twins may find
herself so overwhelmed by long hours at work and the necessities
of keeping the family functioning that it's almost more than she
can manage to get the laundry from the washer to the dryer.

In the worst of all instances parents can feel that a kid just doesn't measure up, and they can find themselves wondering if they did the right thing. Sometimes, when relationships are strained during a child's adolescence (and they nearly always are) if can be tempting, when there is an absent genetic parent to blame and a faltering sense of entitlement between parent and child, to think, "This can't be my fault. My natural child wouldn't behave this way."

Super parent syndrome is a phenomenon of the baby-boom generation. Lots of parents, not just the infertile, have nearly ridiculous expectations of both themselves and their children. And so you will run into dozens of parents who have enrolled their two-year-olds in ballet class, have already signed their newborns into the very best private kindergarten, have scheduled their second grader for Brownies on Monday and Suzuki piano on Tuesday and soccer on Wednesday and play dates on Thursday and French lessons on Friday.

It's possible that those who take longer to become parents are slightly more inclined to push in this way because their expectations for themselves and their children inflate just a little each year. And yet I look around me and I see that a lot of parents who became parents entirely by accident are caught up in this whirlwind, too. Still, since we who are infertile have more time to think about it when it's taking so long to become parents, might we also have time to figure out whether being the superparent of a superkid is a good idea at all?

The reality is that nobody gets guarantees and kids don't come with warranties. And the reality is that you can't ever know what really goes on inside another family's walls to be certain that they really are more perfect than are you. The reality is that parenting is hard... and so is being a kid.

New Roles, Old and New Relationships

When infertility is "over" we somehow expect that we'll just fit right in to our new roles as parents. And sometimes we do. But sometimes infertility has gotten in the way of a few things.

Are we just like other parents? Maybe. Maybe not. We sure don't fit into the swim-n-gym locker room talk about failed birth control. Some of us can't contribute to the labor-and-delivery or breast-feeding war stories. Sometimes our "differences" can make us feel awkward.

But then again, at least with other parents we can feel free to joke occasionally in the very normal way, "He's driving me crazy! Ya want him?" We couldn't say THAT to a member of our infertility support group.

Finding where we belong is one challenge. Sometimes mending fences damaged during the infertility battles is another. Now that we have children, perhaps that neighbor who was pregnant every summer has more appeal, but will she want anything to do with us after we've avoided her for so long? Now that we have children, perhaps we do have things to talk about with our brothers-in-law... but have we driven them off completely and irretrievably by now?

And what about our relationship with our partner? Parenting changes everything. Are we together in this? Can we make time for one another again? Will we ever be alone? In some ways, after parenthood, the relationship is new. Marriages take work. Parenting in a marriage takes even more.

What's Normal, What's Not

Good parenting is not an instinct we are born with, and in this society, we aren't taught how to parent effectively. Moreover, unlike the African cultures whose philosophy taught us that "It takes a whole village to raise a child," in an increasingly transient society, most of us are on our own. The result is that unless we make the effort to learn, we tend to parent as we were parented (whether that was good or bad) and we tend to fly by the seat of our pants.

As an infertile person preparing for parenthood, you've got time to get ready. If you can make the leap of faith required to believe that you will indeed become a parent in one way or another, one of the nicest gifts you can give yourself and your children-to-be is some parent preparation beforehand—reading books, taking classes or attending seminars.

But I'm not crazy. I know how hard it will be for many, if not most, infertile people to subject themselves to such a routine. So instead, if you're feeling comfortable enough to at least read this chapter about as far as it is reasonable to go is to suggest to you two things: that support and information are plentiful (as if you hadn't noticed, with much pain, the magazines and the TV programs and the shelves full of books at the library and the announcements of activities in your house of worship's bulletin) and that normal has a very broad range. If you can (and it probably won't be easy) relax and enjoy!

Resources

Since the overwhelming majority of the readership of this book is most likely made up of people who have not yet become parents, suggesting specific good general parenting materials probably doesn't make a whole lot of sense, as new and better materials come out every year. In fact, you may have noted that few of the resources listed in any of the chapters were more than five years old. What worked well for Dave and me with our now 18-year-old isn't the same stuff we found helpful when our now 9-year-old was a baby and then a toddler.

Still, I can't resist telling you that I have found very helpful the parenting books and columns of Dr. Lawrence Kutner (who, as an adoptee, is adoption sensitive though not adoption focused) and the practical (and entertaining) books and tapes from the *Parenting with Love and Logic* series by Foster Cline and Jim Fay.

Some things that I can suggest that you will want to learn about and look for include basic information about how children learn (for example the most up-to-date version of Piaget, the series of child development materials by Louise Bates Ames and Frances Ilg of the Gesell Institute.) To keep abreast of specific information about special issues for your family such as surrogacy or donor insemination or adoption, stay in touch with OPTS and AFA, etc.

The following organizations and reading materials will be helpful for some of the special situations described in this chapter.

Only Child Association (9810 Magnolia Ave., Riverside, CA 92503) a group dedicated to dispelling the myth that to be sans sibling is to be spoiled, lonely and selfish.

Wanting Another Child: Coping with Secondary Infertility by Harriet Fishman Simons (New York: Lexington Books, 1995). Support and answers for unique problems and concerns of those who find themselves unable to conceive or carry to live birth after having done so before.

The Long Awaited Stork: A Guide to Parenting after Infertility by Ellen Sarasohn Glazer (Lexington, MA: Lexington Books, 1990). One writer's view of how infertility issues may rise again for couples who pursue quasi or tradition adoption or give birth after struggling with infertility.

ParentAge: The Publication for the New Parent Over Thirty-Five (19 w 21st St. New York, NY 10010, $29.95 annually) is a monthly newsletter for "older" parents.

Mother-Infant Bonding: A Scientific Fiction by Diane Eyer (Stanford: Yale University Press, 1992.) A critical look at the impact that bonding and attachment theory has had on families, the women's movement, etc.

When Partners Become Parents: The Big Life Changes for Couples by Carolyn Pape Cowan and Philip A. Cowan (New York: Basic Books, 1993) reports the findings of a 10 year study which followed 100 couples into and through the first years of parenthood and how it changed relationships.

Chapter 12

WHAT SHOULD WE TELL OUR KIDS?

Johnny, age 4, rushed breathlessly in from play to ask his mother, "Where did I come from?" His mother was surprised, but she'd been preparing for this one for years. She looked up from her computer and sighed and pulled Johnny onto her lap, whereupon she began a long, well-rehearsed (in her head, at least) discourse on human reproduction—sperm, ova, penis, vagina, nine months, birth... As she finished, she asked her squirmy son, "So, does that answer your question?" and his reply was, "I guess. Did you know that Timmy is from Chicago?"

Sex education is a challenge for nearly all parents. Sometimes for the infertile it feels even more complicated. Should our children know about our infertility? If so, what should they know and when? Many infertile people who want to become conscientious parents are thinking ahead about how their own infertility will color their children's lives and wondering whether or how to talk to their children about the long quest which resulted in their becoming parents.

For most young children, their own arrival stories become a favorite piece of family lore which they love to hear repeated over and over. The pleasure that parents exude as they share not just the facts, but the aura of joy and excitement that they, and their extended families and friends, felt on the day each child became part of their family—whether by birth or adoption—is a valuable part of a growing child's development of feelings of belonging and self worth. Should their parents' infertility, the rigors of testing, treatment with assisted reproductive technologies, explorations of family building alternatives become part of this story?

In exploring such issues we are not operating in the theoretical vacuum that some have led us to believe is a natural consequence of rapid-fire pharmaceutical and technological development in the scientific field that is infertility. While it may be true that some issues related to reproductive technology are complicated by the difficulty of helping ethics and law keep up with science, that's not necessarily the case when it comes to how children learn and what children need to know.

In the past infertile parents may have looked to the wrong professionals for guidance about talking to children about infertility. While many specialists in reproductive health care are quick to express their views about these issues, their opinions should be understood as just that— opinions. Their area of training and experience and thus expertise is medicine—not child psychology, education, or parenting. Talking to children about infertility-related issues is a parenting issue rather than a medical issue. Decisions about if, how, and when education about infertility and alternatively formed families should happen are best made using the advice and expertise of those whose training and experience is in child development, child psychology, education, and parenting.

Significant facts have emerged from research and testing in the fields of education and child psychology during the twentieth century to offer us some reliable anchorage from which to begin to explore answers to questions about what children should know, and when, about their parents' infertility treatment and alternative choices. From this knowledge base answers begin to seem much less difficult to find, and we discover two principles to guide us:

1. Children need to have complex information of any kind shared with them in age-appropriate ways which respect their level of intellectual development.

2. Children deserve the truth. They want and need to know all facts which pertain specifically and permanently to themselves as they explore who they are.

How Children Learn

The Swiss psychiatrist Jean Piaget and his many students and followers have taught us much about how the minds of children grow and mature. Piaget, who began his life's work at the age of 25 in the early 1920s, spent his entire career focused on the cognitive development of children—learning about how they think, how they experiment, how they react to and learn from their environment, how they come to be able to reason. What he discovered and shared with the world and evolving research following his early work have colored childrearing practices, education and curriculum development, psychology and psychiatry, and even logic and philosophy through much of the last half of the twentieth century.

It is difficult to summarize such important work without risking distortion, but in the interests of simplification, two important pieces of Piaget's theory can be shared in two sentences. Young children see the world and all of its phenomena in terms of the limitations of their own concrete experiences and their own developing emotional needs. Their ability to reason—to change their free form ideas to conform with objective reality— occurs very gradually throughout childhood, is influenced by physical and emotional development, and is almost never in place (even in gifted children) until age eleven, twelve or older.

The work of Piaget has influenced many researchers. Significant among them for purposes of our discussion here have been Dr. Anne Bernstein, whose doctoral research involved determining what children understand at various ages about human reproduction and was first published in the book *The Flight of the Stork* in 1978, and Dr. David Brodzinsky and his team of researchers at Rutgers, who, in the 1980s, completed a landmark study of what children (both adopted and nonadopted) understand about adoption at various ages. The Brodzinsky work, published in various professional journals and in several related essays in his book *The Psychology of Adoption*, also influenced the writing of his consumer-oriented 1992 book *Being Adopted: The Life-Long Search for Self*.

When added to the work of psychiatrists and neuroscientists of the late 20th century, who have made amazing discoveries about how the brain works which have led them to confirm that abstract thinking is a consequence of acquiring the ability to read, this body of Piagetan-based research in closely related fields offers us clear guidelines for deciding what children can understand and should know about sexuality, about alternatively formed families, about infertility testing and treatment at various ages.

Keeping Information Age-Appropriate

When an issue to be shared with children is a difficult one, it is not unusual for parents to deal with it in either of two inappropriate ways. They may oversimplify it to the point of euphemism (witness those stories about storks and cabbage patches and daddies giving mommies seeds) or, in their eagerness to be conscientious, parents may over educate, sharing far more than their children are cognitively prepared to handle (the old joke shared at this chapter's beginning is a perfect example.)

Because the learning process Piaget observed is relatively constant (children observe and take in information, form assumptions and test theories based on their prior experiences and knowledge, and finally learn something from this process which they store for future use), it is somewhat predictable.

Children's minds will only store what they are mature enough to understand and use. When children are given information which is too sophisticated for them, the information just doesn't compute and it isn't stored. What this means is that children aren't usually hurt by information that is above their intellectual level, but they aren't helped by it either. In most cases the information will simply go in one ear and out the other. The danger, then, is that parents will feel comfortable that the information is "out" and will be unaware that their children didn't "get it" and so may forget it.

When we talk to children about reproduction or alternative ways to form families, then, we are challenged by the need to keep the discussion age-appropriate. The more complex the situation, the more important it is to simplify, simplify. Sharing issues which are complex, from where babies come from (including adoption, donor insemination, surrogacy) to issues of rape, incest or sexual abuse, becomes an ongoing process repeated and expanded and embellished each year, over many years, in a series of stages, with just enough information added each time to satisfy a more mature understanding and encourage more complicated questions. And because it is so important that our children be able to trust us, truth must be at the heart of every conversation with our children— a commitment to never sharing information which is inaccurate and so must later be changed.

What Children Need to Know about Their Own Arrival

Because these issues are identity issues that cannot and will not be changed, their adoption, their conception through surrogacy or using donor gametes are the kinds of information to which individuals have a right. These issues, which are <u>central to who they are genetically</u>, are different from and far more significant than mechanical issues surrounding their conception and birth such as a failure of birth control, a medical problem which resulted in a cesarean rather than vaginal delivery, the use of hormonal therapy in order to sustain a pregnancy, or the placing of father's sperm into mother's uterus via catheter rather than through sexual intercourse.

But let me make clear at the outset that in identifying genetic issues as more significant than mechanical issues I am not suggesting that parents never talk to their children about ARTs or keep them a secret. Instead I am suggesting that information about ARTS need not become the kind of burden parents worried about finding the "right time" for that adoption once was.

Secrets are almost universally impossible to keep. An undercurrent of whispers and overheard bits of conversation, of hesitant or evasive answers to questions, combine to drive children into a fantasy world which can be much more disturbing than reality! Parents walk a tightrope in trying to decide how much is too much and how little is too little, but the overriding thing to remember is that secrets are unhealthy in intimate relationships and can be toxic to family systems.

Children who learned late of their adoptions, for example, almost universally report that they "had always known" since childhood that something was "different" and possibly "wrong" about their families, but had felt that whatever that difference was was a taboo subject—one about which they couldn't possibly ask. And though most people who had been given this information late do remember the revelation as shocking and disturbing and initially were inclined to deny it, nearly all of them also report that the most powerful emotion they felt was anger and a sense of betrayal at having been deceived.

Psychiatrist Robert Anderson, M.D., in his hauntingly sad autobiography *Second Choice: Growing Up Adopted* (Badger Hill Press, 1993) writes

"Being uninformed about my adoption did not prevent me from perceiving its effects—one can more easily hide the cognitive than the emotional component of behavior, just as one can more easily conceal the content of a secret than conceal the secret itself. While as a child I did not know specifically that my parents were worried I might be removed from their home, I was able to perceive that something about our relationship troubled them. Similarly, I did not know my mother was depressed because she could not have her own children, and would not have understood what it meant to be depressed, but I could perceive that she was not happy. I did not know my parents kept secrets from me, but my experience indicated we were not close. Being spared the details was not a blessing, for when a child knows something is wrong but does not know what, he blames himself for the difficulties." (Anderson, pp. 20-21)

With adoption in the early part of this century having served as a laboratory, we have learned unequivocally that it is unwise to deliberately choose to keep information about their personal genetic heritage a secret from children in the interests of "protecting" them from the truth. And to add to the anecdotal evidence shared by adoptees themselves, we have clinical and academic knowledge. In observing adoption-built families over many years, the Canadian sociologist H. David Kirk concluded that the families who were most comfortable about openly and consistently acknowledging the differences that adoption brought to the lives of all of its members were the ones with the healthiest, most empathic, most communicative parent-child relationships. In his classic book *Shared Fate: A Theory of Adoptive Relationships* Kirk offered encouragement for families willing to acknowledge the "role handicaps" and the losses they shared with one another by pointing out how such honesty had strengthened the relationships within the families in his longitudinal studies. Clinicians have reported extensively on the damage to self esteem and to relationships which has occurred when adoptees have stumbled across the facts of their adoptive status or had it revealed late in childhood or beyond. Such revelations nearly always resulted in feelings of betrayal by and anger with parents that were all but impossible to heal completely. Reactions to and revelations about the negative effects of this once universally recommended secrecy about adoptive status in the past have been an important impetus in the trend toward more openness in late twentieth century adoptions.

Families formed via various forms of surrogacy, donor insemination, donor oocytes or donated embryos are, genetically, adoption-expanded families, too (for want of a better term, I often refer to these as quasi-adoptions), and they can learn much from what is no longer even an issue of debate among those involved in traditional adoption. In a technologically advancing age, "secrets" concerning the genetic connectedness of families are increasingly likely to be revealed at some point despite best efforts to conceal them. Parents who choose not to tell their children about such origins risk great damage to their relationships with their children later when their children discover the truth that has been hidden from them.

The majority of physicians offering donor insemination as a part of their practices continue to call for total secrecy around the use of this alternative. They present three arguments for their position. They claim that what children don't know won't hurt them. (The above paragraphs dispute that argument.) They fear that a loosening of the pledge of full confidentiality might result in fewer available donors, since most men who donate sperm would be unwilling to take the risk that they might someday be possible by the children they fathered genetically. (A concern that may be true with some donors. However, several clinics and sperm banks which have surveyed their participating donors have found that the majority of them expressed a willingness to be contacted for further information later. So changes in confidentiality might more likely result in different donors rather than fewer donors being recruited.) Furthermore, they feel that there is no need for infertile men to be "exposed" in this way when there is an alternative. (An argument which denies the need to fully resolve the losses of genetic continuity that infertile men experience and seems to reflect a sexist bias, since similar attempts at cover up are not promoted for infertile women!)

The most important question parents can ask themselves concerning whether or not to tell is why would information be kept secret? From what are we attempting to protect our children?

Is the issue your concern about what other people will think and your fear that a young child will blurt out such information inappropriately? This problem has solutions. Even very young children can be taught to set boundaries that respect and honor family or personal privacy. Preventive education concerning sexual abuse, for example, includes exercises in boundary setting concerning sexuality.

But perhaps there is something deeper here than concern about privacy. Secrets are usually based in and caused by feelings of shame. Is there something to be ashamed of in the method by which you have chosen to expand your family? If you believe that there is, this may negatively color the way in which you relate to your child. A method of family building about which you feel shame is not a wise choice in the first place. If you are considering an option about which you feel shame or embarrassment, please spend whatever time it takes with a counselor to work this issue through before pursuing this course of action.

Getting Ready

What specifically do you tell and when? There is guidance available in how to talk to children about sexuality issues. Anne Bernstein's book *The Flight of the Stork* (to beupdated and republished by Perspectives Press in October, 1994) is a good place to begin. Dr. Bernstein's research focused on what children understand about reproduction from their earliest ability to verbalize through their intellectual maturation as abstract thinkers. She discovered an interesting pattern to the levels of maturity in thinking about human sexuality that was related to age and intellectual growth. Noting, as had Piaget, that these building block steps in mastering information applied to a slightly open-ended range of ages, she attached colorful labels to each stage:

1. The Geographer (ages 3-7). At this level of understanding children tend to think that babies have always existed and that they come to their families from some *place*, like a star or heaven or a hospital or an airplane, and that all grownups are mommies and daddies.

2.   The Manufacturer (ages 4-8). These children have come to believe that babies are built, like houses or cars, but how? They can only imagine from their own experience and knowledge. Maybe babies were made outside the body and then swallowed, coming out like a bowel movement? If they come from eggs, am I eating a baby for breakfast?

3.   In Between (age 5-10, the stage that Piaget refers to as Pre-Operational). Early reasoning and logical thinking has begun, but the child limits herself to what is technically possible from personal experience and observation. She may have trouble letting go of old beliefs, so that there is still quite a bit of magical thinking, and children continue to think very literally.

4.   The Theoretician (ages 10-13). These children still struggle to understand why the ova and sperm have to get together (Couldn't there be a complete baby just in the sperm or just in the egg?) but are willing to speculate. Now is the time when children are able to understand that parenthood has both a social and a biological component. For some children this is the last stage of intellectual growth—as sophisticated as they will become. (Pat's note: ancient Greek scientists reasoned about reproduction at about this level!)

5.   The Reasoner (11 or older). Finally able to think abstractly as does an adult, children at this level can put it all together. Clearly understanding sperm and ovum as different entities which can combine to form another separate entity, children who have achieved this level of intellectual growth can think morally and socially.

Several books on talking to children about adoption can offer help for families expanded both by traditional adoption and by quasi-adoption alternatives. Lois Melina's *Making Sense of Adoption*, for example, includes specific information about the third party reproduction forms of adoption. This and other of the newest books for adoptive parents reflect the influence of David Brodzinsky, a professor at Rutgers whose research about children's developing understanding of adoption from the 1980s paralleled Bernstein's work about reproduction.

David Brodzinsky, his wife Anne Braff Brodzinsky, and several others, interviewed two groups of children—the members of one group had joined their families by adoption and the members of the second group were being raised in their families of birth. In every other respect these families were matched for economic status, educational background, etc.

The results of the study showed that adopted and nonadopted children tend to be able to understand the concepts which underlie adoption at the same time, though children who were themselves adopted do learn the language of adoption faster than do their non-adopted peers. The children in this study progressed in stages parallel to those that Bernstein identified in children's understanding of reproduction. By ages 3 to 5, children might know the words and parrot their own arrival story effectively, but, because their thinking is still very literal and concrete, they could not understand the concepts this involved. Few five year olds in the Brodzinsky study, for example, could differentiate between birth and adoption. They thought that people were either born *or* adopted. These five year olds were unable to understand the motives that underlie adoption at all, and so were likely to misinterpret explanations they had heard.

By about six, however, kids knew that birth and adoption were different. They were still having trouble with how adoption works and couldn't quite grasp its permanency, though. During this stage, which is colored by rich fantasies and a great deal of magical thinking for all children, adoptees were likely to have some fears about being abandoned by their adoptive parents. After all, they reasoned poorly, I was bad enough that my birthparents, who supposedly loved me, let me go.

This knowledge has some important ramifications for parents considering how to impart their children's arrival stories. Many adopting parents and quasi-adopters who want the message to be clear that their children's genetic parents are good people worthy of respect and affection tell their children that their birthparents loved them very much and so chose adoption for them. To a child unable to reason and think abstractly, this story doesn't wash! Thinking concretely, children told this story are likely to make a thought progression which goes something like this: If my birthparents loved me and so chose to let me go when things were hard, then since my adoptive parents love me, too, if things get hard (and they are very likely to, somewhere along life's way) they, too may need to find new parents for me.

Educators have noted in several studies that when children of this age are given information that is potentially painful, they may actually come to feel that curiosity in general is potentially painful, so that they try to suppress their curiosity, leading to some school problems.

Somewhere during the middle childhood span of ages 7 to 11, children begin to understand adoption's permanence, even though they are often still unable to understand the function of intermediaries in the process. Since children of this age do lots of fantasizing with their friends, envisioning what it would be like to have idyllic, permissive parents, children who were adopted experience a conflict. For them, there really *are* another set of parents out there, so for adopted children—especially those in confidential adoptions—the typical fantasies of middle childhood (maybe my mom's really Madonna and my dad's really Joe Montana) are also possibilities.

The Brodzinsky study found that somewhere beyond the age of 9, as they move toward adolescence, children begin to understand permanence in adoption and can begin to understand what a transfer of parental rights is all about. Finally, as teens struggling with identity issues common to all teens, adoptees put it all together. They can begin to understand the social issues that are a part of adoption and the motivations of both sets of parents.

Parent groups—in particular adoptive parenting groups like Adoptive Families of America—are good places to stay up-to-date on current books and tapes for both adults and children. Another benefit of parents groups is that talking to parents whose children are slightly older than your own will give you the opportunity to observe how children think and to ask their parents what kinds of questions they have raised.

Bottom Line: Whose Issue Is It?

Think about how far we have come from the old days of the "bad seed" theory, when we held children responsible for the sins of their parents and shamed them with "you're just like your father" beratements. We understand now that one of the things which caused many young adoptees great discomfort for many years was the concept of being "special" and "chosen" by their parents. It was not uncommon in years past for a child's adoption arrival story to include some focused information about how lonely and unhappy Mommy and Daddy were without children and how very happy they had been about the arrival at long last of this very special baby after a terribly long wait. Many school aged children embroiled in the rich fantasy life common to elementary-aged youngsters reprocessed this information in unhappy ways—worrying that they were personally responsible for their parents' happiness and feeling inadequate to live up to such a responsibility, worrying about what would have happened had they not been the one selected, and more. Young adoptees often mistranslate information about why their birthparents planned adoption for them. From the common, but inappropriate, explanations that "their birthparents loved them so much that they gave them up" or that "the birthparents weren't able to take care of you" children unable to think abstractly often develop worries that if one set of parents who loved them "gave them away" perhaps their adopters will too or that perhaps poor behavior now would be a reason for his parents to select new parents for him.

Consider what we have learned about the impact on children of the once common tendency of some mothers to encourage their children to behave differently by making them feel guilty with stories about how "I almost died when you were born." We understand now that even when this is true, it is not appropriate information to share with a young person still thinking concretely.

What we have learned from all of this becomes another guiding principle: children should not be placed in the position of feeling that they are somehow responsible for making or keeping their parents happy.

Most of the discomfort that nearly all parents have in sharing information about human sexuality with their children comes not from an unwillingness to do this teaching, but instead from their concerns that they won't do it well. With infertility issues, an additional factor is that the issue that produced the perceived need for information was one which caused the parents a great deal of frustration and pain, and from which they may continue to experience residual feelings of loss which occasionally confuse their feelings of genuine joy about their role as parents. These kinds of internal conflicts—conflicts born of experiences much more sophisticated than any child's—often lead parents who have dealt with infertility to be overly concerned about sharing specifics with children at a very early age.

Parents who have experienced especially stubborn cases of infertility which have led them to choose invasive and expensive high-tech treatment options such as IVF or GIFT resulting in a pregnancy with their own gametes have recentrly begun to seek ways to share this information with pre-schoolers. Books have begun to appear which attempt to explain assisted reproductive technologies to pre-school and elementary aged children. The question is, is this age-appropriate or necessary?

In my opinion, the concerns parents have about how best to share the fact of a standard IVF or GIFT or ZIFT conception which has resulted in a child genetically related to the people he calls Mom and Dad are more often rooted in the parents' frustrations and the naturally self-centered pain of crisis and loss than in needs expressed or questions raised by their children. Such information is the parents' information, weighing on adult minds, and, while it may affect the adults' parenting styles in subtle ways, it does not affect the genetic identity of the child.

Children younger than eleven or twelve are universally unable to think abstractly, and so are unable to understand and process the reasoned thinking which seems to burden their parents with a need to share their past infertility treatment experience. Furthermore, concrete thinkers take everything very literally, very personally, in a self centered manner, so that they often misinterpret sophisticated information.

Ultimately, the deciding factor in what children need to be told about their own conception and birth and when is that the information should be their own information and that the information be age-appropriate. Your children should have accurate information about their genetic origins and any factors which directly influence them. For example, when a problem at birth has resulted in an ongoing problem (cerebral palsy or oxygen deprivation resulting in learning problems, for example) children need this information. But while a parent may have found a cesarean birth traumatic or disappointing, unless that birth has resulted in physical complications for the child, this is parent information.

Unless there are life-long complications for the child, the mechanics (as opposed to the genetics) of his conception and birth are as parent-personal as are his parents' favored positions for sexual intercourse. You may or may not choose to share this. Only older children will derive and retain useful information from such material. In sharing his arrival story, there is no more necessity for telling a concrete-thinking pre-schooler whose birth involved only his parents' genetic material and reproductive capacities about his IVF conception, than there is to tell a same-aged child about his parent's treatment for some long-ago-cured sexually transmitted disease or the number of sexual partners his parents had before marriage or his conception after a night of heavy partying and sloppy birth control. While many might choose to share this kind of information in an age appropriate fashion with an adolescent as an expansion of his general knowledge base or part of preventative infertility education (whether you share things of such a personal nature is a matter of personal style and choice), to think of this as the child's vital personal information and allow oneself to feel burdened with a weighty responsibility for finding the right moment for sharing is inappropriate. The result of such pressures is the development of needless burdens on both parent and child.

I am not suggesting keeping secrets or telling lies about ARTS. When GIFT or IVF come to a child's attention, his questions should be answered directly. What I am suggesting is that these issues are too sophisticated for most young children and so parents must think carefully about when and how and why to explain these techniques. The first questions pre-school-aged children ask result in their being satisfied with knowing that sperm come from male bodies and ova from females. Mechanical questions about how these come together come at a later stage.

Explaining Ongoing Treatment or Adoption Efforts

Unlike attempts to conceive through natural intercourse, many treatment options and attempts at adoption create significant changes in normal household routine. There may be numerous trips to the doctor or even the hospital. Moms who are on hormone therapy are often ill or moody. Monitoring equipment may be left where children can see it. Children may overhear one side of phone calls that sound alarming. Social workers may visit the house and even ask children questions.

Something is obviously up, and children will speculate about "the secret." Because young children think egocentrically and because they can only theorize based on their limited experience, their fantasies about what they see or overhear or experience may cause them to become alarmed.

"Mommy's been so mad (or so sad) for
several days. What did I do wrong?"

"Mommy cries and Daddy seems angry. Will
they get a divorce?"

"I heard Mommy tell Grandma she's going
to the hospital? Why? Is she sick? Will she die?"

"They called the adoption agency and the
social worker is coming. Are they going to send me
away?"

"Mommy says she's sad because she wants
another baby. Aren't I good enough?"

Most parents will find that if they are participating in an
ART or pursuing an adoption, their children will cope best if they
know something about what is going on. Information shared
needs to be limited to small pieces of age appropriate information
at a time, and the information should be accompanied by a
discussion of family privacy boundaries. What is it OK for the child
to say to others and what should she keep to herself?

Preparing for the Arrival of a Sibling

Many children's books are now available which will help
families prepare for the arrival of a sibling by birth or by adoption.
Some of these, such as Jane Schnitter's *William Is My Brother* and
Stephanie Stein's *Lucy's Feet*, are even designed for families where
one child was born to the family and another adopted.

Family expansion by collaborative reproduction presents a
more difficult challenge. There are few books so far and no sibling
arrival books. The first children's books are not well crafted to hold
the attention of a child and tend to deal with adult issues and
concerns. A family-created book may be more useful than a poor
commercial alternative.

One important thing to consider is what age-appropriate
information, if any, the sibling should have concerning the
conception of his sibling-to-be. In adoption it is usually advised
that a child's personal information is his own, to be shared at his
own discretion. If this is a transferable model, parents need to
think carefully about whether or not an older child should have
information about their young sibling's donor conception or
surrogate birth before the child himself does.

Veronica was one excited six year old! Her mommy was having a baby! She wanted to tell everybody she knew. And Veronica's parents predicted that this would be the case, so they had shared information with her very carefully. Veronica did not know about the donor eggs that had produced her mom's pregnancy. She hadn't asked (because she wasn't sophisticated enough to think about doing so.) Randi, her mom, had been careful in choosing her words. There were no lies to retract later... just absent information.

It is important not to try to protect a child from possible disappointment by keeping him in the dark too long about the fact that you are expecting, whether by birth or by adoption. Just as it is important to the attachment process for parents to allow themselves to feel excitement in anticipation of the arrival of a baby, siblings need this preparation too.

Children can and should become part of the process of nesting behaviors: planning and stocking the nursery, talking about names, stocking the freezer with prepared-in-advance foods to be pulled out later, and more.

Talking about the Loss of an Expected Sibling

Sometimes a baby doesn't come home. After a miscarriage or a neonatal death or the change of mind of a birthmother when her baby is born, families who have been caught up in the excitement of a pending arrival will all need to mourn their loss. Children need to hear their parents' sadness and to be allowed to grieve along with them. They need to understand that they are not in any way responsible for the loss (often their ambivalent feelings of jealousy about a sibling-to-be may have triggered some magical thinking.)

As more and more materials become available about death and about pregnancy loss, some of those materials include information developed for children. Nothing is yet available for explaining a lost adoption to a child.

Your discussion about adoption loss should be affirming. For example

"Stephen, we were all excited when we thought we might get to be Sandra's baby's family. When she was pregnant Sandra didn't think she was ready to be a mom, even though she wished she could be. It was fun for us to paint the nursery and buy sheets for the baby bed. But Sandra has figured out that she can parent her baby. Her mother is going to help her, and she will get a job. We are all really disappointed and sad for us, but we are happy that Sandra's baby will have plenty of love and someone to care for him every day and every night."

"But, Mommy, will my birthmother change her mind, too?"

"Stephen, your birthmother made an adoption plan for you five years ago, when you were a baby. She knew that it was a forever plan when she chose Daddy and me to be your parents. The judge has said that we are a forever family now, and that can't ever change. Sandra hadn't gone to court to talk to the judge about making us her baby's forever family. All she had done was talk to us about it. This is not the same as your adoption. You'll always be our child."

If a baby arrives and then is lost, either through death or through an adoption disruption, you should expect that your child will experience a mixture of fear and sadness that may be long lasting. Since you as parents will be grieving, too, it is easy to overlook a grieving child. You will want to be particularly careful about being aware of this, drawing the child into the circle of your embrace and finding outside help for all or some of you if necessary.

The Heroes

Parents who have struggled to build a family often have especially strong feelings of gratitude about certain special professionals: attorneys or agency workers in adoption, doctors in treatment. These feelings sometimes lead them to make these people a heroic part of their personal saga of infertility and the quest for parenthood. These are adult feelings. Children should not be expected to try to understand why Dr. Smith or Ms. Jones sometimes seems to stand next to God in his parents' eyes and to feel grateful to these heroes for their parents or for their very existence. Use moderation in describing the role of these helping professionals in your family's life.

Preventative Education

Most of us who have gone through infertility would certainly like to find ways to prevent our children's having to go through such a difficult experience. All adolescents—not just the children of the infertile—need information about the impact of sexually transmitted diseases, use of medicinal and "recreational" drugs, delayed childbearing, uninformed medical choices, misused birth control, etc. on their future fertility. There's no doubt about it, this is an important kind if education.

Most parents will have at least referred to their own difficulty in building a family fairly early in their child's life as a part of his "arrival story". The need for preventative infertility education, however, will likely begin during the transitional grades between elementary school and high school and is perhaps best introduced by sharing concerns in a broad, universal way rather than describing the personal circumstances of the child's parents.

By this time, a tone has been set in the family regarding intimacies. The message has already been sent (most often indirectly) that parents are either open and approachable, encouraging questions and discussions of intimate issues, or they are embarrassed or emotionally edgy about difficult issues.

Children whose parents have encouraged openness may ask very intimate questions and expect direct answers. Children whose parents have seemed more closed off will likely retreat to fantasy and become dependent on others—friends, teachers, the media—for their information (and misinformation.)

Having already been told the barest facts—the truth—about their own genetic heritage, young people exploring their own emerging sexuality may be curious about infertility and its impact on their own future. Is it contagious? Is it genetic? Does it effect sexuality? Are there behaviors that cause it or prevent it?

These are important questions! Certainly most of us who have been through infertility wish that we had known to ask them many years before! But here we are dealing with kids who have come to a time in their lives when their parents are often the very last people they want to listen to! By having worked hard much earlier at becoming the kinds of parents who encourage questions, we can help our children prevent or deal more effectively with a possible fertility impairment in their future. But it won't be easy.

Fears about sexuality are common among teens. Most, for example, are homophobic and may go out of their way to establish themselves as proudly and publicly heterosexual (even when they are not.) Some children (both those born to their parents and those who were adopted) may find their parents' infertility threatening. They may feel a need to distance themselves from this frightening specter. Occasionally children who are not genetically connected to both of their parents may try to cope with their fears by refusing to identify with their infertile parents or even by finding ways to remind their parents of their "not real" status by overidentifying with their known or fantasized parents of origin.

The work of adolescence is separating, and it isn't much fun for parents. But then, you may well remember from personal experience that it wasn't much fun being an adolescent kid, either. It gets better.

Practice makes perfect, they say, and as you parent you will have lots of practice in answering difficult questions from your children. Questions about infertility may someday seem among the easiest to answer!

RESOURCES

For the best of books and tapes for yourselves and your children, stay in touch with the organizations that will be most likely to stay up-to-date on what's new, including Adoptive Families of America and Organization of Parents through Surrogacy. AFA, for example, has a wonderful mail order bookstore carrying adoption-sensitive books and toys for all ages. Also see resources in adoption section.

Not in Front of the Children... How to Talk to Your Child About Tough Family Matters by Lawrence Balter, Ph.D. and Peggy Jo Donahue (New York: Viking, 1993). A child psychologist and well known advice columnist talks to parents about how young children (from toddlers through early school-aged) learn and how they perceive difficult issues and "family secrets." Infertility and its alternatives are not addressed specifically, but general guidance provided here can be valuable.

The Flight of the Stork (revised edition) by Ann Bernstein (Indianapolis: Perspectives Press, 1994). How children learn about and come to understand sexuality and reproduction. (The updated and expanded version of this book, specifically addressing ARTs, third party reproduction and adoption will be published by Perspectives Press in October, 1994.)

The Long Awaited Stork: A Guide to Parenting after Infertility by Ellen Sarasohn Glazer (Lexington, MA: Lexington Books, 1990). One writer's view of how infertility issues may rise again for couples who pursue quasi or tradition adoption or give birth after struggling with infertility.

Parenting in Adoption, a series of three audio cassette tapes with Pat Johnston, from Perspectives Press.

"Discussion with Children about Their Donor Conception" by Kris Probasco ACSW, LSCSW is a fact sheet available from the author (a counselor who specializes in this field) at Adoption & Infertility Resources, 144 Westwoods Dr., Liberty MO 64068. Kris also distributes a British picture book written for DI-conceived children and a video of a symposium on DI issues for adults.

Making Sense of Adoption: A Parents Guide by Lois Ruskai Melina (New York: Harper & Row, 1989). Advice on how to talk with kids about adoption, surrogacy and donor insemination.

Raising Adopted Children: A Manual for Adoptive Parents by Lois Ruskai Melina (New York: Harper & Row, 1986). A somewhat "Dr. Spockish", encyclopedic handbook on adoption issues.

Your Baby's Mind and How it Grows: Piaget's Theory for Parents. by Maryann Spencer Pulaski (New York: Harper & Row, 1978). Developmental psychology of children.

A Mighty Time: Talking to Your Adopted Adolescent about Sex by Randolph W. Severson (Dallas: House of Tomorrow Productions, undated). A helpful little booklet for parents dealing with "the hormone years" which does a good job of helping to identify what's "normal" and what's "adoption."

Chapter 13

LIFE GOES ON

Mrs. Minifred said once that life is made up of circles.

"Life is not a straight line," she said. "And sometimes we circle back to a past time. But we are not the same. We are changed forever."

I didn't understand what she meant then. I remember steam whistling in the radiator under the window in the school library, and the way Ms. Minifred's hair brushed the side of her face when she leaned forward. But I liked the sound of her words, and I remember saving them for later.

Patricia MacLachlan
from Baby, *p. 108*

Not long ago, as I thumbed through national RESOLVE's newsletter, my attention was caught by a headline and I stopped to read an article on menopause after infertility. The article made me incredibly sad for its author (who was experiencing menopause as a resurgence of the grief of her infertility). I was also sad for her children, who had been adopted, but who, it would seem from the tone of her article, had never been "enough." Finally, I was alarmed for the many readers who, caught up in the pressure and anxiety of ongoing treatment or only recently having put treatment behind them, would see this view as "the way it will be."

At 47 I was beginning to watch for signs of menopause. In fact I'd begun to use its approach humorously as I spoke ("It could arrive any day now... Is it hot in here?") But I was not feeling afraid of menopause.

It's true that I've never been pregnant, but I feel fully female. It's a fact that I've never given birth, but I feel incredibly fertile! Though I'm a little anxious about aging, the fertility aspect of menopause was almost an afterthought! The reality of my life is that I have faced infertility, I have battled it, and I have won! And so can you.

The Fertile Infertile

The overwhelming majority of infertile people don't get a diagnosis of sterility. With diagnoses like low (but not zero) sperm counts, and kinked (but not blocked) fallopian tubes, and poor (but not absent) ovulation, and hormones that are out of balance (but still flowing), and "unexplained" infertility they are subfertile more than infertile. What this means is that for a significant number of people who have been fertility impaired at some time in their life, the serious possibility exists that changes in their hormones or in their lifestyle or whatever could result in an out-of-the-blue pregnancy. Surprise!!

Large numbers of drifters (the opposite of take-charge folks) almost count on this possibility. Though treatment didn't work and they actively end it, one or the other of the couple (often without ever mentioning it to their partner) never really gives up hope that someday they might just spontaneously become pregnant. He or she continues to count the days and schedule "spontaneous" intercourse appropriately. Other fertility-impaired couples leave treatment so discouraged that their lack of success convinces them that such a thing could never happen. The end result for both of these kinds of couples is the possibility of an unplanned pregnancy.

Obviously the author of the article on menopause fell into the first of these two groups. Every month for years and years the glimmer of hope that resided in the back of her mind was extinguished. She parented, but her children were not all that she had hoped for. And now, at menopause, she was being forced to face that she would never have what she had really wanted all along. In addition, in going so public with her grief, she had also let her children know that they were second best.

Every child deserves to be wanted for who he is.

Alicia fell into the other category. The mother of two children, one who had been adopted and the other conceived through a complicated treatment regimen, Alicia's husband had made it clear that two children were all that he wanted. I stood next to her while she asked several reproductive endocrinologists at a symposium we were attending together whether a problem like hers meant that she was unlikely to become pregnant without treatment. Each doctor clearly said that that could not be depended upon and advised her to use birth control. She didn't, but she didn't tell her husband what the doctors had said. She became pregnant spontaneously a few years later and her husband felt so betrayed that their relationship disintegrated. They divorced. Alicia is the bitter single parent of three.

Even take-charge couples will of course be astonished at the initial thought that perhaps birth control should be a part of their plan to take charge of infertility, but it should.

As you and your partner make a plan about your infertility—a plan to continue treatment, a plan to adopt, a plan to use a surrogate or a sperm donor, a plan to live childfree—the plan should include the future. If parenthood is a part of the plan, how many children do you wish to parent, and how long will you try to give birth to or to adopt that number of children before revamping the plan? In order to assure that each child gets his own space (both emotional and physical) in your life, what form of birth control will you use just before and after an adoption or after the birth of a child and for how long?

Don't discount this. It is a real issue! Fertility after infertility can be just as difficult as the infertility experience itself. And perpetual infertility is the total absence of resolution! Take charge of your life!

Menopause

Earlier in the spring of the newsletter article I had been sent by my internist to a gynecologist because I had, for the first time in many years, experienced a strangely late and then strangely long menstrual period. Hmmm, I remember thinking one morning as I realized that I was over two weeks late, could this be the beginning of "The Change?" I had had no other symptoms that I could recognize—no unusual moodiness or restlessness, no headaches, no hot flashes or night sweats. The sudden lateness of a period that had been amazingly predictable during the 12 years since we had ended treatment for the last time (a wryly amusing irony, since my periods had almost never been regular during nine cumulative years of treatment) was a surprise.

After the results of the blood work, the pelvic exam, the endometrial biopsy were in, the diagnosis from the gynecologist was that, yes, this was likely a very early symptom of menopause. We talked about what to expect, when I would see him again, what treatments I might want to consider several months or even a couple of years down the road as this process progressed.

I sat in my car for a while outside that building and let thoughts and memories wash over me. I remembered my last visit with this same doctor nineteen years before. The results of a hysterosalpingogram had shown that surgery done then to correct a blockage in my only remaining fallopian tube had not worked. This was before Baby Louise, before Norfolk, before major cities were dotted with IVF/GIFT clinics competing with one another. I had spent a whole year grieving intensely after that failed surgery, mourning failures, lamenting losses, letting go of expectations, coming close to drowning in sorrow.

But allowing myself to wallow in that awful process had been worth it. Finally, I had been ready to begin the work of moving on. Examining what we wanted most, my husband and I had decided on adoption. As I sat outside the gynecologist's office last spring our oldest son was about to turn eighteen and graduate from high school. Two weeks before I had experienced another milestone doctor's appointment with him—the last visit with the pediatrician who had examined him first at 12 days old— premature and fetal-looking, weighing less than five pounds.

Part way through writing this book during the summer of 1993 my reproductive life took another detour. I had four nervous weeks to prepare for an oophrectomy/hysterectomy. For the first time in a long time I found myself coming round in that circle. I was afraid of what lay ahead and worried that perhaps I had not been right after all: perhaps infertility would not be as "behind me" as I had thought. Perhaps this hormonal shift and physical trauma would bring it all back.

I read several books on menopause, including two new ones by "gurus" of feminism in my era, Gail Sheehy and Germaine Greer. I had expected these to tell me that hysterectomy and menopause were something very manageable. I was surprised by how devastating they made menopause sound, how angry they were at the loss it represented for them. This frightened me.

So I started to make phone calls to everyone I knew who had had a hysterectomy, and in "interviewing" them I thought I saw a pattern developing. My observation is not the result of academic research, of course. It is strictly anecdotal. And you'll remember from Chapter Five how cautiously I suggested you react to anecdotal observation as compared to the results of a carefully structured and controlled study. That caveat offered, my observation is this:

Among the women I spoke to, those who had experienced a hysterectomy and surgical menopause after going through the experience of infertility with the support of a group (either something organized like RESOLVE or IAAC or something less formal such as a group of well informed friends) were on the whole much more positive about themselves, about their recovery from surgery, about the intactness of their femininity and sexuality than were women who had never experienced infertility. A third group of women who had experienced infertility by denying its impact and not allowing themselves to grieve about it found hysterectomy or menopause difficult, too.

Of the three groups, the women most likely to have experienced strong grief after hysterectomy or as part of natural menopause seemed to be those who for the first time were being forced to acknowledge that they would not be giving birth in the future. These included both those who had never been infertile and the infertiles who had tried not to examine infertility's losses before and were grieving the final loss of their fertility now, like the author of the article in the newsletter. For these two groups of women, post-surgery and post-menopause had become a time of grief and loss. My RESOLVE sisters and I, on the other hand, had dealt with that grief long before.

In the spring of 1993 I attended the American Booksellers Association Convention in Miami, where my book *Adopting after Infertility* was a finalist for a Benjamin Franklin Award given there to the best new book in the field of Parenting/Family Issues (it didn't win.) I wandered the huge trade show's floor, admiring all of the new books. The marketing staff at Indiana University Press was passing out buttons to promote their new book, *Menopause: A Life Passage*. The buttons read

"Those Are Not Hot Flashes. They're Power Surges!"

I love it!

Resolved

Often over the past dozen years I've thought back to the Thanksgiving weekend car trip of 1978. My son strapped into the carseat behind us, my husband driving, I was reading a book plucked along with several others on infertility and adoption from a library shelf as part of my quest to expand our family. The book, with its boring sounding title (*Infertility: A Guide for the Childless Couple*) and straightforward descriptions of medical issues in its first section, was by Barbara Eck Menning, RESOLVE's founder. Because I was really pursuing adoption, had I not been compulsive, I might not have finished the book. But I am compulsive and I had forced myself to read on.

Several pages into section two, "The Psychosocial Aspects of Infertility," I was set on the path that changed my life forever and brought this book to you. I learned here that I was not crazy, that I was not alone. Later, as I became involved in RESOLVE, I learned from reading, from attending conferences, from speaking with a plethora of infertile people (including a number of mental health professionals) who were willing to explore their grief rather than deny it, who were willing to take charge of their lives rather than become victims of loss, that life could be full and good— if I were willing to allow it to be.

Now, I recall how at 33 I feared menopause not so much as a signal of my aging, but as a cliff over which I might drop—still infertile after all these years. I recall conversations and columns where those of us within RESOLVE shared our fears about this looming final outcome. I think about you, feeling that fear now.

I remember those fears—and I smile. Because what I feared at 33 couldn't be farther from how I feel today. A few would say that it was the finality of my diagnosis at a time when I had no medical options that made my resolution "easier." They are wrong. I was an excellent candidate for IVF/GIFT for a number of years after my unsuccessful surgery at age 29. I chose not to try this treatment. Furthermore, some of my dearest friends from within RESOLVE have not had so permanent a diagnosis but are—at close to my age—in the same place. They include a woman whose several miscarriages ultimately led to the birth of one healthy child but no more. Treatments did not produce another much wanted child, but she now practices birth control judiciously and, in her work as a clinical psychologist, encourages others to explore why this needs to be a part of a truly healthy resolution. Another couple (diagnosis: unexplained infertility) who share my perspective have embraced a childfree lifestyle and chosen a permanent birth control method. They have been willing to teach others the communication skills by which they reached this lifestyle choice.

Why do people like us hang around RESOLVE or IAAC, you might wonder. If we truly have "resolved" infertility and left it behind as a factor in our day-to-day lives, why would we not have put the group behind us too. The answer is clear, but it certainly isn't simple.

The reason is you. We've been where you are, but there were no role models ahead of us then. Many of our fears about what infertility would, could, or should mean in the context of our whole lives were a result of past generations having lived in a closet with their infertility, resulting in an information vacuum.

RESOLVE is an organization of the baby-boom generation, and those of us at the front edge of the boom have been throughout our lives pioneers of a sort in the reproductive revolution that we ushered in—birth control pills, sexual freedom, delayed parenting, high-tech family building options. As the explorers, we must help our younger partners understand the long term consequences and benefits of the challenges we faced and the choices we made. We wish we had had a perspective like ours when we were youngsters like you.

On the "outside" RESOLVE is sometimes criticized for what appears to be a single minded focus on the goal of achieving pregnancy and advocacy directed almost exclusively on medical treatment options. Those critics wonder what this says about the organization's view of what success after infertility really is.

"Resolution" has always been an ambiguous and controversial term. How it is measured and how it is accomplished is something we've too often not taken the time to debate.

People like me believe that resolution is a process that demands hard work but that ultimately results in contentment no matter what the medical outcome or alternative choice. We believe that infertility need not be a life-consuming "condition," that life itself need not be impaired by a fertility impairment. We believe that as we move on past the childbearing years whether or not we have borne or parented children need not become the measure either of our success or of our pleasure in life.

No coulda, woulda, shoulda's for us. And so we hang around and sometimes serve as irritants as we question, question,

question in order to help you hear our message: Life is good! It offers choices! Dive into it!

And so we have come full circle, back to where we began, but, as Ms. Minifred said, we are not the same. We have changed forever. There has been pain, but from the pain, growth.

I am an infertile woman. Though I would not wish infertility on my worst enemy, I would be no other woman that the one I am today. This journey has been a powerful journey, its discoveries wondrous. Among the most wondrous discoveries of Dave's and my journey through infertility are three children we did not give birth to, but who are the perfect children for us, the children we were meant to parent.

Your journey will be different from ours. It may or may not include children, but it, too, can be a wonderful journey if you are strong enough to take charge of it rather than to allow yourself to be lost in the thicket. The danger in this crisis is clear. Only you can find your opportunity. I leave you to continue your journey with words which have been attributed to Helen Keller.

"When one door of happiness closes, another opens. But often we spend so much time looking at the closed doors that we cannot see the doors that have opened for us. We must all find these doors, and, if we do, we will make ourselves and our lives as beautiful as God intended."

INDEX

Abbey, Antonia, 108
abortion, 219
acupuncture, 100
adhesions, 137
adolescence
    and identity, 243
    and sex education, 209
Adopted Child, 48, 206
Adopting after Infertility, 110, 199, 257
adoption
    acceptance of difference in, 203-5
    ad for, 152
    and age, 199
    agency, 200
    assisted. 226
    and attachment, 156, 194-96
    and attorneys, 106-7
    and bondng, 156, 194-96
    in Canada, 112
    child's understanding of, 235,
        241-42, 244-45
    as choice, 84
    choice of agency, 95
    communication issues, 158
    consequences of, 147
    and control, 114
    denial in, 114-15
    differences associated with, 226
    direct, 105
    domestic, 201
    education issues, 106, 198, 206,
        236-43
    egg. *See* egg donation

embryo, 138, 172, 184
    and age limitations, 189
    chance of success, 184
and entitlement, 197, 199, 225-27
exploitation in, 110
and extended family, 205-7
feelings about, 157
gamete, 57, 103. *See also*
        adoption, quasi; donor
        insemination; egg donation;
        gamete intrafallopian
        transfer; *in vitro*
        fertilization; surrogacy
    as choice, 84
    donor insemination, 88
    in vitro fertilization, 89
    as means to parenting, 168
    surrogacy, 90
identified, 105
independent, 106, 198, 200
infant, 202
inracial, 202
international, 199, 201
loss of control in, 21, 111
loss of genetic connection in, 196
as means to parenting, 168
needs of child in, 155
nonagency, 199
noninfant, 190, 199, 202
open, 90, 198, 201
options available, 74, 148, 172-73,
        198-203
and packaged infertility services,
        146-48

perspectives on, 110-12
planning for, 203-5, 255-56
and postnatal depression, 220
privacy issues, 187, 198, 201
private. *See* adoption, independent
professionals, 104-5
quasi, 154, 171ff, 226, 239, 241-42
    See also adoption, gamete
requirements for, 82
and self esteem, 238
social workers and, 105-6
societal view of 193-94, 226
special issues, 224
special needs, 199
traditional, 88, 154, 200, 241
transcultural, 202
transethnic, 157, 201
transracial, 198-99, 201
adoption advocate, 112-113. *See also*
    advocacy groups
adoption consultant, 95, 107-8
Adoption Council of Canada, 202
adoption intermediaries, 104
adoption language
negative, 197
positive, 166, 206
adoptive embryo transfer, 78
Adoptive Families of America (AFA),
    74-75, 194, 202
Adoptive Parents Committee of New
    York, 75
Adoptnet, 48, 206
advocacy groups, 74, 105, 113-14, 202.
    See also adoption advocate;
    infertility advocate
and education, 106, 115
seminars and meetings, 125
AFA. *See* Adoptive Families of America
AFS. *See* American Fertility Society
AIDS, 176
American Academy of Adoption
    Attorneys, 107
American Booksellers Association, 257

American Fertility Society, 74, 98, 139
and donor insemination, 176
journal of, 109
Psychological Special Interest Group,
    102
seminars, 102
as source of information, 126
American Tissue Bank Association, 176
Anderson, Robert, 127
Andrews, Frank M., 108
ART. *See* Assisted Reproductive
    Technology
artificial insemination. *See* donor
    insemination; husband
    insemination
Assisted Reproductive Technology
    138-43
alternatives to, 141
Clinic Specific Outcome Assessment,
    139
and education of children 246-48
legislation and regulation, 139
new procedures, 144
and packaged infertility services,
    146-48
physical impact of, 141
rate of success, 141, 152
attachment. *See* bonding
attorney, 106-7
and adoption, 204
choice of, 95
as intermediary, 104, 106

Baby Louise. *See* Brown, Louise
baby blues. *See* postnatal depression
Baron, Bonnie and Lawrence, 160
Bebbington, Dr., 124
*Being Adopted: The Life-Long Search for
    Self*, 235
Bernstein, Anne, 235, 240, 242
*Beyond Infertility: Understanding the
    New Reproductive Options*,
    172

birth control, 15, 255, 258
  permanent, 259
birth defects, 145
birth experience, 175. *See also*
    pregnancy
  loss of, 23-24
birthmother. *See* birthparents
birthparents, 189, 198, 203, 226, 242-48
  and adoption, 245
  fantasies about, 243
blocked fallopian tubes. *See* fallopian
    tubes, blocked
Bombardieri, Merle, 39, 48
bonding, 205
  and adoption, 194-96
Bothun, Linda, 48, 206
Braverman, Andrea Mechanick, 183
breast feeding, 24, 230
Brodzinsky, Anne Braff, 241
Brodzinsky, David, 235, 241
Brown, Louise, 138, 256

Carter, Jean and Michael, 38, 160, 169
cesarean section, 237, 245
childfree lifestyle, 160, 163-66, 225
  choice of, 38, 67-68, 76, 84, 89, 153-
    54,259
  embracing, 163ff
  plan for, 255
children
  and adoption efforts, 246-47
  cognitive development of, 240-41
  education of, 235-36
  identity issues, 237
  preparation for a sibling, 247-48
chiropractic, 100
chlamydia, 137
Clapp, Diane, 48
clomiphene citrate, 130, 152. *See also*
    Clomid
collaborative reproduction. *See*
    adoption, embryo; adoption
    gamete; donor insemination;
    egg donation; reproduction,
    assisted
Collins, John A., 124
communication
  in adoption, 158-59, 187, 197
  between partners, 36-41, 45, 60, 71
  with children, 234
  and fear of impasse, 61-62
  importance of 40, 42
  and sharing, 69-71
compassion, loss of, 28
consumer groups. *See* advocacy groups
control. *See also* adoption, and loss of
    control.
  abdication of, 27
  in Canadian medicine, 111
  and decision making, 59, 165
  and image of victim, 27-29
  loss of 19-20
  regaining, 78, 155
Cooper, Susan, 172
cost. *See* resources, financial
counselor. *See also* psychiatrist,
    psychologist, social
    worker
  and adoption, 101
  choice of, 95, 101-4
  as intermediary, 104
  need for, 62
Covey, Stephen, 56

Dawson, Roger, 56
decision makers, traits of, 56
decision making, 55-56, 58, 121. *See*
    also infertility, treatment of,
    decision to stop; planning
    process
  alternatives, 83-4
  and assisted reproduction, 173-74
  choosing service providers, 95ff
  about drug therapy, 133-35
  lack of, 168
  motivation for, 56

resources for, 164
DeWolf, Rose, 56
diethylstilbesterol, 134
Donahue, Phil, 38
donor gametes, 44, 138, 148, 216, 241.
    See also egg donation; gamete
    intrafallopian transfer; *invitro*
    fertilization; sperm donation
donor insemination, 67, 74, 78, 146,
    152, 172, 174-82
    See also, adoption, gamete
choice of donor, 180-82
and confidentiality, 177
fresh vs frozen, 176
openness about, 239
procedure, 175
secrecy issue, 239
and societal attitude, 177-80
statistics/success rate, 175-76
teaching children about, 236
drug therapy, 133-35. *See also* infertility,
    treatment of; drug therapy

eating disorders, 41
Ebersold, Donald, 124
education. *See also* infertility, education
    about; information; sex
    education
about adoption, 115
of children, 233 ff
about fertility, 249-50
preventive, 249-50
sexual, 249-50
sources of information, 122-27
egg donation, 67, 147, 172, 182-84. *See*
    also donor gametes; adoption
    gamete
and age limitations, 189
source of donors, 183
success rate, 183-84
embryo adoption. *See* adoption, embryo
embryos
cloning of 148-49

disposition of, 142
donated, 142, 239
freezing of, 182
multiple, 142
emotional resources. *See* resources,
    emotional
endometriosis, 70, 135-37
entitlement, 225-27
and self esteem, 226

FACE Facts, 48
Fairness to Adopting Families Act, 194
fallopian tubes
    blocked, 137, 254, 256
    reconstruction of, 135
Family and Medical Leave Act, 194
Faulkner Center for Reproductive
    Medicine, 159
FDA. *See* Food and Drug
    Administration
FerreFax, 124
fertile partners, 43-46
fertility
    and age, 189-91
    control over, 19-20
    factors affecting, 128-29
    and sterility, 109, 124-25, 140, 183
fertility impairment. *See* infertility
financial resources. *See* resources,
    financial
Fluker, Dr., 124
Food and Drug Administration, 134, 144
Freeman, Arthur, 56

gamete intrafallopian transfer, 28, 90,
    97, 123, 136-38, 143, 258. *See*
    also Assisted Reproductive
    Technology
clinics, 256
and multiple pregnancy, 133
and sex education, 244
success rate, 140
unsuccessful, 158, 181

gender-based differences, 36-39
genetic connection, 22, 59, 78, 89, 171.
    See also genetic continuity
    and egg donation, 184
    and embryo adoption, 184
    and entitlement, 226
    in families, 239
    importance of, 67
    lack of, 250
    loss of, 175, 196
    need for, 143, 228
    partial, 173-74
genetic continuity, 21-22, 44, 70, 140.
    See also genetic connection
    and donor insemination, 174
    need for, 88-89
genetic parents. *See* birthparents
George Washington University, 148
gestational care. *See* surrogacy,
    gestational
*Getting the Love You Want: A Guide for
    Couples*, 40
Glazer, Ellen, 172
goals
    of adulthood, 25
    determining major goal, 77-78
    objectives and strategies, 77-78
"Grandchildfree", 46
grandparents
    and adoption, 206
    disappointment of, 22, 46, 50
Gray, John, 37-38, 41
Greer, Germaine, 256
grief
    and communication, 61
    over hysterectomy, 257
    and infertility, 66, 256
    and loss, 28-29
    over loss of sibling, 248
    over menopause, 254
    need for time in, 153
    reactions to, 44
    resolution of, 26-27, 57, 259

Hallarn, Rose Kegler, 131
Hallenbeck, Carol, 166
Halman, L. Jill, 108
Hendrix, Harville, 40
hMG. *See* human menopausal
    gonadotropin
Holmes, Pat, 48, 206
homeopathy, 100
homestudy. *See* parent preparation.
hormone imbalance
How Can I Help?, 48
Humagen, 130
human menopausal gonadotropins,
    130, 152
husband insemination, 138, 237
hysterectomy, 256-57
hysterosalpingogram, 136, 256

IAAC. *See* Infertility Awareness
    Association of Canada
impaired fertility. *See* infertility
in vitro fertilization, 28, 97, 124, 136-38,
    143, 147, 258. *See also*
    Assisted Reproductive
    Technologies
    and age, 189
    clinics, 256
    and egg donation, 183-84
    and embryo donation, 184
    multiple pregnancy, 132
    and sex education, 244-45
    success rate, 140
    and surrogacy, 185
    unsuccessful, 182
infertility
    and childfree lifestyle, 163ff
    choices and decisions about, 30, 67
    as couples issue, 43-46, 120, 128
    denial of, 16-17, 25, 99, 114
    education about, 48-52, 73-77
    and family, 46-52, 84
    and friends, 46-52, 84
    grief over, 257. *See also* grief

266

health care issues, 21, 75, 85, 111, 134, 143, 157, 184
linking/packaging services, 112-12, 146-48
losses associated with, 19-25, 29, 62, 168, 196
and parenting, 223ff
reaction to, 29, 35-36, 226
secondary, 159, 224-25
and secrecy, 178-80
and sex education, 243-46
and sexism, 178, 239
stages of experience, 57
and stress, 41-43, 101
treatment of, 26-27, 79, 99, 119ff
    alternative, 100-01
    assisted reproduction, 129
    basic work-up, 127-30
    beyond, 115
    decision to end, 84-87, 120-21, 151ff
    hormone therapy, 21, 127, 129, 130-35, 144-46, 237 246
    perspectives on, 110-12
    references, 143-44
    satisfaction with, 108-9
    sources of information, 122-27
    surgical, 129, 135-37
    testing, 128-29
unexplained, 159-60, 225, 254, 259
Infertility: A Guide for the Childless Couple, 26, 258
Infertility Awareness Association of Canada, 29, 74-75, 258-59
as consumer advocate, 125
Insights into Infertility, 159
International Federation of Infertility Societies, 124
IVF. *See in vitro* fertilization

Johnston, Spencer, 56

jointly conceived child, 89, 152, 228
expectation of, 23
loss of, 44, 173, 175
Journal of the American Medical Association, 125

Kass, Leon, 120
Kastner-Roundy, Barbara, 46
Keane, Noel, 185
Keller, Helen, 260
Keye, William R., 166
Kirk, H. David, 238
Kubler Ross, Elisabeth, 26
Kues, Jack, 124

Lancet, 125
language, positive use of, 165-67. *See also* adoption language
laparoscopy, 129, 133, 135-36
and *in vitro* fertilization, 138
laser surgery, 135
Lauritzen, Paul, 120-21
loss
    acceptance of, 18
    associated with infertility, 19-25, 62
    of assumed child, 83
    coping with, 18-19, 28-29, 57, 115, 155
    denial of, 164-65
    experienced by birthmother, 204
    as learning experience, 17-18
    ranking and weighting, 63-66, 69, 77, 121
    reaction to, 152
    resolution of, 26-27, 57, 259
low sperm count, 70, 88, 254
Lucy's Feet, 247
Lupus Foundation, 124
Lupus Journal, 124

Making Sense of Adoption, 241
Mason, Mary Martin, 161
mediator. *See* counselor

medical research, 144-45
Melina, Lois, 241
Men Are from Mars, Women Are from Venus, 37, 41
Menning, Barbara Eck, 26, 258
menopause, 254-57
    books on, 256
    fear of, 258
    grief over, 254
Menopause: A Life Passage, 257
men, viewpoint of, 37
microsurgery, 135
miscarriage, 145, 152, 160, 217, 219-20, 248, 258. *See also* pregnancy, loss of
Mothers of Twins Clubs, 219

NACAC. See North American Council on Adoptable Children
National Council for Adoption (NCFA), 194
New England Journal of Medicine, 218
News of FAIR, 48
North American Council on Adoptable Children, 105, 202

obstetrician/gynecologist, (OB/GYN), certification, 97. *See also* physician
oocytes, donor, 239
oophrectomy, 256
Organization of Parents through Surrogacy (OPTS), 74
OURS: The Magazine of Adoptive Families, 48, 75, 206
ovarian cysts, 135
ovarian dysfunction, 41, 89, 130, 182, 254
ovum donation. *See* egg donation

parent preparation, 90, 197, 203, 210
parenting
    of adolescents, 227, 229
    by adoption, 224
    by assisted reproduction, 224
    alternatives to, 25
    choices about, 122, 143
    disappointment in, 228-29
    education about, 175, 230-31
    and entitlement, 226
    expectations of, 15-16, 55, 227-29
    experience of, 190
    as goal, 78, 111, 157, 196
    after infertility, 229-30
    opportunity for, 24-25
    readiness for, 122
    superparent syndrome, 229
parent groups. *See* advocacy groups
Perspectives Press, 126, 169, 206, 240
physical resources. *See* resources, physical
physician. *See also* obstetrician/gynecologist; psychiatrist; urologist
    attitude of toward treatment, 124
    beginning treatment, 128-30
    choice of, 95-98
    infertility specialist, 96, 99
    satisfaction with, 108-9
    and specialized treatment, 135-37
    as source of information, 123
    subspecialists, 99
Piaget, Jean, 235
planning process, 57-58
    evaluation, 87
    following the plan, 84-85
    need for time, 152
    outline, 59-60
    setting goals, 77-84. *See also* goals
    strategizing, 84
    and treatment, 129-30
postnatal depression, 220, 228
pregnancy
    and assisted reproductive technology, 216
    and attachment, 156

control over, 174
ectopic, 137, 217
and egg donation, 184
expectations of, 215-16
experience of, 141, 152, 168, 171
fears about, 216-17
high-risk, 217-18
after infertility, 216
loss of, 22, 24, 39, 44, 88
        and mourning ceremony, 160
and medication, 216
multiple, 131-34, 140, 142, 217-19
        and gamete intrafallopian
            transfer, 218
        and *in vitro* fertilization, 218
and "older" mothers, 218
psychological, 195
as shared experience, 24, 184
spontaneous, 254-55
successful, 120
pregnancy reduction, 133, 141-42, 219
prepared childbirth, 24
pressure. *See* stress
privacy, sexual, 20
psychiatrist, 101
psychologist, 101
*Pursuing Parenthood: Ethical Issues in
    Assisted Reproduction*, 120-21

quadruplets. *See* pregnancy, multiple

ranking and weighting system, 63-66
reflection, as part of planning process,
    62-63
reproduction. *See also* fertility
    assisted, 153, 171ff, 241, 247.
            See also adoption, gamete;
            assisted reproductive
            technology; surrogacy;
            and counseling, 174
    collaborative. *See* adoption, gamete;
            adoption, quasi; donor
            insemination; egg donation;

        reproduction, assisted;
        surrogacy
control over, 15
marketing implications of, 20, 24
third party. See reproduction,
    assisted
reproductive endocrinology, 98-100. *See
    also* physician, infertility
    specialist
resolution, 26-27, 57, 259
RESOLVE, 26-27, 39, 45, 48, 74, 194,
    258-59
    as consumer advocate, 125
    and donor insemination, 181
    and mourning ceremonies, 160
    and peer support, 114-15, 174
    physician referral, 98, 181
    positive language, 166
    as source of information, 129, 131,
        254
resources
    emotional, 72, 82-83, 100, 145
        and adoption, 200
        and egg and embryo
            donation, 184
    financial, 72, 80-81, 100, 132-34,
        136-37, 141, 145
        and adoption, 200
        and childfree living, 168
        and donor insemination, 168
        and egg and embryo
            donation, 184
        and ending treatment, 154
        and packaged infertility
            services, 147
    inventory of, 71-73
    limitations of, 87
    personal, 121, 135-37
        and adoption, 199-200
        depletion of, 154
    physical, 72, 79-80, 100, 137, 145
        and adoption, 200
        and egg and embryo

donation, 184
and ending treatment, 154
time, 72, 81-82, 87, 100, 137, 141
and adoption, 200
and egg and embryo
donation, 184
and ending treatment, 154
retreat weekend, 60, 68-69
retrograde ejaculation, 136
Riley, Pat, 168
rituals, value of, 160-61
Roots & Wings, 48, 206
Rubin, Theodore Isaac, 56

SART. *See* Society of Assisted
Reproductive Technology
Schnitter, Jane, 247
Schwartz, Judith D., 20, 24
Second Choice: Growing Up Adopted,
237
Seibel, Machelle M., 159
self-esteem
and adoption, 238
and decision making, 83
and entitlement, 226
and fertility, 44-45
and genetic connection, 173
loss of, 20, 27
and terminology, 167
semen analysis, 129
semen, frozen, 176
Serono Symposia, 74, 159
seminars, 102
Serophene, 130
sex education, 16, 179, 233-34
sexuality, fears about, 250
*Shared Fate: A Theory of Adoptive
Relationships*, 238
Sheehy, Gail, 256
siblings
loss of, 248-49
preparation for, 247-48
Simon, Harriet, 224

Smith, Jerome, 197, 225
social workers, 198, 203
and adoption, 105-6
certification of, 101
as intermediaries, 104
Society of Assisted Reproductive
Technology, 139, 142
Spencer, Marietta, 166
sperm banks, 176, 239
sperm count, low. *See* low sperm count
sperm donation, 147, 255. *See also*
donor gametes
statistics, comparison of, 123
Stein, Stephanie, 247
sterility, 254
stress, 41-43
and medical choices, 120
and medical research, 144
subzonal sperm injection, 138, 145
support groups. *See* advocacy groups
Supporting an Adoption, 48, 206
surgery. *See* infertility, treatment of,
surgical
surrogacy, 74, 78, 138, 146-48. *See also*
gamete adoption
aspects of, 185-87
and confidentiality, 187
evolution of, 172
financial consideration, 185-86
gestational, 172
as means to parenting, 168
openness about, 239
perceptual problems in, 187-89
plan for, 255
similarity to adoption, 186
teaching children about, 236
SUZI. *See* subzonal sperm injection
*Sweet Grapes: How to Stop Being
Infertile and Start Living
Again*, 38, 160, 169

Takas, Marianne, 25
Tannen, Deborah, 36-37, 40

testicular biopsy, 129
The Confident Decision Maker, 56
The Flight of the Stork, 235, 240
*The Miracle Seekers: An Anthology of
        Infertility*, 161
"The Mommy Trap", 20
*The Mother Puzzle: A New Generation
        Reckons with Motherhood*, 20
The New England Journal of Medicine,
        125
The Psychology of Adoption, 235
*The Winner Within: A Life Plan for Team
        Players*, 168
therapeutic donor insemination. *See*
        donor insemination
therapist. *See* also psychiatrist;
        psychologist
  as intermediary, 104
time factor. *See* resources, time
To Love a Child, 25
triplets. *See* pregnancy, multiple
tubal ligation, 182
Twenty Minute Rule, 39-40, 43
twins. *See* pregnancy, multiple

ultrasound, 133
  and *in vitro* fertilization, 138
*Understanding: A Guide to Impaired
        Fertility for Family and
        Friends*, 48, 52
urology, 97

varicocele, 135, 181
von Ende Communications, 75

Warner, Edward, 25
When Friends Ask about Adoption, 48,
        206
William Is My Brother, 247
Williams, Wendy and Rob, 160
women, viewpoint of, 37

*Woulda, Coulda, Shoulda: Overcoming
        Regrets, Mistakes, and Missed
        Opportunities*, 56
*You Just Don't Understand: Women and
        Men in Conversation*, 37, 40
You're Our Child, 197, 225

ZIFT. *See* zygote intrafallopian transfer
Zouves, Dr. 124
zygote intrafallopian transfer (ZIFT),
        124, 140, 244

ABOUT THE AUTHOR

Patricia Irwin Johnston, M.S., is an internationally known infertility and adoption educator. Her personal experience in a family which dealt with two generations of infertility led her to become a volunteer for the consumer groups in the fields of infertility and adoption.

Over the course of fourteen years Pat was a RESOLVE chapter co-founder and president, was a regional chapter representative to RESOLVE's national board, and spent three years as that board's chairman. (RESOLVE's annual volunteer of the year award was named in her honor.) She was also among the initiating members of the National Advisory Board for Adoptive Families of America and has been an advisor for several other national organizations and publications. She was one of the North American Council on Adoptable Children's 1989 Adoption Activists of the Year. In 1992 she was named a Friend of Adoption by the Adoptive Parents Committee of New York.

Her earlier books, also from Perspectives Press, include *Perspectives on a Grafted Tree, Understanding: A Guide to Impaired Fertility for Family and Friends, An Adoptor's Advocate*, and *Adopting after Infertility*.

LET US INTRODUCE OURSELVES

Since 1982 Perspectives Press has focused exclusively on infertility, adoption, and related reproductive and child welfare issues. Our purpose is to promote understanding of these issues and to educate and sensitize those personally experiencing these life situations, professionals who work in these fields and the public at large. Our titles are never duplicative or competitive with material already available through traditional publishers. We seek to find and fill only niches which are empty. In addition to this book, our current titles include

FOR ADULTS
Perspectives on a Grafted Tree
*Understanding: A Guide to Impaired Fertility for Family and
        Friends*
Sweet Grapes: How to Stop Being Infertile and Start Living Again
Residential Treatment: A Tapestry of Many Therapies
A Child's Journey through Placement

FOR CHILDREN
Our Baby: A Birth and Adoption Story
The Mulberry Bird: Story of an Adoption
Real for Sure Sister
Filling in the Blanks: A Guided Look at Growing Up Adopted
Where the Sun Kisses the Sea
William Is My Brother
Lucy's Feet

COMING SOON
Flight of the Stork (advice for adults on sex education)
Family Pictures (for the young friends of childfree couples)
Let Me Explain (for children conceived by donor insemination)
Birthparenthood (living with the adoption decision)

If you are writing on our issues, we invite you to contact us with SASE to request our writer's guidelines, which will help you to determine whether your idea might fit into our publishing plans.

Perspectives Press
P.O. Box 90318
Indianapolis, IN 46290-0318